PENGUIN BOOKS

BOGEYS AND BANDITS

Robert Gandt, a former Navy pilot and now a
captain for Delta Airlines, is the author of
three previous books, including *Skygods*. He
lives in Daytona Beach, Florida.

BOGEYS AND BANDITS

THE MAKING OF A FIGHTER PILOT

★ ★ ★

ROBERT GANDT

PENGUIN BOOKS

PENGUIN BOOKS
Published by the Penguin Group
Penguin Putnam Inc., 375 Hudson Street,
New York, New York 10014, U.S.A.
Penguin Books Ltd, 27 Wrights Lane, London W8 5TZ, England
Penguin Books Australia Ltd, Ringwood, Victoria, Australia
Penguin Books Canada Ltd, 10 Alcorn Avenue, Toronto, Ontario, Canada M4V 3B2
Penguin Books (N.Z.) Ltd, 182–190 Wairau Road, Auckland 10, New Zealand

Penguin Books Ltd, Registered Offices:
Harmondsworth, Middlesex, England

First published in the United States of America by Viking Penguin,
a division of Penguin Books USA Inc. 1997
Published in Penguin Books 1998

1 3 5 7 9 10 8 6 4 2

Photographs courtesy of the author unless otherwise indicated.

THE LIBRARY OF CONGRESS HAS CATALOGUED THE HARDCOVER AS FOLLOWS:
Gandt, Robert L.
Bogeys and bandits: the making of a fighter pilot / Robert Gandt.
p. cm.
ISBN 0-670-86721-7 (hc.)
ISBN 0 14 02.6412 4 (pbk.)
1. United States. Navy. Strike Fighter Wing.   2. Fighter pilots—Training of—
Florida—Jacksonville.   3. Hornet (Jet fighter plane).   I. Title.
VG94.6.S77G36   1997
359.9´4´092—dc21   96–51439   [B]

Printed in the United States of America
Set in Bodoni Book
Designed by Susan Hood

To the memory of

Lieutenant Commander Scott Speicher   USN
Lieutenant Kara Hultgreen   USN
First Lieutenant Michael Blaisdell   USMCR

PREFACE

U.S.S. Nimitz: *Santa Barbara Channel, March 1995*

It was all vaguely reminiscent: the hard lurch of the arrested landing, the wind and din of the flight deck, the orderly violence of the catapults hurling jets off the bow.

I climbed down from the C-2A turboprop that had just delivered me to the deck of the *Nimitz.* The scene had an old familiarity: fighters perched like hawks in a row with their wings folded, clouds of steam wisping from the catapult tracks, yellow-and-green-jerseyed deck crewmen in survival vests and Mickey Mouse ear protectors, scuttling between the shrieking jets.

It was a place I remembered, like a long-ago hometown.

But it wasn't until I had ducked through a steel door and started down a ladder that it hit me—*the smell*! I stood there, frozen on the ladder, stupefied by the scent—an evocative mix of oil, steel, jet fuel, paint, machinery, sweat—the peculiar internal atmosphere of a ninety-ton aircraft carrier.

A flood of old memories, anxieties, forgotten glories swept over me. *I was back!* I'd been transported in time, over a quarter of a century. Back to another life.

★

I had just turned twenty when my mother came to Chase Field, in the hill country of Beeville, Texas, to pin on my Navy wings. In a year and a half I had metamorphosed from college dropout to officer and aviator in the U.S. Navy. In a few more months, before I had yet reached legal drinking or voting age, I'd be launching off aircraft carriers with nuclear weapons hung on my jet.

Which seems unimaginable today. No one that young gets near a Navy cockpit or is allowed such immense responsibility. Today's naval aviation candidates are all college graduates *before* they are even considered for flight training. Most have degrees in engineering or the sciences, and many have graduate degrees. To win their wings and fly Navy or Marine Corps jets, they incur obligations that keep them in uniform into their thirties.

It wasn't always so. By the age of twenty-five I had completed my service and bade farewell to the Navy. I would be an airline pilot, instructor, journalist, husband, father, air show pilot, writer of aviation and military books. And, always, frustrated fighter pilot.

Now I wanted to write a book about modern Navy fighter pilots—who they were, where they came from, what they did. My motives, of course, went beyond just reporting. I wanted to get back in the cockpit of a Navy jet. This was going to be a sentimental journey.

For such a journey, I needed inside help. Most of my old squadron mates who stayed in the Navy were now retired. One of the few still on active duty was Dick Allen, a fellow graduate of the old naval aviation cadet program. Allen and I had arrived together as fresh young pilots in Carrier Air Group Three, and we twice deployed together on extended cruises aboard the carrier *Saratoga*. Because of his freckle-faced, cherubic looks, Allen drew the nickname, Sweepea, after the cartoon character in *Popeye*.

Sweepea survived Vietnam, Tailhook, and the perils of military politics. He rose in rank to command a squadron, an air wing, an aircraft carrier. And he kept going. Now Sweepea wore three stars and commanded all the naval air forces of the Atlantic Fleet. I had my inside help.

With Admiral Allen's endorsement, I received official authorization to check into the Navy's FA-18 Hornet fleet replacement squadron at Cecil Field on January 23, 1995. Cecil Field was where I (and Sweepea) had spent four years flying the A-4 Skyhawk—then the Navy's state-of-the-art attack jet.

For the next six months I attached myself to a class of students in strike fighter training. I sat in on their mission briefings and debriefings as they progressed through each phase of the strike fighter curriculum—familiarization, strike, fighter weapons, all the way to the big one—carrier qualification. With them, I endured endless lectures on subjects ranging from instrument flight procedures to carrier deck protocol to AIDS prevention. I pored over FA-18 systems and procedures and logged numerous sweaty hours in the *very* realistic flight simulators.

Like everyone who flies Navy jets, I underwent flight physiology qualification: aeromedical exam, ejection seat training, high-altitude pressure chamber, and water survival qualification (wherein you are strapped into an aircraft cabin, inverted, and plunged to the bottom of a twenty-foot pool, ramming something like forty gallons of water up your nose). Somehow I survived the survival test.

With my tutor and fighter pilot friend, Lieutenant Tom Bacon, I flew the Hornet through all its realms—supersonic flight, aerobatics over the Atlantic, low-level navigation over the Florida hinterlands, dive-bombing on the Pinecastle range, field carrier landing practice at Cecil Field.

I accompanied the students on training detachments, most notably to the anything-goes Key West fighter weapons facility. On half a dozen mosquito-swarmed days and nights I stood in the weeds at the end of practice runways while they rehearsed day and night carrier landings. I stood again on the landing signal platform of the U.S.S. *Nimitz* while they did the real thing.

But mostly I listened. During hurried lunches in the squadron duty office, over beers in late-night bars, on the back porches of the students' rented Florida homes, in the eerily red-lighted ready room aboard the aircraft carrier—I listened to them talk. In snippets, small pieces at a time, they told me about themselves, their wives and husbands and children, their passions and fears, their larger-than-life dreams.

This book is their story.

★

Certain usages in the book deserve explanation.

These days the matter of pronouns can produce a migraine. *He, she, him, her, it?* Though it is now acceptable (and even fashionable) to use the female pronoun when generalizing about aviators, it can be confusing. Only a few women naval aviators were in uniform before the nineties, and *none* had joined fighter squadrons until after April 28, 1993 (when Secretary of Defense Les Aspin signed the order lifting the ban on women in combat).

Thus, an arbitrary decision: For clarity of understanding, when referring to military aviators in the aggregate, I have opted for the traditional male pronoun.

In the interest of readability, the time lines of some of the pilots in training have been compressed. The FA-18 strike fighter syllabus takes about five months, but the students' actual progress varies according to weather, medical problems, mechanical status of their jets, and available deck time on aircraft carriers. Though all my subject students of "Class 2-95" were in the FA-18 training pipeline at the same time, their actual beginning and finishing class assignments were staggered throughout 1995.

For reasons of privacy, certain of the characters' names and identifying characteristics have been changed. In two instances, the identities of separate persons have been merged into single composite characters.

★

I owe thanks to numerous officers and aviators of the Navy and Marine Corps. My old fellow cadet, Commander P. J. Burke, USNR, pushed the right button to get the project off the ground. Admiral R. C. "Sweepea" Allen, Commander, Naval Air Forces Atlantic, gave the crucial green light. Successive commanding officers of VFA-106, Captains Matt Moffit and George "Rico" Mayer, made me feel welcome in their squadron. Hornet pilots Commander John Wood,

Lieutenant Commander Allen "Zoomie" Baker, and Lieutenant Tom "Slab" Bacon perused the text for technical and literary errata.

The staff of the Strike Fighter Wing Atlantic, commanded by Captain John "Flamo" Fleming, extended unfailing courtesy and assistance with my many requests. I am indebted to the superb instructor pilots and the squadron landing signal officers of VFA-106 for allowing me to join their briefings, for patiently answering my questions, and for taking me to sea with them. Thanks to the officers and crew of the U.S.S. *Nimitz* for the sentimental cruise in the Pacific.

Special gratitude goes to my agent, Alice Martell, of the Martell Agency, and to Mindy Werner, executive editor at Viking Penguin, for their patient and professional guidance.

Most of all, thanks are owed to the men and women—strike fighter pilots—whose lives I shared for six months, and for whom I developed a profound admiration. I salute them all.

RG
Summer 1996

PART ONE
NUGGETS

★ ★ ★

nug-get (nŭg′ĭt) n. 1. A small, solid lump,
especially of gold. 2. Neophyte naval aviator,
wearer of shiny new gold wings. 3. Occupier of
lowest stratum in naval aviation hierarchy.

PROLOGUE

His squadron call sign was "Mongo," an inevitable mutation of his real name—Nick Mongillo. Mongo was an unlikely hero. He was what they called a "nugget," which meant the same thing as "rookie"—a naval aviator on his first squadron assignment. He had only been in the squadron three months when they were sent to the Red Sea.

As a nugget Mongo had already done most of the knuckleheaded nugget things: being out of position as a wing man, missing frequency changes, losing sight of his flight leader. It was all part of learning to be a fighter pilot.

But no one had prepared him for his new role: Nick Mongillo—hero. Suddenly he was supposed to act like some sort of celebrity, grinning and spouting one-liners for the fans back home. He was supposed to be cool.

Instead, Mongo was standing there like a zombie. He couldn't think of anything cool. He looked like he was still scared to death from the five-hour mission. And, in fact, he *was* scared to death—but it wasn't from anything out there over Iraq. At the moment, Mongo was scared to death of Christiane Amanpour and all those freaking CNN cameras and lights that were trained on him like a battery of howitzers.

Here she was, dressed up like Ernie Pyle in her war correspondent bush jacket, sticking that goddamn microphone in his face, peering at him with those big brown eyes, asking the kind of question television reporters think they have to ask to prove that *they* comprehend the ghastliness of war.

Her question was: "What did it feel like to kill another man?"

Mongo stared at her blankly. The question had come off sounding like an accusation, which, of course, it was. For the life of him, he couldn't come up with a good answer. But he knew what *not* to say. In a tiny, flea-speck portion of his brain, Nick Mongillo knew that it definitely wouldn't play well back home in millions of living rooms if he stood there and blabbed the truth: *It felt GLORIOUS! The guy flying that MiG was trying to kill me. But I smoked the fucker first. . . .*

He didn't say it. Mongo just shrugged and tried to look anguished about having performed such an execrable act of aerial homicide. He mumbled something about just doing his duty . . . war was hell, you know . . . they were all in it together . . . he hoped it would be over soon . . .

And other such balderdash.

Later the Navy would complain that they "lost the media war." This was because their heroes in Desert Storm, they claimed, didn't receive the same treatment by the media that had been given the Air Force. But that was nothing new; it had always been so. The Air Force always managed to outplay the Navy in the public relations department, somehow coaching their heroes to deliver the apple-pie, Boy Scoutish, Rotary Club answers to inane questions. For whatever reasons, Navy pilots just didn't know how to talk to reporters like Christiane Amanpour. They never seemed to have the right answers to questions like, "What did it feel like to kill another man?"

It felt GLORIOUS . . .

★

The reason it felt glorious was because the war had become very personal for the fighter pilots aboard the U.S.S. *Saratoga*. During the previous night, on the first strike of Desert Storm, one of them had become the first American casualty.

No one knew—officially—what happened to Scott Speicher. He had been number four in a flight of FA-18 Hornets thundering through the darkness toward the target. On the way to the target, something happened. Speicher disappeared.

So the next day, there was Mongo, a nugget on his first squadron tour, on his way to bomb the enemy. He was busy—almost too busy—to be scared. Almost.

"It was like juggling crystal," Mongillo remembered. "They kept throwing new pieces to juggle. You were scared that you were going to drop one." It was hard to keep up with all the frenetic activity around him. He had to keep sight of the other three fighters in the flight. He had to keep track of where they were going, how much farther they had to go to the target, had to interpret data from the airplane's mission computer, had to listen to all the hysterical radio calls flooding the tactical frequency.

That was the hardest part: listening to the nonstop hysterical jabbering on the radio. The frequency was a cacophony of madness. Everyone was yelling. No one was transmitting in a normal voice. You could *smell* the adrenaline pumping through each cockpit.

The airborne strike controller in the Air Force E-3 AWACS (Airborne Warning and Control System) jet was trying to call out information to the strike fighters:

"Bogeys twelve o'clock, forty!"

"Where? Where? Say again!"

"Manny, one-eight-zero, thirty-five."

"Quicksand Four hundred," the controller said, using the lead strike fighters' call sign, "bogeys are at Manny, two-zero-zero, thirty . . ."

"Manny?" Mongo tried to remember what the hell Manny was. It was a spot on the ground, an airfield or something up north, that they decided to use as a reference point. The technique was called "Bullseye Control," referencing everything around a geographical point, or "bullseye." All unidentified aircraft would be called out in relation to the point called "Manny." If something was south of Manny at thirty miles, you were supposed to give the bearing and distance: "Manny, one-eight-zero, thirty." Trying to orient everything around "Manny" was a mental gymnastic that was getting very difficult.

The chatter was incessant, overwhelming. None of it was making any sense to Mongo. He was Dash Two—the number two position in the four-plane flight—stuck out there on the left flank of the formation. They had only forty miles to go to the target.

Four more minutes. Mongo stopped trying to make sense of the radio chatter. It was time to think about bombing.

A "bogey" was an unidentified airplane. By the stringent ROE (rules of engagement) applied by the allied coalition command to the Navy strike fighters in Desert Storm, you couldn't take a shot at a bogey until he had been labeled a "bandit," which meant he had been positively identified by an airborne electronics ship, either a Navy E-2 Hawkeye or an Air Force E-3 AWACS, as a bad guy. The only other way you could legally shoot was after a VID (visual identification), which meant you had to get close enough to *see* that the bogey was, indeed, a bandit. Of course, the bandit might already have reached the same conclusion about you. The confrontation then became an aerial quick draw.

The restriction made sense, considering the skies over Iraq were now more congested than the New York air traffic control area. They were crammed with coalition warplanes, all hell-bent on shooting something—anything—as long as it might be an enemy.

The problem was, the Iraqi fighter pilots suffered no such restrictions. They could point their missiles in almost any direction and be sure they were aimed at a coalition warplane.

Which explained, at least in the Hornet pilots' minds, what happened to Scott Speicher the night before. Inbound to their target, Speicher's flight leader had reported obtaining a radar lock on a bogey. The bogey was coming head-on. On the Hornet's air-to-air radar, the bogey showed up electronically as a supersonic MiG-25.

That wasn't good enough to mark the stranger as hostile. According to the ROE, they had to obtain a confirmation from the AWACS. Or they had to make a visual identification, which was not possible in the pitch-blackness over the desert.

The bogey, therefore, was not a bandit. Not legally. No one took a shot. Within seconds, the bogey, whoever he was, passed behind the flight of Hornets and disappeared.

Minutes later, the Hornets arrived over their target. But now there were only three in the formation. Scott Speicher, who had been number four, was missing. He was never seen again.

The next day the coalition command issued the report that Speicher has "probably" been downed by a Russian-built SAM-6 surface-to-air missile.

The pilots knew better. They knew in their guts what really happened: The bogey was a real-life bandit—an Iraqi MiG-25—who performed what was called a "stern conversion." He had executed a well-timed turn to fall directly behind the flight of Hornets. He locked on to the number four Hornet and fired an AA-6 air-to-air missile.

And took out Scott Speicher.

★

All this was on Mongo's mind now. The flight of Hornets was inside the Iraqi border. Thirty miles to the target. Mongo's head was moving like it was on a swivel—left, right, up, down, sweeping the sky, the desert, the horizon. There were nasty things out there, things that would kill them: SAMs, antiaircraft, enemy fighters, *friendly* fighters.

They were going like hell now, nearly supersonic. Mongo had to keep "tapping" his afterburner—jamming the throttles past the full power detent—to stay up with the formation. In combat, speed was your best friend. Speed was life. The more, the better.

The babble on the radio was getting worse. It sounded like feeding time at the monkey zoo.

And then through the clutter of radio transmissions came a call from strike control. It cut through the babble like a knife:

"Quicksand Four hundred, *two bandits* on your nose at fifteen."

A spike of adrenaline surged through Mongo. The controller had said *bandits*. Not bogeys. *Bandits*.

Or had he? Mongo felt a stab of uncertainty. In the radio garble, could he have heard wrong?

Mongo forced himself to switch his attention inside the cockpit—something he *hated* doing at this critical moment—just for a second. He switched his mission computer to air-to-air mode.

Two sweeps later, there on his radar display, he could see one of the bandits. The radar was electronically identifying the target as a MiG-21 Fishbed fighter. The MiG was at supersonic speed, two thousand feet below.

It was coming directly at him, twelve miles away.

The bandit was well inside the range of the Hornet's Sparrow antiaircraft missiles. No one in the flight was shooting. Why the hell not? Had he heard wrong? Hadn't the strike controller said *bandits?* Or did he say something else?

Mongo selected a radar-guided Sparrow missile on his arming display. His finger went to the trigger on his control stick.

For a millisecond, he wrestled with his conflicting thoughts: *Maybe he'd heard what he wanted to hear. Maybe it wasn't a MiG. . . .*

If it *was* a MiG, the Iraqi pilot would be taking *his* shot. *Just like the MiG did last night on Speicher.*

Mongo squeezed the trigger.

Whoom! The five-hundred-pound Sparrow missile left its rail like a runaway freight train. Mongo watched the missile accelerate. It was flying in an arc toward—*there it was*—a speck, growing larger . . . the MiG!

They were closing fast. Mongo got one good glimpse of the fast-moving Soviet-built fighter—just in time to see it erupt in a bright flash. The Sparrow had hit its target.

Mongo rolled up on his right wing. He could see it clearly—the tan, desert-colored paint scheme, the insignia of the Iraqi Air Force. The MiG was a mess, crumpled in the middle, burning fiercely, trailing thick smoke, descending like a shotgunned pigeon.

"Splash One!" Mongo called on the radio.

"Splash Two!" called someone else.

Two? Mongo had forgotten for a moment: The controller called out *two* bandits. Someone had just taken out the second one. Over on the opposite side of the formation, the second MiG was trailing fire and smoke, going down like a gutshot crow. Lieutenant Commander Mark Fox, who was Dash Four out on the right flank of the formation, had reached the same conclusion as Mongo: *Shoot.* Shoot the bastard before he shoots us.

Two MiGs, two kills. No one saw parachutes from either of the stricken MiGs. That meant a couple of Iraqi fighter pilots that day were keeping an appointment with Allah. And no one in the flight of Hornets was feeling any particular remorse about it. It was an outcome that suited the squadron mates of Scott Speicher just fine.

How did it feel?

It felt GLORIOUS . . .

★

Three minutes. That's how long it took, from the initial bandits call of the strike controller until the missiles dispatched the MiGs. Three minutes of air-to-air action.

And less than two minutes after that came the air-to-ground action. The Hornets hit their *real* target—an airfield in western Iraq. Each of the FA-18s rolled in on the complex of buildings and hangars. Their Mark 84 two-thousand-pound bombs ripped through the roofs of the complex like an ax through an orange crate. When they pulled off the target and headed toward the *Saratoga* in the Red Sea, they could look back and see the smoke from the ruined Iraqi airfield billowing into the desert sky.

Their success in obliterating the airfield, however, was quickly eclipsed by the greater event. The *big* news—as reported by Ms. Amanpour and her CNN crew—was the air-to-air, high noon shootout with the MiGs.

As it turned out, the two MiGs they downed that day were the *only* air-to-air kills achieved by Navy fighters in the Gulf War. Air Force pilots accounted for several more. But after the first week or so of war, MiG hunting became a fruitless activity. There were no MiGs, at least none in the sky. The pilots of the Iraqi Air Force displayed a keen interest in self-preservation by taking off and hauling ass out of the country.

Thus did Mark Fox and Nick Mongillo become instant cult heroes around the ready rooms of the Navy. The MiG killers! Each was decorated with a Silver Star. Mark Fox was ultimately promoted and given command of his own squadron.

As for Mongo, the nugget fighter pilot, the Navy had something equally appropriate. He would return whence he came. He would be assigned as an instructor back in the strike fighter training squadron—the place where fighter pilots were made.

CHAPTER ONE

ROAD

First Lieutenant Ilya "Road" Ammons, U.S. Marine Corps, returned the gate sentry's salute. He drove the old Porsche on through the main gate of the Cecil Field Master Jet Base, down the long, straight Avenue "D," between the stands of Florida pines toward the base complex and the great drably painted jet hangars. On the left he passed the row of retired Navy warplanes, parked on display like artifacts from another era.

Halfway down the long avenue, Road Ammons heard them. Even with the windows up in the Porsche, he heard the sound rising in pitch like an approaching tornado. Ammons looked up and—*there they were*! Four of them, FA-18 Hornet fighters, tucked together in a tight right echelon formation, screeching over the runway at six hundred feet. They were doing, Ammons guessed, something over four hundred knots.

Ammons pulled over and stopped. He watched the lead Hornet in the formation break abruptly to the left in a hard turn. Vapor from the moist morning air spewed from each wing. At three-second intervals each of the fighters banked hard to the left and followed the leader into the landing pattern. As they passed low over where

Ammons sat in his parked car, each jet made a howling, air-ripping noise like an enraged beast.

Sitting there by the roadside, ears ringing from the thunder of the passing fighters, Ammons felt a glow of satisfaction. A grin spread over his round face. *Well, Grandpa, I made it. I'm gonna be a fighter pilot!*

★

Whenever he wanted, Road Ammons could close his eyes and freeze with perfect clarity the instant back in time when he *knew* that someday he would be here. It was an image he carried around in his head, like a secret talisman.

He had been nine years old. His grandfather had taken him to visit the Marine Corps air station at Beaufort, South Carolina. The boy was introduced to a man named Frank Peterson, who was a major in the Marine Corps, a fighter pilot, a decorated hero from the Vietnam War.

Peterson was black, like Road and his grandfather. The boy stared at the officer. He had never seen so handsome a human being, black or white. Major Peterson's perfectly tailored uniform had creases like razors down each breast. Six rows of campaign ribbons covered the left side of his chest. His close-cropped hair carried flecks of gray, like ocean foam, on each temple. He looked like he had been cast for his role by Hollywood. But Frank Peterson was no actor. He was the real thing.

The officer took the nine-year-old out to the flight line. Rows of F-4 Phantom jets, the hottest warplanes in the world at the time, were poised like killer angels on the tarmac, sleek noses aimed at an invisible enemy.

Emblazoned on one of the fuselages, just beneath the canopy rail, was the pilot's name: MAJOR FRANK PETERSON.

They climbed the access ladder, and the major hoisted the boy inside the cockpit of the Phantom fighter. It was a world of magic: consoles loaded with luminous dials, an instrument panel that displayed everything about the jet's path of flight, throttles that commanded the two mighty engines, and a control stick bristling with buttons, switches, and a trigger for the Phantom's nose-mounted cannons. The kid breathed the sweet intoxicating cockpit smells, a redolent mix of oil, gunmetal, leather, jet fuel, parachute cloth, canvas, sweat.

The kid's eye caught something loose in the cockpit. Lying on the right console of the cockpit was the pilot's flight vest. It was an SV-2 harness containing survival gear—rations, flares, flashlights, emergency radio—all the gear a downed combat flyer would need to stay alive.

And then he saw it . . . something dark and shimmering and beautiful. Buckled to the survival vest was the most impressive objet d'art that any kid had ever gazed upon. He was staring at Frank Peterson's personal sidearm—a holstered, nickel-plated, pearl-handled .45 pistol.

Holeeeee cow! The boy stared, transfixed. At that instant, there in the oil-leather-gunmetal-sweat-smelling cockpit of Frank Peterson's jet fighter, he glimpsed his destiny: *Someday . . . I'm gonna grow up and be a Marine fighter pilot . . . just like Frank Peterson . . . and in my cockpit I'm gonna have a pearl-handled pistol . . . JUST LIKE THAT ONE.*

The image never left him. And now he was almost there. Road Ammons *was* an officer in the Marine Corps. And here he was at Cecil Field, about to fly the hottest damned fighter in the world.

All he needed now was the pearl-handled .45.

★

Teeth. That's what you noticed when you first met Road Ammons. Road had a grin like a Yamaha keyboard. In a room full of flight suits and short haircuts, you'd look for some distinguishing feature, and it would jump out at you like a beacon. There would be good ol' Road Ammons, grinning that big toothsome grin that told you, shucks, man, I'm nothin' special, just another Marine like all the others, just here to do a job.

Road was twenty-six years old. He had the burly structure of a running back, which he had been for four years at Tennessee State University, where he earned a degree in computer science. Briefly, but only briefly, he had deliberated over an offer to play professional football. Instead, he went into the Marine Corps. And he married his college sweetheart.

With the possible exception of professional sports, the military was the most equal of all equal opportunity employers. The volatile subjects of race and discrimination and ethnicity, at least around the ready rooms of naval aviation, had dissolved into such nonissues that the color of one's skin was scarcely noticed. As a burning issue, race relations had been replaced by the hot-button subjects of the nineties—gender integration and homosexual rights.

But still, you didn't see many black faces in fighter cockpits. No one could say exactly why. It had mostly to do with the fact that, still, an appallingly small percentage of black kids were graduating from universities, and an infinitesimally smaller percentage of those were applying for military flight training.

So there was good ol' Road Ammons, the only black face in sight. Road was so congenial, so noncontroversial, so middle-of-the-road, that he was practically imperceptible. Colorless. It got to be a joke among the instructors back in flight training. It was enough to make them wish that Road would come out with *something*, anything outrageous, some in-your-face epithet to identify himself as one pissed-off black dude who wasn't taking any shit from the system. People would *try* to engage Road in the controversies of the day: affirmative action, Clarence Thomas, Rodney King, O. J. Simpson.

Not Road. He wouldn't take the bait. He'd just flash that Yamaha grin and go about his business. It was almost as if someone had briefed Road to keep his head down and stay focused.

In fact, someone had.

★

It would have been a very long shot for *any* black kid from a town like Greenwood, in the delta flatlands of Mississippi, to grow up to be a military officer and fighter pilot. About as remote as flying off into space. It would have required an inordinate amount of luck.

Road Ammons had something better than luck. He had mentors and role models. Chief among the mentors was his grandfather, the one who had taken him to meet Frank Peterson.

Grandpa Ammons knew something about being a fighter pilot. During World War II, he had been one of the famed Tuskegee Airmen and had flown P-51 Mustangs in combat over Europe. And he remained active in the Tuskegee Airmen Association, an organization that fostered aviation training for black kids. Grandpa Ammons saw to it that Road spent every summer after his thirteenth birthday at a camp run by the Tuskegee Airmen. Road learned to fly, and by his seventeenth birthday he had earned his private pilot's license.

Another role model, since that day when Road was nine years old, was Major Frank Peterson, who became Colonel Frank Peterson, and who continued to ascend to the rank of lieutenant general and to the status of "Silver Eagle," the senior aviator in the Marine Corps. Frank Peterson, with the pearl-handled .45, represented *everything* Road Ammons wanted to be.

Road had another connection. He had a godfather named Charles Bolden, whose own father had been a Tuskegee Airman and had flown with the senior Ammons in the war. And now Charles Bolden, who held the rank of colonel in the Marine Corps, had just come down from space. Literally. After making five shuttle flights as an astronaut, Bolden had resumed his military career and had just been selected for promotion to brigadier general. And he maintained a keen interest in the career of his godson.

So there *was* more behind the toothy grin and the congenial manner. It took a while to figure it out. You had to know Road Ammons before you understood that behind that keyboard grin and colorlessness and the aw-shucks-I'm-just-doin'-the-best-I-can manner was an ambition as huge as outer space.

CHAPTER TWO

THE FINE MESH

There was a sameness to naval air stations. If you could close your eyes and be transplanted from one air station to another, it would be difficult when you opened your eyes to say where you were. They all had the same enormous slab-sided hangars with arching roofs, painted either standard Navy gray or an indefinable hue the sailors called puppy piss yellow. The hangars were half a block long. Inside the structures, along each two-story wall, were the resident squadron's working spaces—maintenance shops on the bottom deck (floor, for the unnautical) and administrative offices on the upper deck (second floor). From the upper deck you could look down from an open passageway (hall) onto the spacious hangar deck and the maintenance crews working on the jets.

VFA-106 occupied such a hangar at the southeast corner of the Cecil Field Master Jet Base, five miles west of Jacksonville, Florida. "Master Jet Base" was a suffix applied to Cecil back in the Cold War days to distinguish it from all the lesser Navy jet bases around the southeastern United States. It meant that Cecil Field was the center of a galaxy of outlying bases, target complexes, and operating areas. Cecil had four intersecting runways, one an incredible thirteen thousand feet long, with arresting gear and all the accoutrements for tailhook-equipped jets. It was also the shore-based home to half the carrier air wings that deployed from the East Coast.

The designation "Master Jet Base" used to have a certain cachet, but it didn't mean much anymore. In the Incredible Shrinking Navy, Cecil Field was the *only* jet base, Master or otherwise, in that part of the world. And even that was about to change. The word had just come down that Cecil was on the "hit list" of the Pentagon's base closure committee.

The Hornet training squadron's official label was Fleet Replacement Squadron, or FRS. But nobody called it that. In the perverse way that the Navy renames its institutions, then continues to call them by the old name, almost everyone still called the FRS the "RAG." RAG stood for the now-obsolete Replacement Air Group. Never mind that the signs on the buildings, the letterhead stationery, the covers on the manuals all said FRS. If you wanted to get there, you asked anyone in uniform how to find the RAG.

In fact, there had been no such thing as an Air Group, let alone a Replacement Air Group, and certainly not an Air Group Commander, for well over twenty years. Those were ancient acronyms. But in the Navy, ancient acronyms carried almost as much sentimental weight as ancient airplanes and warships. So the skipper of a modern Carrier Air Wing, which in olden times was called an Air Group, was still universally known as the CAG (commander, Air Group).

The Navy had three Hornet RAGs. Two were in California, one at Naval Air Station (NAS) Lemoore, stuck out in the cotton-and-soybean farming boondocks of the San Joaquin valley. The other was at the Marine Corps Air Station El Toro, which was now nearly surrounded by the sprawl of Los Angeles and already on the base closure hit list.

The "VFA" in VFA-106 was another example of Navy shorthand. It stood for Strike Fighter Squadron. All Navy squadron designations began with "V." The "FA" stood for fighter/attack, the official prefix for all units and airplanes in the strike fighter community.

Which was one more quaint term in naval aviation: "Community" referred to the squadrons and units associated with any particular type of Navy airplane. The F-14 Tomcat people had their own community. So did the A-6 Intruders, the S-3 submarine hunters, and the FA-18 Hornet units. Each community included at least one RAG—a training squadron—that produced replacement pilots for the fleet squadrons. By its very nature, the RAG was the cultural and spiritual matrix for its own community.

And so it was with the FA-18 Hornet community. VFA-106 was the only FA-18 RAG on the East Coast, and it was there they trained fighter pilots for all the Atlantic Fleet FA-18 Hornet squadrons.

★

The McDonnell Douglas FA-18 Hornet was the newest, hottest fighter in the world. The Hornet was designed to perform *both* the classic missions of tactical aviation: air-to-air (fighter against fighter) and air-to-ground (strike).

Historically, the Navy had a dedicated type of aircraft assigned to each mission. It had the big Grumman-built F-14 Tomcat fighter, which had reigned for twenty years as the Navy's principal air superiority weapon. The Tomcat was an exotic jet. It had a variable-sweep wing that extended straight out for takeoff and landing and slow speed maneuvering, then folded back into a sleek delta shape for supersonic flight. The Tomcat had always been the weapon of choice of *real* fighter pilots, like those portrayed in the movie *Top Gun*.

The Tomcat was still considered a hot fighter—one of the few in the world that could rip along at more than twice the speed of sound. But it was getting long in the tooth, its 1970s technology outclassed by the hot new stuff in the modern fighters. And although the Navy was still sending new pilots through the F-14 RAG, the end was in sight. The Tomcat's day had come and gone.

Likewise with the venerable A-6 Intruder, also built by Grumman. For thirty years the Navy's all-weather attack mission had been performed by the homely A-6, which when loaded down with bombs and stores looked like a walrus with wings. Now the tough old A-6s were being retired, replaced by FA-18 Hornets.

The Navy had bet its tactical future on a new concept—the strike fighter. It was a matter of economics. Gone was the day when you could afford a specialized vehicle for every mission. A modern fighter like the FA-18 cost over $30 million per copy. With its state-of-the-art mission computer technology, the Hornet possessed the capability for both air-to-air *and* the air-to-ground mission. Built into the Hornet was a quick-change upgradeability feature—an aerospace version of the plug-and-play feature of a desktop computer. The idea was, as new technology evolved, so would the Hornet.

The Hornet's defining moment came on January 18, 1991. That was the day Nick Mongillo flew his first combat sortie—to bomb an Iraqi airfield. En route, Mongillo and his squadron mate, Mark Fox, took on two MiG-21 Fishbed fighters—while carrying *eight thousand pounds of bombs* aboard each of their jets. In previous wars, a strike aircraft pilot under threat from enemy fighters would jettison his bomb load, yell for fighter cover, and dive for the deck.

No more. With their bombs *still on board*, Mongillo and Fox engaged the MiGs—and shot them down. Then they continued to their assigned target—an Iraqi air base—which they duly flattened.

The strike fighter concept had been validated. The FA-18 had proven that it could fight its own way to an objective, obliterate the target, and fight its way out. The Hornet was the fighter of the future.

★

Road Ammons and the other members of Strike Fighter Class 2-95 (so named for the month they commenced training) spent their first morning of instruction sizing each other up. Like Ammons, most were nuggets. Only a few weeks ago they had completed initial flight training and pinned on their wings of gold. Each had graduated in the top of his flight training class, which had earned him the most elite assignment in naval aviation: strike fighter training.

They were sizing each other up not just out of friendly curiosity. It was a reflexive activity. During their military careers they had become so accustomed to competing with their peers for *everything*—grades, class ranking, honors, assignments—it didn't matter now that the competition was supposed to be over. Each of them, by definition, was already a winner. They had all beaten out the other nuggets and gained entrance to the Valhalla of naval aviation.

But here they were, assessing the competition. It was the same thing they had done since the first day they competed for a Navy scholarship, and it had been that way ever since. You sized up the other guy, then you figured out how you were going to wax his ass. That was just the way it had always been in naval aviation. You had to beat somebody out for every damned thing you wanted.

On this, the first day of strike fighter training, they were wearing their Navy or Marine Corps khaki uniforms, shiny gold wings pinned over the left breast pocket. After today, like all the other students, instructors, and staff officers at the training squadron, they would wear the ubiquitous gray-green Navy flight suits. The only markings would be name tags, the bright orange Gladiators patch (official emblem of the training squadron, VFA-106), and their insignia of rank on each shoulder.

Class 2-95 was a cross section of the "new" military: Five class members were Navy, three Marine Corps. Six were men, two were women. Road Ammons was the only African-American.

Of the Navy bunch, the least talky was a smiling, bland-faced young man named Chip Van Doren. Both women students were also Navy: Lieutenant Angie Morales, a diminutive 105-pounder, and Lieutenant Sally Hopkins, a Naval Academy graduate who had already completed a tour of duty flying jets in a utility squadron in the Far East.

Two redheaded Navy lieutenants had everyone doing a double-take. They looked nearly identical. In fact, when you studied them up close, they *were* identical: the McCormack twins, Russ and Rick, who had won their wings at the same time and received orders to the same class here at strike fighter training.

Of the three Marines, Ilya "Road" Ammons and David "Burner" Bunsen were both nuggets and Marine first lieutenants. The most atypical of the class was Marine Captain J. J. Quinn, ex-helicopter pilot and the graybeard of the bunch. At age thirty-five, Quinn had nearly a decade on his classmates.

★

They kidded each other about being Navy squids or Marine jar-heads. Someone joked about bristle-headed Marine haircuts, and the Marines retorted about long-haired Navy sloppiness.

But mostly the talk was about Hornets:

"The next two carriers will be deploying to the Adriatic, to overfly Bosnia . . ."

". . . new FA-18 squadrons will replace the A-6s . . ."

"The Hornet will outturn a Tomcat at any speed above . . ."

"The A-4 has a better roll rate than an FA-18—"

Someone called out, *"Attention on deck!"*

The chatter ended abruptly. All in one motion, the class snapped to attention. Into the room strode a youthful-looking, trimly built officer in khakis with eagles on his collar.

"Take your seats, please," said Captain Matt Moffit, the com-manding officer of the RAG. The captain was a pleasant man who smiled a lot. He told them they would enjoy their training here. He wanted them to know that they were the *chosen*, the pick of the Navy's litter, so to speak, which was why they were here in this room. "You are the best of the best," Moffit assured them.

Then he reminded them that the nation's taxpayers had invested a great deal of faith in them, not to mention money. The fleet needed them. He was counting on them to perform at their very best.

And so on.

Captain Moffit wished them luck and left the room. Again the class rose as one to its feet. The formalities were finished. It was time to go to work.

★

The flight suits and short haircuts worn by both men and women aviators had a democratizing effect in the ready room. The same flying attire was worn by junior and senior, male and female, from the commanding officer to the newest nugget, producing a oneness of appearance that transcended rank and gender. The only observ-able distinctions were the tiny emblems of rank sewn on the shoul-ders of the flight suits.

Another democratizing tradition was the use of call signs—the fra-ternal nicknames assigned to all fighter and attack pilots. They were used in the air as radio identification. On the ground, they were used in lieu of name and rank. When addressing a senior officer by his proper name, particularly a lieutenant commander or above, you were expected to say "sir" or "mister" or prefix his name with his rank. Or you could simply address him by his call sign. No other niceties were required.

Call signs were acquired early in an aviator's career, usually when he or she did something noteworthy. Or noteworthily stupid. If a pilot had an aerial incident—say, a landing gear problem—he might thereafter be called "Wheels." Or if he tried to strafe the wrong target, his call sign would forever be "Sniper."

Sometimes a pilot's call sign was simply a play on his real name. "Roller" Rink. "Slab" Bacon. "Pearly" Gates. "Comet" Haley. Certain raunchy name combinations were often irresistible: "Squirt" Seaman; "Buster" Cherry; "Lingus" Cuny; "Butt" Hoale.

But in PHT (post-Tailhook) times, even the matter of call signs had come under review. After all, ladies *were* present now, and a certain level of decorum had to be maintained. Squadrons had been directed to clean up their pilots' monikers. The "Linguses," "Busters," "Squirts," and other tainted appellations were vanishing from the rosters.

★

Ilya "Road" Ammons was one of the few nuggets who arrived at the RAG with a call sign already attached to his name. "I got it out in Kingsville," he explained. "They hung it on me after my first solo in the T-2 Buckeye."

It had been one of those standard west Texas summer afternoons: distant cumulus towering like nuclear eruptions, heat waves shimmering from the brown-baked landscape, dust devils swirling prairie dirt into the hazy atmosphere. Ammons strapped into the front seat of the Buckeye. He took a moment to twist himself around and look back at the empty rear seat where the instructor usually sat. He grinned. *Look at you, man! You're a jet pilot now.*

The T-2 Buckeye was a basic trainer, the first jet a student naval aviator gets to fly after he completes primary training in the propeller-driven T-34C Mentor. *I'm a jet pilot now*—that was a big deal in the career of a young naval aviator like Ilya Ammons. And his first solo in a jet—that was a *very* big deal.

He blasted off into the haze and headed west, toward the practice area. He went through the maneuvers on the syllabus sheet: steep turns, slow flight, then the basic aerobatics—barrel rolls, loops, Immelmanns.

And that's when it happened. Ammons was just pulling up into an Immelmann—the first half of a loop with a half roll on top, returning to level flight going the opposite direction—when everything went to hell. He heard a *Zzzzztttt* in his earphones, then silence.

The radio was dead. So was the Tacan, his navigation radio. The instruments on his panel all showed red flags, indicating they too were dead as dirt.

The Buckeye was without electrical power.

Ammons looked around. *Shit. This ain't good. You'd better get your butt back home.*

That was a good idea. But which way was home? Without the Tacan, he had no idea where Kingsville Naval Air Station might be. Looking around at the scorched brown landscape, he had no idea where *anything* might be. He didn't even know how much fuel he had left. The fuel gauges were dead too. What to do?

What he did was revert to basic instincts—and to lessons learned back when he was flying Cessnas in college. Down there was a highway—one hell of a big, four-laned artery—which he knew *had* to be Route 77, the major thoroughfare that meandered through south Texas—*and* right past Kingsville.

Down he went. Ammons locked on to the winding concrete strip of Route 77 and flew eastward, right on the deck, following every curve and bend. And sure enough—voilà!—there it was, dead ahead, looming out of the haze like an oasis in the desert—the spectacularly gorgeous sight of Kingsville Naval Air Station.

Back in the ready room, Ammons told the duty officer what had happened. The duty officer, who was an instructor in the training squadron thought it was a great story. "No shit, you followed a road? Your first solo, and you found your way home following a frigging *road?*"

"Yes, sir. A big road. Route 77."

The instructor couldn't wait to blab the story around the squadron. From that day forward Ilya Ammons was known as "Road."

★

These kids are different.

That's what you heard from all the senior officers, especially those over forty, like Captain Moffit. What they meant was, the current crop of students was the product of a much finer screening process than the one they themselves had undergone.

Back in the sixties and seventies, when Vietnam was swallowing aviators like a voracious beast, and while the Cold War still demanded a constant supply of trained warriors to deal with the Red Menace, it hadn't been so difficult to get into Navy flight training. You had to be healthy, of course, with 20/20 vision and no obvious physical deformities. You were supposed to have a couple years of college to get into the Naval Aviation Cadet program, but even that could be circumvented if you came from the enlisted ranks and could pass all the Navy's aptitude tests for flight training.

The idea in those days seemed to be that Navy pilots ought to be smart, but not to the point of geekiness. Advanced education was nice, but it was something that could be acquired later, after you'd learned to fly and proven to the Navy that you were worth keeping. After all, flying a Navy fighter wasn't something that required a degree. It was more important that pilot candidates have good hand-eye skills and understand a little about machinery. If you were a bright kid with good eyes and a fondness for motorcycles, you were a naval aviation recruiter's dream.

Even flawed social backgrounds didn't eliminate cockpit candidates. There was once a time when a local judge would glower down from his bench at a teenage lawbreaker, then give him two options: jail or the military. *Pick a service, kid, it doesn't matter. Sign up and get the hell out of my town.*

So off the miscreant kid would go to boot camp, where he would have to take the battery of basic tests given to every recruit and—Eureka!—he might be found qualified for officer training. Maybe even flight school. To the astonishment of parents, teachers, and the judge, the adolescent terror would by some incredible process metamorphose into a naval aviator as well as—*could it be?*—an officer and a gentleman.

But that was in another time. Along the way the world changed. Down came the Berlin Wall, and with it the Red Menace, and the military became a shrinking community. The flow of candidates to Navy and Air Force flight training slowed to a trickle. And the competition for the few flight training slots intensified to the extent that *only* college graduates would be considered. Eventually only college graduates would be considered who were already in a military program, meaning either ROTC or one of the service academies.

The Fine Mesh got even finer. The screening process tightened so much that only the top-ranking students of any college graduating year were even considered for flight training. By definition, these were the superstars. While still in high school each had competed with the entire nation's crop of college-bound students for the coveted ROTC scholarships or for appointments to Annapolis.

None of these kids had been a teenage delinquent. None had ever stood before a glowering judge. None had ever been arrested, flunked a course, done drugs, wrecked a car, failed a test.

What did it mean? In the "new" Navy, it meant no more walk-ins to flight training. No more deliverees from benevolent magistrates. A coal miner's son like Chuck Yeager could never become a fighter pilot and a national hero. Gone was the old Naval Aviation Cadet program that had produced more than half the Navy's wartime aviators, including an eighteen-year-old named George Bush. Gone forever was the chance for a bright kid with good hands to escape the mean streets and fly a Navy jet.

These new kids, the Fine Meshers, were undeniably smart. And educated. They graduated from prestigious universities, most majoring in the sciences. Many already held graduate degrees. They were super-achievers, at least to the extent that they had excelled throughout their academic careers. When each won his wings, he had graduated in the top ten percent of the class, which was what earned him the assignment to strike fighter training—the apex of naval aviation.

But how did all that connect to being a fighter pilot? How did a degree in, say, astronautical engineering relate to staying cool during a night catapult launch? Or diving your jet through a wall of flak to bomb an enemy?

These were unexplored questions. No one had yet proven that it was to a fighter pilot's advantage, when he went one-on-one with a MiG at thirty thousand feet, that he happened to be a rocket scientist.

What it meant to the old hands, the senior officers who had come up in the old system, was that *they* wouldn't have made it through the Fine Mesh. "I was a ski bum," said Captain Matt Moffit, whose own naval career was rising like a rocket. "Hell, with my college grades, I wouldn't even get into flight training today. These kids are different."

★

Just how different they were struck Commander Moe Vazquez one day. Vazquez was a forty-something fighter pilot instructor in the RAG. He was nearing the end of his career. His retirement was scheduled for mid-1995.

Moe couldn't believe what he had just heard in the ready room. He stopped Major Bull Durham, the training officer, in the passageway. "You're not gonna believe this. What would you guess a bunch of twenty-four-, twenty-six-year-old fighter pilots would be bull-shitting about in there?"

"Getting laid?" ventured Bull.

"Of course. Something like that. Or fast cars. Or telling lies about how shit-hot they are in an airplane."

"So what are they talking about?"

"Bonds."

"Bonds?"

"Their goddamn investments!" roared Moe. "That kid in there, who is a lieutenant jaygee three years out of college, is reading *The Wall Street Journal* and discussing—get this—*the yield on thirty-year bonds.*"

"Are they listening?"

"They're all doing it. That's what they're talking about—frigging stocks and bonds! Unbelievable! These kids are going to be fighter pilots?"

★

There was no question about it: These kids *were* different. They were not like the nuggets from Moe Vazquez's generation, nor from any previous generation of Navy fighter pilots.

This was the Fine Mesh generation. They were better educated, smarter, distinctly more serious. They talked more about getting rich than getting laid.

That these kids were different, everyone agreed. But no one had yet supplied the answer to the most important question about the super-serious, overeducated Fine Meshers: *Were they better fighter pilots?*

CHAPTER THREE

WOMEN WARRIORS

Lieutenant Angelina Ramona Morales was accustomed to not being taken seriously. With her dark, bobbed hair and tiny stature, she looked like somebody's kid sister. Angie Morales had brown eyes and a pretty, oval-shaped face. Even in the gray-green flight suit, twin bars on each shoulder, clunky black flying boots on her feet, she looked so . . . *kidlike*. How could a baby-faced little girl like her fly a supersonic fighter? How could she be a warrior? She looked like someone's baby-sitter.

Even her manner was diminutive. In the boisterous ready room talking-with-your-hands bull sessions—". . . there I was behind the ship, on this black frigging night, when all of a sudden . . ."— Morales would listen politely. In such bull sessions she never took the lead. She listened with interest, laughed in the right places, and accorded the storyteller what amounted to a polite deference.

Such deference she learned from her mother, who came from the border town of Reynosa, Mexico, and who, as a teenager, had migrated to the hill country of Texas. It was in San Antonio where she met and married Angie's father, a third-generation Mexican-American, who was an Air Force sergeant stationed there.

Angie Morales's parents were enormously proud of what she had accomplished. Her father, who retired as a master sergeant after thirty years' service, could hardly believe it: His tiny little girl, the smart and bashful one, was an officer! And flying those supersonic jet airplanes!

It was her mother who was having trouble. She was a worrier. Though she had become thoroughly Americanized, learning the peculiar customs of her new country, she was still bewildered by her daughter's nontraditional choice of a career. She worried constantly about Angie.

So when Angie Morales finished Navy flight training and received her wings, her mother was there to congratulate her. She seemed extraordinarily cheerful that day, beaming and smiling, patting her daughter on the back. Angie had never seen her mother so happy.

And then she realized why. Angie's mother was overjoyed that she had *finished* Navy flight training, because she thought the whole dangerous business was behind her. Now her daughter could get on with her life, raising a family and being a woman. No more of those dangerous airplanes.

"Uh, Mom, this isn't the end of my flying. It's just the beginning."

"Beginning?" The mother was perplexed. What did she mean, just the beginning? Wasn't it over? There was more?

"This was just the training, Mom. Now that I have my wings, I'll go to the fleet and be a *real* aviator. I'm going to be a fighter pilot."

Oh, dear. The smile vanished. The mother's brow furrowed just like it always did when she thought about her daughter flying those Navy airplanes. Now she *really* had something to worry about.

★

Angie went to the University of Texas on a Navy ROTC scholarship. While she was there she met Roger Yeates, whom she dated for four years. They married six months after they graduated. Both had goals: He was a teacher and aspiring writer. She was a naval officer and aspiring fighter pilot.

She was lucky. Roger was her greatest fan, giving support and encouragement. Best of all, he didn't mind the sometimes subservient role he had to play as the spouse of a Navy pilot. He even had fun playing the role.

"My wife, the fighter pilot," he liked to say, introducing her to friends. He liked to watch the perplexed looks: *Fighter pilot? This half-pint kid who looks like she ought to be selling Girl Scout cookies?* They just *knew* it had to be some kind of joke.

Angie was a math major. She graduated in the top ten percent of her class, something she managed to accomplish wherever she went: the top ten percent. The Fine Mesher percentile. It was that distinction that won for her the top assignment for newly graduated and commissioned Navy officers: assignment to Navy flight training.

Two years later, when she won her wings, there she was again: the top of her class. Which then earned for her the most coveted of flying assignments: FA-18 Hornet strike fighters.

The Fine Mesh. That was the way it worked. You went through it at every phase of training. If you made the top ten percent, you moved on. Then you had to make the next top ten percent. And so on. Of the several thousand who had begun the journey with Angie Morales as newly commissioned officers in the Navy and Marine Corps, that's what it came to: Fewer than a hundred were going to fly Hornets.

Lieutenant Angie Morales was, by definition, a winner. She had made it through the Fine Mesh. But it wasn't over yet. The hardest part was yet to come.

★

Sally Hopkins's call sign was "Shrike."

"I got it at postgraduate school," she explained. "One day I was bitching about things—the Navy or the school or something—and an instructor told me I sounded like some kind of shrieking bird. A shrike. The name stuck, so I guess it fits."

Like other professions whose progeny tend to continue the family tradition, the officer corps included a disproportionate number of military offspring. Sally Hopkins's stepfather had been a Navy enlisted man, and then a warrant officer. She finished high school in a small town in Tennessee, just outside Memphis, where she graduated third in her class and won an appointment to the U.S. Naval Academy.

After commissioning and graduation with a degree in mathematics in 1988, she won an assignment to flight training. She completed advanced training in jets and pinned on her Navy wings at the Meridian, Mississippi Naval Air Station in 1990. Like her male classmates in the jet pipeline, she should have been eligible for an assignment to a seagoing fighter squadron.

But that was before complete gender integration reached the Navy. The ban on women in combat squadrons was still firmly in place.

So Sally went off to a utility squadron based in the Far East. She was flying the A-4 Skyhawk, a Navy attack jet, and that was good. But her job was to fly *support* missions, and that was not good. Utility squadrons were supposed to provide services to fleet squadrons, serving as radar targets and adversary aircraft in mock attacks on ships. Assignment to a utility squadron meant you were, in effect, relegated to the scrub team. You hadn't made the varsity.

Sally looked around for something better. In 1992 she was accepted in the Navy's postgraduate school at Monterey, California, where she earned a master's degree in astronautical engineering. And during the time she was off in grad school, away from the cockpits and ready rooms of the airborne Navy, a phenomenal thing happened. The new secretary of defense, Les Aspin, signed a crucial document on April 28, 1993. "The services shall permit women to compete for assignments in aircraft," the secretary's memorandum said, *"including aircraft engaged in combat missions"* (italics mine).

It was the breakthrough Sally and her female comrades had been waiting for. The wall of discrimination had been breached. It meant they could fly *real* pointy-nosed fighters on *real* missions, not the scrub team roles they'd been assigned before. It meant they could fly off carriers. They could fly combat missions. They could be killers.

Killers?

That was the part that was making people say the stupidest things. Things like: *Women just don't . . . well, you know . . . they get all sort of queasy about . . . I mean, the gentler sex and all that . . . they're just not into blood and guts . . .*

One thing Sally Hopkins could never get over was how people always thought *women* were somehow incapable of killing. She'd heard it enough times, it made her furious.

One of those times was an evening in the Miramar officers' club. It wasn't long after the ban on women in combat had finally been lifted, and Sally had her orders to strike fighter training.

A Navy commander whom she recognized as the CO of the Top Gun school—the polishing school for the Navy's shit-hottest fighter pilots—came up to her at the bar. At first she thought he might be trying to be friendly. But the commander stared at her with eyes like lasers and fired the question that seemed to be roiling the guts of every male fighter pilot in the business: "Lieutenant, do you *really* think you have what it takes to kill another human being?"

The thought occurred to Sally that this would be a wonderful opportunity for her to do something smart—and keep her mouth shut. But that wasn't Sally's style. She looked the commander in the eye and asked, "Do you have a gun?"

★

It was clear that Angie Morales and Sally Hopkins were not destined to be soul mates. They were as different as hawks and geese. Despite their common minority status—they were the *only* two women in strike fighter training—they might as well have come from different planets.

Morales tended to be invisible. She was quiet by nature, slight of stature, and in a room full of hulking, flight-suited aviators she blended into the surroundings like a bird in a forest. Sally Hopkins, by contrast, was a one-woman blitzkrieg. She would barge into a male-filled ready room, full of chutzpah and hubris, and within a minute have every one of the inhabitants grinding his teeth like a mill saw.

In the drab and baggy Navy-issue flight suit and the clunky flying boots, her blond hair pulled back in a helmet-fitting bun, Sally was far from gorgeous. Her plain-featured face was made plainer by the absence of makeup or mascara or lipstick. Cosmetics, in any case, were a no-no with flight gear, especially oxygen masks. Oxygen and any grease-based cosmetics, even lip salve, made an inflammable mixture. Sally knew one *guy* who tried out a trendy new hair gel and, while wearing his oxygen mask during a flight, set his scalp on fire.

Sally was on the short side, about five-five, and had the solid build of a weight lifter, which she was. She was also a jogger, roller-blader, and lover of ballroom dancing.

She had a sometime boyfriend whom she had met back in postgrad school. His name was Bruce, and he was a helo pilot based at North Island in San Diego. Sally and Bruce had a relationship that sputtered on and off. "Bruce, well . . . he and I are different. He's sort of a narrow, unspontaneous kind of guy. Not like me, you know."

★

Women aviators in the Navy were a small group. Because they were so few in number, most knew each other, or knew about each other. As they fanned out to assignments around the world, most stayed in touch. Each had experienced her own share of the Gender Thing—the hostility, discrimination, the exclusion. Each had gone through flight training knowing that no matter how good she was at flying Navy jets, she wouldn't be getting one of the glamour jobs—the assignments to pointy-nosed fighters that flew off carriers. Those slots were reserved for the *guys* in their class.

So when the ban came off in 1993 and women were finally authorized to fly combat airplanes, the Navy reacted with a typical military scattergun approach: *Find women pilots and train them. Get them in fighters now!*

★

Sally Hopkins had two friends from back in flight training with whom she stayed in touch: Kara Hultgreen and Bonnie Detweiler. They were the Terrific Trio. All were early-nineties graduates of Navy flight training, and each, because of the ban, had been assigned to noncombat aviation units. The Terrific Trio stayed in touch, monitored each other's progress, exchanged hopes and aspirations for the future.

Kara Hultgreen, who was nearly six feet tall, tough, and outspoken, had been flying EA-6 Prowlers in Key West. The Prowler was not a glamorous jet. It was an unarmed, electronic warfare version of the A-6 Intruder attack jet. It had four crew members on board and, weighted down with surveillance gear, flew like a turkey.

When the ban was officially lifted, Kara Hultgreen was the first of the Terrific Trio to get orders. She won her dream assignment: F-14 Tomcats in a West Coast squadron. Hultgreen was going to be the Navy's first operational woman fighter pilot.

Bonnie Detweiler was next. She was assigned to an A-6 Intruder squadron on the East Coast and had already started her training by the time Sally arrived at strike fighter school.

The last of the Trio was Sally Hopkins, who was still finishing her postgraduate studies at the Navy's postgraduate school in Monterey, California. She received orders to FA-18 training on the East Coast.

By the end of 1994, when Sally Hopkins reported for strike fighter training, things had changed. The Terrific Trio was no longer a trio. Soon it wouldn't even be a duo.

★

The Gender Thing.

It was the hottest, messiest, most controversial topic in the Navy. Nothing had inflamed passions in the ready rooms and coffee messes and officers'-club bars like this since the torpedoing of the *Lusitania*. No one was neutral on the subject. Depending on which side of the issue you sat, integration of women into combat units was either inevitable and overdue or it was unbelievably cockeyed stupid.

Some of the nastiest resistance women encountered came from their own classmates, the guys with whom they had gone through the Naval Academy and flight training. In a shrinking post–Cold War Navy, these young men saw precious flying billets being reserved for a favored group—at their expense.

Some saw the whole thing as a social experiment being forced onto the military by a liberal government. This view was widely held because the military service, at its core, was deeply conservative both in politics and culture. The military officer corps has always tilted to the starboard side of center. This whole business of women in combat, well, hell, it just wasn't . . . you know, *natural*.

The argument always boiled down to a traditionalist attitude: Women were supposed to be the nurturers, the life-givers, the homemakers. That was the way it had been for several thousand years, and it worked just fine. Leave it to the men to go out and kill, burn, pillage. To let women join the killer team—that just got everybody confused about roles.

Contributing to the debate was a deep-seated feeling that women were not being evaluated on the same scale as men. Male officers were convinced that women were being accorded special concessions in training, that a double standard was being applied that allowed women to get away with mistakes that, in a man's case, would get him disqualified.

For a squadron commanding officer, the Gender Thing was a nightmare. If you flunked a woman for poor performance, you could be accused of discrimination. If you recognized her for superior performance, you took flak for giving special treatment. If you criticized her, it could be construed as harassment.

"I wish we didn't have them," said the commanding officer of a RAG. Then he caught himself and quickly added, "But, of course, we *do* have them. It's the law. Now I wish we had a lot more. I wish we had as many women as men."

To which his listeners said, *"Whaat?"* Did he really mean that?

"Definitely," he said. "Here's why. Because then each one wouldn't be unique, a cause célèbre. We could treat everyone alike—flunk them or pass them on their performance and not their goddamn minority status."

Which sounded good—in theory. The trouble was, most of the male pilots in the Navy believed the problem was more fundamental than just performance and evaluation. Among most was the gut feeling that flying combat jets was something women were inherently *not* qualified to do, no matter how many of them you threw into the equation.

In other words, flying was a man's game. This premise was an extrapolation of the more cherished theory that *war* was a man's game. Gender integration amounted to a double assault on their manhood: First you had women thinking they should join in the manly sport of war, and now they wanted to fly your goddamn airplanes too!

What you heard in the men-only ready room conversations was:

"It's like replacing one of the Washington Redskins with a woman. You can dress her up in the uniform, shoulder pads and helmet and all, and throw her in there. And she might even be able to keep from getting killed. But it doesn't mean she can do the same job as the other players. In the meantime, what have you done to the team?"

"It's the left brain–right brain thing," volunteered a lieutenant commander and instructor in the FA-18 RAG. "Women see things differently than men. They see things in a more abstract way. And there's nothing abstract about air-to-air combat or low-level weapons delivery. The rules out there are hard and fast."

"Women don't have situational awareness," declared another instructor, a Marine captain. "In the three-dimensional arena out there, they'll lose it and get disoriented. Women pilots are like women drivers."

"We're still old-fashioned enough to think we ought to *protect* our women," said a graying Marine colonel. "With a woman flying on your wing in combat, you've gotta worry about her. It's just natural. You're gonna feel a need to keep her from getting shot down. It's gonna take away the combat edge."

Ah, the *combat edge*. There it was. No evidence existed that women were any less qualified than men to *fly* airplanes. But you could still argue that they couldn't fly in *combat* because, well . . . they just weren't *killers*.

That's what it always came back to. Women couldn't perform in combat. Women couldn't kill.

All of this sounded like a replay of the arguments heard back in the seventies when women began integrating into the big city police forces around the country. *Women aren't tough enough . . .*

*women can't kill . . . women won't back you up when the going gets
rough . . .*

After a few years passed, you stopped hearing such talk. Women
did prove themselves to be tough and capable police officers. And
they even proved that they could kill. No problem.

★

All of this Angie Morales and Sally Hopkins and the women of the
Terrific Trio had heard many times. They heard it in every happy
hour bull session they attended. They heard it in muted dialogues
in the ready room. They saw it in anonymous notes on the bulletin
board. They *felt* it in the company of their male peers.

"We're trailblazers," said Sally. "The women who come along
after us will have it easier. They'll be more and more accepted until
the time comes when no one even thinks about it anymore. Women
are here to stay. But for us, it's sometimes very lonely."

Lonely indeed. The loneliness went with the job. Every woman
aviator knew what it was like to walk into a ready room full of guys
in flight suits. The pilots would be drinking coffee, talking about
flying, laughing at somebody's wisecrack, and suddenly—silence.
It was as though someone had hit the mute button. Their space had
been violated. A woman. She was the intruder, the outsider, the
unwanted. A woman in the ready room was as welcome as a cat at a
dog show.

That was the hard part. Some women in the Navy couldn't deal
with it, the loneliness and isolation, and they left the service
as soon as their contract was up. It just wasn't worth it, being a
trailblazer.

Sally couldn't contain her feelings. In her exasperation she
would sometimes remind everyone in the ready room that she could
be making a hell of a lot more money doing something else. After
all, with her credentials in astronautical engineering she could be
working somewhere in the aerospace industry, where at least she'd
feel *welcome*.

"Well, why don't you?" someone would say from across the
ready room. "Do everyone a favor and quit."

"I'd miss you guys too much," she would say. "This is like a home to me."

When Sally got into one of these exchanges in the ready room, her female colleague, Angie Morales, ducked for cover. A gulf was widening between the two women strike fighter students. Angie Morales was making it clear that when it came to being a cat at the dog show, Sally Hopkins was on her own.

Sometimes Sally would come back to her little rented bungalow after a twelve-hour day at the squadron feeling like a zombie, numbed from the strain of the intense concentration. Even more numbing was that cold sense of *aloneness*. The silent hostility of the ready room. It was dispiriting.

After she had peeled off the sweat-soaked flight suit and settled into the hot bath, the thought would sometimes flit through her mind: *Why am I doing this?*

Why? Sometimes she had to think. And then she'd remember: *Because you have a goal. Remember? You're going to the stars.*

Sally Hopkins had aspirations that extended far beyond the range of an FA-18. It was an ambition as huge as the universe. It was a dream she had clutched to her like a talisman since she was a kid in high school.

Sally Hopkins wanted nothing less than to fly off into space. She wanted to be an astronaut.

So far she was on track. In high school she had earned the grades and taken the courses that would gain her an appointment to the Naval Academy. At the academy she'd done the tough courses— not something easy like the political science route—majoring in mathematics and the sciences, graduating in the top of her class.

And that had earned for her the assignment to flight training. And then selection for jets. And then orders to FA-18 training. And along the way, she picked up that most golden credential for astronaut status, the MS in astronautical engineering.

Sally Hopkins was a *real* rocket scientist.

She was right on schedule, qualifying in the most advanced jet in the Navy's inventory. After a squadron tour in FA-18 Hornets, she intended to apply for the Navy's Test Pilot School at Patuxent

River, Maryland. After she had qualified as a test pilot, then she would become a candidate for the astronaut corps. The prize would be won.

Yes, thought Sally Hopkins, soaking in the hot bath after a long day at the squadron, *that* was why she was here. Nobody said it would be easy. Sometimes it was a bitch. But it was worth it.

Still, it was very damned lonely.

CHAPTER FOUR

THE DUPLICATES

Everyone in the squadron went through the same initial experience with the McCormack brothers. You walked into a ready room, and there was this freckled, grinning, redheaded guy in a flight suit making wisecracks and laughing at his own joke. Then your eyes would catch an image of another guy—an *identical* freckled, grinning, redheaded guy, wisecracking and laughing at *his* jokes.

The reaction was always the same: *Whuhhh? Is this some kind of act?* . . . until it sunk in that the two grinning redheads not only looked alike, they were identical. The McCormack twins, Russ and Rick, were as identical as carrots from the same patch. So alike, in fact, that even their mother back in California used to have trouble distinguishing which of her hell-raising kids to wallop for any particular offense.

The McCormacks team-laughed like Heckle and Jeckle, the duplicate magpies in the old movie cartoon. One of the duplicates would crack a joke. The other would cackle at his brother's joke: *Heh-heh-heh-heh-heh.* To which the first would respond: *Haw-haw-haw-haw-haw.* Back and forth, like Heckle and Jeckle: *Heh-heh-heh-heh. Haw-haw-haw-haw. Heh-heh-heh-heh* . . .

It was catching. The whole room would crack up, not so much at the corny jokes but at these two redheaded clowns cackling like magpies.

But it soon became apparent that the sameness went beyond team-cackling. After a while, everyone in the class reported having a similar experience with the McCormacks. You'd be talking to one of them, Rick or Russ, discussing something—an airplane matter, or an instructor, or just telling a joke—and then you'd become aware of the *other* twin, well out of earshot across a huge room, looking at you, *knowing* what you'd just said to his brother.

It was uncanny. The twins were data-linked, as though they communicated through the ether on their own private bandwidth. And as their classmates found out, the data-link reached beyond the classroom. It extended into the sky.

Not even the saltiest sailors around Cecil Field could reach back in their Navy experience and recall such a thing. Many sets of siblings, even twins, had gone through naval aviation, and several had even managed to be at the same station, aboard the same ship, or in the same combat theater together. But never could anyone recall identical twins who not only went through fighter training together, but had done *everything*—boot camp, the Naval Academy, flight training, then strike fighter training—together. Always together. Russ and Rick McCormack were inseparable.

They grew up in a place called Canyon Country, California. Their mother was a nurse and a single parent. It had been tough, making ends meet, working forty-hour weeks, raising a set of replicated hellions like Rick and Russ McCormack. Her method was to apply a mixture of tough love and an Irish faith that if she could just somehow keep them out of jail until adulthood, they'd be all right. She even hoped that at least one of them might follow her into the medical profession. It was her fondest wish: *My son, the doctor!*

It didn't happen. Although they stayed out of jail, neither wanted to be a doctor. Worse, they didn't even want to go to college. In high school, neither McCormack had been a superstar. The twins were into typical California-kid pursuits: sports, girls, beer drinking, cars with pinstripes and Glasspack mufflers.

When they graduated from high school, they announced that they were enlisting in the Navy. Together, of course.

It was the worst possible news to a mother whose hopes were pinned on watching a son take the oath of Hippocrates. The Navy? Not only were her sons bypassing college educations and white-collar professions, they were going to be . . . enlisted men. She figured the ungrateful termites would probably even get tattoos.

While the twins were still in boot camp at San Diego, the Navy learned something about them that had escaped everyone's notice, with the possible exception of their mother: *These were smart kids.* So smart, in fact, that they were selected for the Navy's nuclear energy school, the toughest technical course in the military. The McCormacks graduated from the year-long course at the top of the class. Russ was number one. Rick was number two.

It was about then that the notion of being something besides a high-tech enlisted man entered the realm of possibility. There was even a chance, maybe, for them to become *officers*. And way out there at the far rim of possibility was a chance, an unimaginable long shot, that they might be considered for an appointment to the Naval Academy.

"Forget it," said the counseling officer at the technical school. He was a Navy lieutenant—and a Naval Academy graduate himself—whose job was to screen applicants for officer training. He took his screening job very seriously. "Your SAT scores from high school are to low. It's obvious that you couldn't do the work at the academy. You'd never make it." As far as the lieutenant was concerned, that was it. How presumptuous it was of the McCormack brothers to even *hope* for such an appointment.

The twins looked at each other. Their data-linked brains exchanged a wordless message: *Ignore this asshole. We'll do it anyway.*

They ignored the lieutenant. They went ahead with the application process. They took all the tests, underwent the physical exams, obtained the required references and endorsements.

When the selection list came out, it sent a seismic shock through the counseling office. Both McCormacks were on the selection list.

The Heckle and Jeckle twins each received orders to the Navy's academy prep school, where potential academy appointees are groomed and prepared for the arduous four-year curriculum.

The prep school turned out to be a screening ordeal in itself. About half the candidates were civilian, and about half, like the McCormacks, were military enlisted personnel. Of the 360 students who began the course, only 160 finished. Most of the finishers were the enlisted students from the Navy and Marine Corps. Among the finishers were Rick and Russ McCormack, still inseparable.

Four years later, each McCormack graduated—with honors—from the U.S. Naval Academy. They were ten numbers apart in class ranking. Each received the same degree—a bachelor of science in oceanography. Each became a commissioned officer in the U.S. Navy.

With their degrees and commissions in hand, new gold stripes glistening on their sleeves, the brothers had one unfulfilled fantasy: It would be *wonderful* to go back and visit the technical school. They would walk into the office of the counselor—the asshole who told them they would never make it. They'd be wearing their new officer's uniforms, gold stripes glistening like neon on the sleeves. *Hello, Lieutenant. We're the McCormack brothers, the ones you said would never make it. Remember us?*

★

Somewhere along the way, the McCormack brothers had changed. They had matured from roustabout teenage kids to collegiate scholars. In less than five years they had been transformed from civilians to sailors to naval officers. With their success came a new confidence. They could be anything they wanted.

What they wanted now was to be fighter pilots. They wanted to do it, of course, the same way they had done everything in their lives: together.

They applied for flight training. After half a year's wait, each received orders to the U.S. Navy's Air Training Command in Pensacola, Florida. When they commenced training, they were one class apart. A year and a half later, when they finished the last phase of jet training and received their wings of gold at the Naval

Air Station at Kingsville, Texas, the twins were together again. They graduated on the same day, same class.

The identicalness went even further. In total scores, which amounted to several hundred cumulative grade points over the year-and-a-half course, the McCormacks were, incredibly, only *three points* apart.

Their mother was there to pin on their new wings. By now she had gotten over the fact that they would never go to medical school. She had an immense pride in their accomplishments. After all, they *had* gone to college. They became naval officers. Now they were naval aviators.

And to the best of her knowledge, neither had gotten a tattoo.

★

It took another redhead to separate the McCormack twins. Her name was Peggy, and she entered Rick McCormack's life while the twins were still in advanced jet training out in Kingsville. She had auburn hair, flashing green eyes, and in a short skirt she could stop traffic. After a fast-paced courtship, in between training stints and Rick's graduation from flight training, Rick and Peggy were married.

Which made the McCormack duo a trio, of course, because twin brother Russ was never far away. It made them, actually, a foursome, because Peggy brought with her a son by her previous marriage. And then after a year they became a fivesome, when Rick and Peggy produced a son of their own. And the McCormack kids had the same problem everyone else did with the Heckle and Jeckle pair: Who was the redheaded guy who cackled like a magpie? Their father or their uncle?

Of course, such asymmetry between the McCormacks—one married and with a family, the other single—couldn't last. And it didn't, at least not long after the McCormacks checked in to Cecil Field. That was when Russ, the bachelor, was smitten by a petite, smashing brunette whom he met one night at a social at the officers' club. She was a Jacksonville girl named Tracy. They were married in December 1994, just as Russ was beginning strike fighter training.

Rick and his little family lived in a house in a shady suburb in

Orange Park. And Russ and Tracy, of course, moved into a nearly identical house just around the corner.

The twins were back in symmetry.

★

Five members of Class 2-95 were married—Road Ammons, Angie Morales, J. J. Quinn, and both McCormacks—and all lived with their spouses in Jacksonville. They knew they would be there for at least six months—the minimum time it would take to complete the strike fighter curriculum—and possibly as much as a year, depending on uncontrollable matters like health, weather, and airplane availability. And, of course, how they performed in training.

Road was the only one who elected to live in base housing, right there at Cecil Field. He and Lowanda, his wife, reasoned that they would only be in Jacksonville for the six or so months it took him to complete strike fighter training. Like all the Marine families, they expected orders up to Beaufort, South Carolina, where the Marine Corps stationed its FA-18 squadrons. They would skip the hassle of moving in and out of a short-term rental in a Jacksonville suburb.

Most students' wives didn't like the cloistered military residential communities, with the noise of the jets and the constant presence of uniforms and gray-painted vehicles. Lowanda Ammons didn't mind. She and Ilya (she was almost the only one who ever called Road by his real name) lived in one of the tract homes in the wooded neighborhood set aside for junior officers. What she liked about living on the base was the facilities: fitness center, golf course, base exchange, officers' club, and a day-care center for their year-and-a-half-old daughter, Jasmine.

Lowanda already had a degree in communications from Tennessee State. Now she was going back to college to earn a degree in nursing. "Why not?" she told everyone. "It's a transportable skill. Anywhere the Marine Corps sends us, I'll be able to find a job as a nurse."

Captain J. J. Quinn lived in town, in a leased house in Orange Park. J.J., too, was expecting to be assigned up to the Marine base at Beaufort. But he and Dorothy, a tall, gracious woman, had three school-age children. It was important, they figured, to give the kids as much a semblance of a permanent home as they could. They would keep them in school there in Jacksonville until the end of the spring semester, which was when J.J. expected—fate, God, and the Marine Corps willing—to be done with strike fighter training.

Angie Morales lived with her husband, Roger, in a neat three-bedroom home in a suburb of Jacksonville called Mandarin, near the St. Johns River. The neighborhood suited them, with quiet streets and good paths for running and bicycling. Roger was a teacher and a psychologist. While Angie spent her days in strike fighter training, he was taking a sabbatical from teaching. He wanted to learn the craft of screenwriting. "Someday you'll hear about him," Angie told everyone.

★

They were a demonstrative bunch, the nuggets of 2-95. They laughed a lot, argued among themselves, picked on each other's foibles like monkeys hunting fleas. When they assembled in a classroom, it didn't take long before the din reached street riot proportions. You'd hear the McCormacks Heckling and Jeckling— *Heh-heh-heh-heh, Haw-haw-haw-haw*. Burner Bunsen would be issuing some cogent speculation on the sex life of a barmaid he had met at Hop's Bar downtown. Shrike would be lambasting someone about the latest male sexist pig outrage. They would all be talking at once, at and around and through each other.

Chip Van Doren was the exception. Van Doren would sit there with a silly half-smile on his bland face, pale blue eyes following the action, but he seldom joined in. It was as though he were taping the whole scene for some future playback.

Van Doren was the computer freak of the class. In the JansSport backpack he hauled around, along with his training manuals and class paraphernalia, he had a notebook computer. On his wrist he wore a Buck Rogers–style watch that looked the size of a lunch pail. It beeped and glowed in the dark and was equipped with a micro-keyboard with which Van Doren could insert and retrieve data.

"Chip, what the hell is that thing on your wrist?"

"My watch. Sort of. Actually, it's a data bank."

"What's it for?"

"Numbers. Addresses. Data. Want to see all the stuff I've got in here?"

"No."

Van Doren was a nerd, at least in the techno-freak sense. But he was an amiable nerd, with a quick smile and a genuine friendliness about him. Everyone decided they liked Chip Van Doren, though no one quite knew how to talk to him.

Though Chip Van Doren was a nerd, he didn't look like one. He didn't walk around with a sheaf of pens in a nerdish plastic pocket holder, nor did he wear a haircut that looked like a badly mowed wheat field. He was an ordinary-looking guy, of medium height and build, with a bland, unlined face. In fact, it was his blandness—that half-smiling, unlined face—that made you look again, thinking, *There must be more to this guy.* And, of course, there was.

It took everyone a while to learn about Van Doren. Not until they got into the ground school portion of their training, learning the intricacies of the FA-18 systems, did it begin to dawn on the members of Class 2-95: This guy Van Doren was *very* smart. Maybe, some thought, too smart.

★

He couldn't remember ever wanting to be anything *but* a fighter pilot. And to be one, even when he was a kid back at Shepaug Valley High School in Connecticut, Chip Van Doren knew he would have to win a service academy appointment or an ROTC scholarship.

In high school he took all the right courses—mostly math and science—that would enhance his chances of getting a service academy appointment. Though he disliked team sports, he joined the cross-country team because he knew it would look good on his academy application.

Even in high school, the two facets of his personality revealed themselves. The summer of his junior year, he soloed an old Piper Cruiser at the local grass-strip airport. By the time he went off to the academy he had logged nearly a hundred hours and earned his private pilot's license. And, of course, he already knew computers. His first one, a hybridized IBM AT, he cobbled together at the age of fourteen from components he scavenged at yard sales.

He was number three of some two hundred plus in his high school graduating class. His grade-point average of 3.88 and combined SAT of over 1400 were impressive enough to win him several scholarships and entrance to half a dozen blue-ribbon universities, including MIT and Yale.

He passed them up. Van Doren already had in his hand the prize he wanted: an appointment to the U.S. Naval Academy at Annapolis, Maryland. Going to the Naval Academy was the surest route he knew to becoming a Navy fighter pilot.

Why the Navy and not the Air Force?

"I was hedging my bet," Van Doren said. "I thought about the Air Force Academy. But there was always a chance I *wouldn't* get into flight training. You know, my eyes could go bad, or feet go flat, something like that. In the Air Force, that meant you were stuck as some sort of ground officer, or at best a nonpilot backseater. In the Navy, I figured that if I couldn't fly, I'd go to subs. The submarine service—that would have been my next choice."

And after you got to know Van Doren, you could see it. That was a role—future commander of a nuclear submarine—that fit the bland-faced young man, with his passion for computers and his inherent streak of techno-nerdiness. Submarines. Next to flying supersonic fighters, it was the ultimate computer game.

★

He was a good-looking kid, with whitish blond hair, close-cropped in the standard Navy way (but not side-walled and bristle-topped, like the Marines). At five-ten and a hundred sixty pounds, Van Doren had the lean and wiry build of a cross-country runner, which was what he had been all through high school and college. Running, in fact, was his *only* athletic interest.

Van Doren had zero interest in organized sports, at least of the home-team, rah-rah variety. His notion of unbearable torture was to be locked in front of a television during a football game. He didn't have the patience for golf. Tennis was too much trouble, requiring appointments for a court and somebody to play with. Weight lifting was a bore, and, anyway, he disliked the claustrophobic sweatiness of gyms.

He was a runner. Long-distance running required no one else's participation, no special equipment, no special place. It was something Van Doren did almost every evening, usually five miles or so. Sometimes, when he was sorting out a technical problem in his head, he would keep on loping for ten or more miles. The space and the solitariness of long, slow jogging suited Van Doren.

Another thing his classmates began to notice about Chip Van Doren: He was a blusher. He had this pale Scot's complexion that reddened whenever anyone poked fun at him. Or when a female spoke directly to him. That's all it took, a female voice. A woman— *any* woman, young, old, foxy, pig-ugly, it didn't matter—would say "Chip . . ." and Van Doren's cheeks would redden like a traffic light. He even blushed talking to women on the telephone.

Back when he was a midshipman at Annapolis, he had dated a girl from Baltimore. Her name was Amy, and after nearly three years of going with her, he was *still* blushing when he spoke with her. She was a nursing student and the daughter of a real estate agent who made it big during the eighties when Chesapeake property values took off like a rocket.

As Van Doren and Amy settled into a steady relationship, her father became nervous. Things were looking too serious to suit him. The father worried that his daughter might wind up spending her life as a Navy wife, living in tacky military quarters, shopping in military exchanges, living a middle-class life.

A couple of months before Van Doren's graduation, she made an announcement: "My father thinks I should make a decision about my future."

"Your future?" said Van Doren. "You mean *our* future?"

"You're going off to flight training, and I'm going to finish my degree in nursing. I think we should take some time to think it over."

That's what they did. They took some time. Half a year, in fact, which was how long it took Amy to meet the intern at Johns Hopkins to whom she became engaged. The next spring, about the time Ensign Chip Van Doren was finishing basic flight training at Meridian, Mississippi, he received the news that Amy and the doctor were to be married. Her father, by all accounts, threw the most lavish wedding anyone had seen for years in Baltimore.

Van Doren got over it. By then he had his Corvette nearly restored. His computer with the 486 CPU and sixteen meg of RAM was up and running. And now he was flying jets in advanced training.

★

The Corvette went with the territory. For any self-respecting fighter pilot, or fighter pilot in training, or aspiring fighter pilot, the Corvette was the *only* automobile. For four decades the low-slung, grossly impractical, overpriced (by Navy pay scales) sports car had been *the* earthbound form of locomotion that most closely approximated flying a fighter. It had that rude abundance of horsepower, the cramped-cockpit feel of an A-4 Skyhawk with absolutely no interior space allotted for nonessentials like kids and groceries. The Corvette possessed the streamlined grace of an artillery shell, and it could burn rubber from a stoplight for half a block. Over the years, countless Chevy dealers near Navy and Air Force bases had cashed in and retired early from the windfall profits dumped on them by Corvette-coveting fighter jocks.

Chip Van Doren bought his Corvette a month after he reported for flight training at Pensacola. It was a dog, a '78 with multiple dings and over a hundred thousand miles on the odometer, but it was the best he could afford. Van Doren lovingly restored the beat-up sports car to a near-pristine condition. He rebuilt the engine, had the body resurfaced and painted, replaced every stitch of the interior. When Van Doren left his Corvette in parking lots, he would come back to find notes from people who wanted to buy his car.

Those were the two sides of Chip Van Doren: the Corvette and the computer. He was a techno-freak who loved blazingly fast machines—electronic, aerial, or earthbound. He had a passion for speed. Like most unchecked passions, it was one that would get him into trouble.

CHAPTER FIVE

THE FACTORY

To be assigned as an instructor in VFA-106 was a distinction. The instructors took a private pleasure in their unofficial appellation: the Fleet's Finest. Being an instructor meant you had been screened and culled from all the Hornet jocks out there in the fleet. It amounted to a large gold star on your career grade sheet.

With such distinction, of course, went a predictable inflation of ego. The instructors *knew* they were good. Sometimes it was impossible for them not to say as much, particularly late at night in the bar, and most particularly in the presence of lesser mortals like the pilots of slow-moving S-3 submarine hunters or P-3 patrol plane pukes.

The lesser mortals had their own opinion. Around the bar you could hear *them* referring to the FA-18 instructors. They didn't call them the Fleet's Finest. They called them the *Fleet's Favorites*—a clear implication that the perks and strokes enjoyed by the Hornet hotshots had as much to do with politics and ass-kissing as it did with talent.

If being chosen as one of the Fleet's Finest amounted to a gold star for an instructor, then being selected as the commanding officer of the Fleet's Finest was like a standing ovation. The Finest of the Fleet's Finest. You had arrived! Being the commanding officer of the Hornet RAG made you, in effect, the spiritual leader of the strike fighter community.

At age forty-three, Captain Matt Moffit had reached the zenith of the strike fighter business. For nearly twenty years he had steadily ascended the invisible Navy ziggurat. Most of that time he had spent in the cockpit of a Navy attack or fighter jet. He had managed to please his superiors and, equally important, dodged the political missiles that had snuffed the careers of so many of his contemporaries. He had avoided all the career wrong turns and dead ends that took you out of the game.

Now he ran the RAG. It was the most highly visible job in the strike fighter business and, depending on your luck, would make or break your career.

Good luck had marked Matt Moffit's career. He came from a Navy family—his father was a two-star admiral—which counted for a lot in the tradition-bound, nepotistic naval service. His older brother, Mike, preceded him by two years in the Navy.

For a couple thousand hours Matt flew A-7 Corsairs, deploying on carriers to the Atlantic and Mediterranean. He was chosen to help devise new strike fighter tactics in a special think tank unit at the weapons facility in Fallon, Nevada. He was one of the first pilots to fly the new FA-18 Hornet, and for a while he served as an instructor in the RAG.

Luck stayed with Moffit. Just after he took command of VFA-131, an FA-18 squadron deployed aboard the U.S.S. *America*, a Middle East dictator handed him the greatest favor he could have hoped for: Saddam Hussein took on the aggregate military forces of the entire Western world.

For Navy fighter and attack pilots deployed on aircraft carriers in the Red Sea and the Persian Gulf, *it was heaven!* For six weeks they bombed, strafed, rocketed, and blew the living shit out of every vestige of the Iraqi army.

It came just in time. The era had been shaping up to be the longest period the country had gone without a war since the dry

spell between World Wars I and II. No air medals, no Distinguished Flying Crosses, no Silver Stars. Now all that had changed.
Now there were chestfuls of medals to be had, and they owed it all
to Saddam, bless his lunatic soul.

★

One day early in the war, Moffit was leading a flight of four Hornets
to a target in the western Iraqi desert. The mission was to bomb a
concrete Scud launching complex. The war had been going on for
a week.

By now you could feel sorry for the troops down there in the
bunkers. You *knew* they sure as hell didn't want to be there, hun-
kered down in the bottoms of their eight- or ten-foot-deep
bunkers, wishing they were a hundred feet deeper, wishing they
were back in Baghdad or Basra or anywhere besides there in the
Kuwaiti desert getting their eardrums ruptured by the ceaseless
bombing.

And you could feel a little bit sorry for the Iraqi fighter pilots,
who didn't have decent radar command control to keep them out of
trouble, and who never knew they were about to die until a
Sidewinder missile suddenly came at them from out of nowhere.
During the first week of the war, the Iraqi fighters were in the air
mostly to keep from getting blown up on the ground, which was a
bad choice because they were felled like clay pigeons.

But nobody felt sorry for the bastards in the antiaircraft sites. They
were a mean-spirited bunch whose work was to kill fighter pilots. And
their efforts had already met with some success: In the first week of
the air war, they had shot down over a dozen allied aircraft.

Now they were trying to raise the score. The flak was thickening as
Moffit and his flight approached their target. But where the hell was it
coming from? You couldn't see them. The antiaircraft positions were
well concealed. In the haze and smoke from already-bombed targets,
they were invisible.

Moffit rolled in on the Scud sites. They appeared to be abandoned, which was no surprise. There were no vehicles around them,
no trailers, no sign of life. The Scud shooters had gotten smart and

hauled ass. Well, here were the Hornets, and their mission was to bomb everything in the place that looked hostile, even if it was empty.

It was then that Moffit, midway through his dive to the target, saw them. Over to the left, several hundred yards from the concrete Scud launching pads: tents and nets and—yes!—an antiaircraft emplacement. It was very busy. The Iraqis appeared to be having a merry old time down there, banging away at a flight of Hornets that was just pulling off another easy target. Flak was spewing into the sky like dirty black cumulus puffs.

Moffit was hurtling toward the desert at over four hundred knots. It would be a hurry-up, improvised change of plan—the kind that rarely worked out. But it was within the scope of their assignment, which was to bomb *any* hostile emplacements in that area. He slewed his target designator—the little lighted pipper in his wind-shield display—away from the Scud pad and over to the left, onto the antiaircraft site. He banked and skewed the Hornet over to the left. He hit the pickle button. It was a snap shot, depending as much on luck as on the Hornet's computer-guided bombing system.

Pulling off the target and peering back over his shoulder, Moffit got a glimpse of all six of his Mark 83 bombs, their long, dark cigar shapes aimed downward directly at the flak site.

KaaWhump! . . . a great orange eruption, a geyser of sand and smoke and flame, shredded debris from the enemy gun position. The flak stopped.

★

The war had been good to Matt Moffit. From it he collected a row of medals, a promotion to captain, and, best of all, the assignment to command VFA-106. The Factory.

Most of the instructor pilots, like Matt Moffit, had flown combat missions in Desert Storm. Most had distinguished themselves, mainly by blasting to smithereens large examples of Iraqi architecture. Which was what strike fighter pilots were supposed to do.

But that, as the fighter pilots say, was air-to-mud stuff. Only a few, a very few, had distinguished themselves in the way that every *real* fighter pilot dreams about.

★

Air-to-air. *That* was what flying fighters was supposed to be all about: You sallied forth, like a knight of old, and met the enemy one-on-one. Eyeball to eyeball. You in your fighter, he in his. Like Rickenbacker had done. And Richthofen, Boyington, Galland. All the great single combat warriors of fighter legend.

There hadn't been much of that in the Gulf War. Early in the game the Iraqi Air Force caught on to a dreadful reality: If they sallied forth to join battle with the enemy, they were dead meat. Which, of course, was a great disappointment for the Navy strike fighter pilots launching from their aircraft carriers in the Red Sea and the Persian Gulf. They felt cheated. In the good old days, in Korea and Vietnam, the air wars had been more sporting. At least the Vietnamese and Korean and Chinese MiG pilots had been willing to play their part. They'd sometimes come up and do battle with the Navy and Air Force, and of course, they *too* were usually dead meat. But not always. Some were skilled combatants, and they managed to take out enough Navy and Air Force fighters to make the game sporting.

It would be argued long after Desert Storm ended that the Air Force had managed to steal most of the glory, at least in the air combat arena. This was thought to be because in the coalition command structure, the Air Force was given the overall responsibility for assigning targets and CAP (Combat Air Patrol) assignments to *all* the allied air units, including the Navy. So it should have come as no surprise that—who else?—*Air Force* F-15s were on station to intercept the first Iraqi MiG and Sukhoi fighters sent up to do battle.

Navy pilots, in fact, accounted for only two MiG kills in the Desert Storm air war. And now both the veteran MiG killers were stationed at Cecil Field, where they dwelled among the new fighter pilots like living icons.

One such icon was Nick Mongillo—Mongo—who as a nugget had earned a Silver Star on the first day of the Gulf War when he downed an Iraqi MiG. Now Mongo was an instructor in VFA-106. He dwelled there among the mortals—the other instructors and the lowly students—like a deified being.

The nuggets all liked Mongo. He was a friendly, laid-back guy who didn't brag or comport himself like a deity at all. In fact, Mongo would soon prove himself to be an undeified, *very* mortal fighter pilot.

★

Navy squadron ready rooms had a certain egalitarian quality. They were versions of Hyde Park, where the denizens could be as opinionated as they wished—within limits. At any given moment you could catch a harangue about something—the ineptitude of Congress, the shortsightedness of Navy brass, the crassness of the American voter.

But at the Strike Fighter RAG ready room, the only *real* denizens, those entitled to express truly outrageous opinions, were the IPs (instructor pilots). They were the permanents. The RPs (replacement pilots) were the temporaries. RPs included not only nuggets but also more senior officers on their way to FA-18 squadrons in the fleet. Regardless of rank, RPs tended to be deferential, in keeping with their status as *students*. Most had the good sense to shut up in the ready room, speaking only when spoken to.

Nuggets were expected to defer to everyone, even the clerks and sweepers. They were there for no purpose except to learn, which meant they kept their impertinent mouths shut and displayed a respectful awe in the presence of the Fleet's Finest. Nuggets were supposed to know their place, which was somewhere between invisible and insignificant.

The VFA-106 ready room was a long, cavernous space with a raised, enclosed desk area for the duty officer. On the wall behind the duty officer was the status board, which showed all the flying activities for the day, the aircraft numbers, pilots, times, and comments about the maintenance status of the jets. The duty officer was an instructor. He was supposed to be the ground-based font of wisdom for questions from the air.

"Base, Roman one-oh-six."

"Go ahead, Roman one-oh-six. This is base."

"Hey, Chunks, this is Dawg. I just had a fire warning on the right engine. I shut the sucker down."

"What's your position?"

"Thirty-five south, angels fifteen. Just leaving Rodman target."

"Okay, Dawg. I'm getting the book out. We'll alert the tower that you're inbound and you're going to take an arrestment. And we'll get an LSO out there to hold your hand."

Chunks O'Mara, the duty officer, had at his desk all the FA-18 Hornet systems and operating procedure manuals. He could look up the problem—any problem—and feed the answer to the pilot on the radio. If it was a problem of such complexity that they needed expert advice, the duty officer could call up engineers at McDonnell Douglas, who manufactured the Hornet.

"Here's the procedure, Dawg," the duty officer said on the radio. "Push the fire extinguisher light on the affected engine. The right one, is that correct?"

"Roger that. It's done."

"Okay, single engine procedure. Half flaps, hook down, straight in to the runway, and Paddles will be up on tower frequency."

"Roger."

Of course, the pilot already knew these procedures, but in the heat of an emergency it was always better to have someone on the ground backing you up.

The drama would be followed by everyone in the ready room. Flight-suited pilots—instructors and students alike—would be standing around, coffee cups in hand, nobody saying much, casually assessing Dawg's coolness in this little matter of an engine fire.

★

One day during a fighter weapons exercise in Key West, another instructor had a problem. This time it was Mongo, of Desert Storm fame. And this time, *everyone* got to watch.

Mongo had just touched down when he decided to take off again. He was too close to the preceding jet on the runway. And as his jet was lifting from the runway, Mongo raised the landing gear . . .

And as the landing gear was retracting, Mongo felt his fighter *settle back* to the runway. He felt the tail scraping the concrete!

What the hell was wrong? There was nothing flashing at him yet on the instrument panel. No red lights, aural warnings, nothing like that. The thing was shuddering, settling, behaving as though it wanted to plunge back onto that sun-baked, mashed-seashell shore and turn itself—with the pilot—into one glorious goddamn fireball.

For a millisecond Mongo's brain processed the confusing data. *What the hell . . . is this sucker trying to kill me? Do I stay with it . . . or punch out?*

It was the classic jet jockey dilemma: Eject or not eject? It was one of those instantaneous choices you made *without* the luxury of careful analysis or weighing all the data. You obeyed your gut instincts.

Mongo obeyed his own gut instincts. He grabbed the ejection lanyard and yanked.

Wham! The ejection seat—and Mongo—left the cockpit like a mortar shell.

And fifty feet down below, pilots sitting in their cockpits, waiting to be cleared for takeoff, were astonished at what they saw: *a jet!* . . . sailing right over their heads, wobbling and floundering as though it had no pilot . . .

Which, of course, it hadn't, as they quickly realized when they saw the white blossom of Mongo's parachute. The chute made one swing, then fluttered down on the soft dirt a hundred yards from the runway.

Meanwhile, the pilotless jet kept flying.

Everyone watched the spectacle, including Mongo, who by now was climbing to his feet and trying to disentangle himself from the parachute. The unmanned fighter continued on its way. It wobbled through the sky like a disoriented duck, dipping and swooping, skimming the earth, then soaring upward. When it came to the expanse of a mangrove swamp, it seemed to find a home. The jet dropped its nose and plunged into the green mire.

Kaaablooom! A brief fireball, a cloud of black smoke floating over the swamp, and the Navy's inventory of fighters was reduced by one.

It was, of course, embarrassing.

In the subsequent investigation, nothing could be found wrong with the jet. It looked like the pilot might have punched out of a perfectly good airplane. If so, it wouldn't look good on his record, dumping expensive equipment in mangrove swamps.

But on the other hand, this was Mongo, not some yahoo who didn't know a fighter from a flytrap. Maybe something *was* amiss with the jet. Clearly, *something* had been wrong, or was giving strong evidence of being wrong, to persuade an experienced fighter pilot like Mongo to pull the handle.

In the end, the investigators decided that, yes, the pilot may have erred in his decision to abandon the airplane. But in any case, it was a judgment call, just as it had been a judgment call that day in 1991 when Mongo squeezed the trigger and downed the oncoming Iraqi MiG.

The Navy, like Mongo's peers, was willing to give him the benefit of the doubt. After all, fighters were replaceable. Guys like Nick Mongillo were not.

★

Jacksonville, Florida—or "Jax," as it had been called by generations of sailors—was a Navy town. More specifically, it was a naval air town, being home to two major air stations, NAS Cecil and NAS Jacksonville, as well as NAS Mayport, which was the air facility immediately adjoining the berthing docks for the supercarriers that home-ported in Jacksonville. Entire squadrons of airplanes could land at Mayport, then be hoisted by cranes, one by one, aboard a carrier.

In the old days, not long after World War II and before the migration of business and industry to the Sun Belt, the Navy was about the *only* serious enterprise Jacksonville had going. The sleepy old river town was headquarters for a small hub of southern insurance companies, and it maintained a steady but lethargic shipping business through its seaport. But for years the paychecks of thirty or so thousand uniformed personnel provided the lifeblood for old Jacksonville.

By the booming eighties, all that was changing. An infusion of prosperity and high-tech industry transformed Jacksonville into a pulsating mini-metropolis. Its downtown area had been razed and replaced with a picture-book riverfront commercial area. A professional football team, the Jacksonville Jaguars, came to town. The rate of violent crime soared, putting Jacksonville in the big league of homicide and mayhem. Even culture had arrived in the form of symphony and theater and an annual jazz festival.

Like most Florida cities, Jacksonville was an amalgam of cypress-shaded elegance, bustling nouveau prosperity, and a subtropical roach-and-mosquito bugginess. Waiting at a stoplight you would see a glistening Mercedes 450 SEL, its tanned and coifed driver chatting into a cellular phone. In the adjoining lane would be a rusty pickup, one fender missing, a yellow-eyed Rottweiler glowering from the back, the bearded driver knocking back a can of Rolling Rock. Those were the two faces of north Florida—upscale yuppiness sharing the same space with the piney-woods bubbas. Georgian mansions gazing across the river at tumbledown trailer parks. The eternal duality of the haves and the have-nots.

Such a dichotomous culture suited the needs of the Navy just fine. Out there in the open flatlands around Cecil Field, where no one complained about the thunder and nuisance of the jets in the traffic pattern, the lower-paid enlisted people could find inexpensive housing—mobile home parks and tract developments. Officers and the senior enlisted ranks drifted toward Orange Park, a graceful suburban village on the banks of the St. Johns, on the southern flank of Jacksonville. Orange Park, if you could afford it, provided a certain country club gentility—good restaurants, bars, golf courses. It even had a Florida staple—a dog racing track.

Life was good in Jacksonville. By comparison to the rest of the country, living was still cheap. The natives were friendly, even if the government payroll didn't have such clout anymore. If you liked water sports, it was heaven. You could spend your off-duty time in the ocean or anywhere on the thousand miles of the St. Johns River and its tributaries waterskiing, fishing, scuba diving, watching cranes and alligators and manatees. The weather ranged from winter-chilly, though it seldom touched freezing level, to a four-month stretch of shirt-sticking, bug-swatting steaminess.

But more than anyone else, the fighter pilots loved Jacksonville.

Unlike out west, at Miramar or Lemoore, where they had to deal with the unbelievable air traffic glut of southern California, Jacksonville was a piece of cake. Jax Air Traffic Control would clear an FA-18 through their air space like he was a local celebrity: "Roger, Roman three-oh-four, great to talk to you again. Where do you want to go today? Out to the warning area? Sure thing. Take a heading of one-zero-five and climb to one-five-thousand feet . . ."

Just offshore were the warning areas—restricted air space for the exclusive use of the military. That was where the FA-18s practiced air combat maneuvering. It was also a place where they could make sonic booms—push the Hornet past the speed of sound—without worrying about broken windows and traumatized old ladies down in the suburbs.

Within five minutes' flying time from Cecil were the Pinecastle and Rodman and Lake George target complexes. You could zip down to the targets, work them over with your practice bombs, then take a leisurely, scenic cruise at a thousand feet or so up the river to Cecil.

Since the entire Florida peninsula was flat as a molten cow pie, low-level flying was a snap. And that was the best part, flying low and fast over the sparsely settled piney woods, not worrying about anything except the occasional civilian bug-smasher airplanes and the television towers that could stick up a couple thousand feet and jumped out at you like apparitions from nowhere.

The flying weather in Florida was of two varieties—perfect or abominable. You flew, or you stayed on the ground and waited for it to clear. In the summer months, Florida thunderstorms swelled to forty-plus thousand feet and looked like the anvils of God. They were evil black things that pulsed and throbbed and possessed the collective energy of several small nukes. You didn't mess with Florida thunderstorms. But they *were* almost always quite localized and well defined. It was possible to find a route around them, or between them, or sometimes over the top. Thunderstorms were like the television towers—just another item you tried not to hit.

CHAPTER SIX

SEMPER FIDELIS

J. J. Quinn's wife figured he was having a midlife crisis. It was the only explanation. "What else could it be?" she asked. "Why would you be doing something so stupid?"

It was a question Quinn was hearing a lot these days from his friends: *Why would you be doing something so stupid?*

"Hornets, for Christ's sake! Don't you know people get killed flying those things?"

"Have you lost your marbles? You had a great career going, and now . . ."

"At your age? Learning to fly fighters is for kids . . ."

J. J. Quinn was not a kid. He was a tall, long-limbed Marine captain who looked like Lurch in the old television show *The Addams Family*. He wore the ubiquitous squared-off Marine crew cut, though not cut as close and white-sidewalled as his younger colleagues. His black hair was beginning to show flecks of gray—another feature that distinguished him from the *real* nuggets.

No one could understand why Quinn, at age thirty-five and otherwise blessed with a successful career as a Marine Corps helicopter pilot, had chosen to transition to fighters.

J.J. was having trouble understanding it himself. He only knew that the answer had something to do with the chemistry of advancing age, male pride, curiosity, the mystique of the fighter business.

He tried explaining it to his wife, Dorothy: "I don't want to wake up someday, sixty-five years old, and wish I had been a fighter pilot."

To which she replied, with characteristic bluntness, that given his new line of work, he wouldn't have to worry about waking up at age sixty-five. He probably wouldn't be waking up at age thirty-six.

★

Until one afternoon in the summer of 1980, J. J. Quinn had no notion what he was going to do with his life. He had never given a moment's thought to the military or the Marine Corps or airplanes. But that afternoon something happened. He was standing there in the July sun, baking on the ramp of the Willow Grove Naval Air Station with several thousand other air show spectators. Silhouetted up there against the Pennsylvania sky, trailing smoke like a swarm of flaming arrows, were the Blue Angels, the Navy's crack aerobatic formation team.

Quinn watched the jets. He appreciated the beauty of the maneuvers. He liked the precision of the whole thing. But more than that, he thought there was a *purity* to their routine. Flying had a logic and a method to it that appealed to him.

Standing there on the scorching ramp, watching the sleek jets, Quinn suddenly knew. *That's it!* That was what he'd been looking for. J. J. Quinn wanted to be a pilot.

He was accepted as an officer candidate in the Marine Corps. After going through Marine basic school, like every Marine officer was required to do, he was on his way to flight training. And it was there that Quinn learned a basic truth about himself: He wasn't the best aviator in the world. He was, in fact, quite average.

And so were his flight grades, a reality that caused him to be assigned to helicopters. He wouldn't fly the jets that he had once dreamed about. Quinn's memory of the Blue Angels trailing smoke against a Pennsylvania sky dissolved. He would be a helo pilot, *whop-whop-whopping* across the fields and swamps with all the other grunts.

★

Marine Corps aviation was divided into four communities. Two were jets: the FA-18 Hornet community, and the vertical-takeoff-and-landing Harrier jets community. The Marines also had multi-engine units consisting mostly of four-engined C-130 Hercules transports. And the Marines operated a large force of helicopter squadrons, whose mission was most closely related to the traditional ground-pounding Marine infantry units.

Over the years each community had developed its own unique culture and traditions. The differences between the communities were as marked as differences between real towns. Fighter pilots, for example, could instantly spot "foreigners" from outside their community by little telltale signs—the tilt of their uniform caps, the fit of their flight suits, jargon on the radio, the way they maneuvered their hands when they told flying stories at the bar.

In the Marine Corps, the distinction between flying communities was a little fuzzier, because in the Corps you were first and foremost *a Marine*. Semper Fidelis, the Halls of Montezuma, the shores of Tripoli. Thereafter it was okay to be an aviator. First you were a Marine, secondly an aviator.

J. J. Quinn had lived his entire Marine life in helicopters. And for most of his thirteen years in the Corps, that had suited him fine. It was something he had done well, and he had risen steadily in the hierarchy of Marine aviation. In a few weeks he would pin on his new gold major's leaves. He was of squadron department head rank, meaning he was only two or three slots away from command of his own helicopter squadron. Quinn had a textbook career going.

And then one day at Cherry Point Marine Corps Air Station, Quinn heard about a strange idea that was coming down from head-quarters. Someone with at least two stars on his collar had been smitten with the notion that this closed-door compartmenting of Marine aviation—helo pilots flying *only* helos, and fighter pilots knowing nothing except how to fly fighters—wasn't healthy. After all, they were naval aviators one and all, weren't they? Such un-democratic elitism wasn't healthy for the Corps. Everyone should share the glory, and they should all experience some of the mud and dirt. And they could all have a taste of danger.

As an experiment, six volunteer helo pilots would be allowed to transition to jets. They would be highly qualified pilots, of course, but it was not necessary that they have any previous jet experience. After all, they *were* naval aviators, just like everyone else.

In theory and on paper, it looked like a reasonable idea, spreading the varied experience of Marine Corps aviation around. It challenged the idea of "communities" in naval aviation. It amounted to multiculturalism of the flying business.

But if you asked any fighter pilot—any *real* fighter pilot who had spent his career in pointy-nosed jets—it was an idea that portended disaster. Multiculturalism in tactical aviation was stupid. It meant that you spread your talent around in a thin film over all the specialized areas of aviation. Everyone would be an amateur, having already left the cockpit of the machine he knew best.

Actually, it went deeper than that. Naval aviation, which included the Marines, had a deeply ingrained caste system. At the apex of the system, wallowing in glory and exhibiting the most highly developed sense of snobbery and elitism, were the fighter pilots. In Air Force, Navy, and Marine ready rooms throughout the world, a ubiquitous plaque could be found stuck on a wall somewhere: *If you ain't a fighter pilot, you ain't shit.*

Fighter pilots gazed down in disdain on the rest of the world, the military, the rest of aviation. They were the varsity. They flew faster and higher, took greater risks, won more glory than any of the others. They were the hunters and killers. All the others—patrol plane pansies, antisubmarine wienies, transport drivers, and especially *helo* pukes—were placed here on earth to support the fighter pilots.

Most fighter pilots, in their secret souls, believed that they were where they were (at the apex of the system), and helo pilots were where they were (pounding sand at the bottom), because of an innate difference in *quality*. Back in flight training, the top students were rewarded with the first choice of assignments. This was almost always pointy-nosed jets. The *bottom*-ranking students got last choice, which was almost always helicopters.

So there it was. As far as the fighter jocks were concerned, it was a merit game. Winners and losers. Of course, there was always the possibility that a top student—a winner—might actually *choose* helicopters, but in a way that was even more damning. It meant he had no balls. *Can you imagine . . . some turkey getting helos . . . because that's what he actually wanted?*

In the Marine Corps, being a helo pilot was the closest thing to being a grunt—a raggedy-ass, crawling-on-your-belly, snake-eating infantryman with a tin pot on your head and a piece in your hand. Helo pilots actually got out there with the grunts, hauling them— *whop, whop, whop, whop*—in and out of the field, eating the same gut-rotting rations, sleeping in the same miserable tents, sometimes getting shot by the same goddamned incoming bullets.

Sometimes a helo pilot would look up from his mud-encaked bivouac. He might gaze skyward, and what he would see, way up there above the fray, sublimely removed from the squalor and mud and gore of the battlefield, would be *contrails*. The lovely thin contrails of the high-flying, oh-so-superior fighter jocks.

And it pissed him off royally. Every helo pilot knew about the contemptuous snobbery of the fighter community. He was well aware of the not-so-subtle class distinctions of the aviation "communities," and of the low regard the fighter jocks had for the untouchables of the helo community. And though he might never say it out loud around his peers, the helo pilot nursed a private fantasy: *I could do that just as well as those assholes up there. I could be a fighter pilot—if they gave me the chance.*

One day they gave J. J. Quinn the chance. It was now or never, he thought. You could spend your life looking up at the contrails, being pissed off, wondering if you could have cut it. Or you could go for it.

He was going for it.

★

The father of First Lieutenant David "Burner" Bunsen hadn't been pleased when he heard that his son wanted to be a Marine fighter pilot. *The Marines?* The kid was supposed to go from Yale on to biz school, then join one of the good firms, Goldman Sachs, Salomon Brothers, something like that. That was the plan, and up until the kid's last year at Yale, he had been on track.

The son had trashed the whole plan. Here he was, wearing that bristly white-sidewalled Marine haircut that made his cranium look like a fuzzed onion. He had gone through Marine officer training and then signed up for flight training, *without any consultation from his father*, obligating himself for *seven more years*. Christ, the kid would be nearly thirty years old before he could even interview with one of the investment firms!

Burner Bunsen was a handsome kid, a six-footer with wide shoulders and a lopsided grin. He possessed a long, prominent nose and large ears that extended like speed brakes from his sidewalled crew-cut head.

Burner was an anomaly. He didn't match the profile of strike fighter pilots. For one thing, he didn't come from the great bluish-white-collar middle class of America like most naval aviation candidates, who went to state universities and military academies on scholarships and who earned their degrees in one of the sciences.

He grew up in Charleston, South Carolina, where his father was a wealthy developer of shopping malls and who had become wealthier in the free-for-all eighties. As a kid, Burner never had a paper route. He never joined the Boy Scouts. He didn't go to public schools. He didn't care a fig whether he won a merit scholarship, and he didn't want to go to a service academy. And he didn't like science.

What Burner did like was team sports, particularly crewing. That was what he did at St. Paul's Academy, a venerable prep school in Concord, New Hampshire, attended by kids who were exceedingly bright or exceedingly blessed with wealthy parents. Burner was both.

At Yale, instead of earning a degree in aero engineering or computer science like most would-be warriors, Burner had studied, of all limp-wristed, unwarriorlike subjects, *philosophy*! By ready room definition, Bunsen was a pointy-headed Ivy League elitist.

It was during his last year at Yale that some rebellious chromosome caused Bunsen to start thinking about the military. The idea had rooted itself in his brain that he ought to belong to some kind of elite combat unit. Why? "Camaraderie," he said. "I liked the team spirit I'd seen in school sports. Crewing—everybody pulling together. I started looking for that kind of esprit outside of school."

One summer he interned at an investment bank in New York. It was there he made a discovery: There was no team spirit among investment bankers. In fact, there was no team. It was every man for himself. Forget esprit.

He considered joining the SEALs—the Navy's "Mission Impossible" specialists—guys who blackened their faces and parachuted and scuba dived and crawled on their bellies. That was the part that appealed to him—the crawling-on-the-belly and parachuting. Then he took a hard look at the Marine Corps and liked what he saw even better. Now, here was camaraderie! Two-hundred-plus years of it— esprit de corps and ample opportunity for parachuting and belly crawling.

After Burner had signed up for the Marine's platoon leader course, which would lead to his commissioning as a second lieutenant, he became aware of another even more appealing job, one he had never previously considered: He could be a fighter pilot.

That was when it all came together for him, like a neatly assembled mosaic. Suddenly he *knew* where he belonged. Being a Marine, wearing the uniform, flying a multimillion-dollar, high-tech killing machine—it all had an elegant logic.

And after he had made the commitment, earned his commission in the Marine Corps, then entered the arduous training to become a naval aviator, he discovered another essential truth about himself: He loved flying. And he was good at it.

CHAPTER SEVEN

FAM

They were like kids on their first day of school. In fact, this bright, cold January morning in 1995 *was* the first day of school for the nuggets of Class 2-95. It was called Fam phase—familiarization—and it would be their introduction to the FA-18 Hornet.

They showed up early that morning, wearing their gray-green flight suits, bright orange new Gladiators patch on the breast. Their frustration level had peaked out over the holidays—waiting, waiting, interminably waiting for their appointed time to come, for them to be allowed to claim the prize they had earned—strike fighter training.

A few, like Angie Morales and Chip Van Doren, had been "stashed" for three or four months before receiving a class date. Being a stash meant you were on hold with nothing to do, waiting for your slot in the training pipeline. In the Incredible Shrinking Navy, it had become a common assignment. Assets and slots were insufficient for the number of bodies to be trained. Stashes were given odd jobs, makework assignments, gofer tasks for the squadron officers. "We're about as useful," said a stashed Marine first lieutenant, "as fur on a frog."

Most of the stashes at Cecil Field spent their time hanging around the RAG, running errands, answering the phones, bumming back-seat rides with instructors just to *feel* what it was going to be like to fly the FA-18. They felt like kids with their noses pressed to the candy store window.

Some jobs were better than others. Angie Morales had been stashed as the "writer" for the squadron landing signal officer (LSO). The LSO watched and graded every practice carrier landing made by his class of students. And while he stood out there at the runway, or on the LSO platform when they went aboard the carrier, he barked his comments to the writer—Morales—to be recorded and used in the debriefing. Angie thought it was fun.

Now the stashing was over. Here it was, day one of their new careers. From this morning forward, until they walked out of the RAG as qualified strike fighter pilots, they'd be working their collective butts off.

On this, the first morning of their new careers, the nuggets of 2-95 could afford to feel a certain smugness. They were feeling the sweet contentment of having arrived. They were going to be fighter pilots!

★

Before they let you fly a fighter—any new fighter—you had to learn the airplane. Whether you were a fighter pilot, airline driver, or astronaut, you went through the same ritual. Before you climbed in and took off in any new flying machine, you first had to acquire an intimacy with every detail and nuance of the beast's peculiar personality. You stared glassy-eyed at electrical system schematics, at multihued diagrams of fuel and hydraulic systems, sat through mind-numbing lectures about maximum hydraulic psi (pounds per square inch), minimum fuel pressure from the engine-driven pumps, limits of exhaust gas temperature and fuel flow and oil pressure. This phase of training was as much fun as a root canal.

Each student sat in his own little booth with his own computer. It was called CAI—computer-assisted instruction—and was supposed to be interactive, meaning the computer presented the material, then tested the student's knowledge of the subject, advancing him to the next phase or redrilling him on a weak area.

This was old stuff to the nuggets. By now they had been through years of such training, from their engineering and math courses in college, all the way through two years of flight training, where they'd learned the plumbing of at least three new jets.

But it was tedious. All day long they sat there with the earphones clamped to their heads, listening to some guy with a voice like a twenty-eight-volt motor go on about electrical schematics and hydraulic pressures and asking questions just to see if they were paying attention. It was like listening to an unending Sunday sermon.

They wanted to *fly*. It was tough, sitting there at their computers, punching the keyboard, listening to the twenty-eight-volt voice, being forced to hear the incessant jet noises from out there on Cecil Field's long runways: *Kaawhoom!*—afterburners kicking in, fighters hurtling down the runways.

Interspersed with CAI sessions were lectures. Some of the lectures were worse than the twenty-eight-volt voice. The nuggets endured lectures on naval aviation maintenance procedures, on the military justice system, on AIDS prevention, on community harmony, on radio protocol, on race relations, on alternate lifestyle "sensitivity." They were happy to get back to the computers.

Of all the class, Chip Van Doren was most at home in CAI. Every morning Van Doren would plop his knapsack in the corner of the booth and sit down at the teaching terminal. A look of sweet contentment would settle on his face as he began to stroke the computer keyboard. For a true techno-nerd like Van Doren, it was heaven. It was as though the FA-18, with its mission control computers and fly-by-wire flight controls and electronic flight data displays, were made just for someone like him.

For everyone else, it was a dry grind. Every morning they showed up at seven-thirty and sat there like gnomes hunched over their keyboards until five-thirty. And sometimes later.

★

In the old days, before computer-aided instruction, airplane systems were taught in traditional classrooms. The schematic diagrams would cover an entire wall, and a stand-up instructor with a pointer in his hand and a monotone voice would torture his pupils: ". . . and this valve opens and lets the pressure go to the accumulator over there, and when the pressure gets up to . . ." It was an ordeal of boredom.

That part of the training hadn't changed. It was still an ordeal. Now it was a computer-aided ordeal.

Sometimes, especially in the afternoon, the whole dry business simply became too much. From a CAI booth would come a *Zzzzzz-zzzzz—snort-chuff* as a fighter pilot trainee lost the struggle to maintain consciousness.

Road Ammons learned how to lean his head on the wall of the booth, his eyes aimed more or less at the computer screen, and become comatose.

The bristly head of Burner Bunsen would tilt back, mouth agape, and emit noises like a fleet of chain saws.

Sally Hopkins would get up and clomp around the room like a roused bear, slap herself on the cheeks, then plunge back into the course with grim determination.

Chip Van Doren, being a computer nerd, was the only one who seemed to *enjoy* CAI. Van Doren would annoy his classmates by finishing up the coursework early, then amuse himself by playing with the computer.

After two weeks of computer tedium, they were finally allowed to see something that looked like a Hornet cockpit. It was a simulated Hornet cockpit—an operational flight trainer (OFT)—in which they could exercise all their newly won knowledge about the inner organs of an FA-18. They would "fly" the simulator for at least eight sessions before the first flight in the real Hornet.

The OFT simulator didn't move. It was planted firmly in the concrete floor, unlike the advanced hydraulic-powered simulators in the building next door that moved on three axes and transmitted all the sensations of flight to the pilot. But here in the OFT all the instruments and flight data displays worked. All the knobs, switches, dials produced the correct effects. A visual display in the windscreen presented a pilot's view of the airport and countryside.

And best of all, the OFT simulator hummed and throbbed just like a real jet.

Sitting there with the canopy closed, hearing the engines thrumming and purring, looking out at the lights of Cecil Field's runway 36 left, they thought: *Maybe this isn't really flying. But it's getting close.*

CHAPTER EIGHT

THE FIRST TIME

It was one of those events you always remember, like a first kiss. The first day of school. First solo. First heartbreak.

A new relationship with an airplane was like a love affair. The whole process was a tumult of joy and discovery. If you were lucky, not until later would come disillusionment, the realization of flaws and foibles.

So it was with the FA-18. The airplane was a joy to fly, light and responsive on the controls. The Hornet had no bad traits—none, at least, of the insidious variety that could get you snuffed in a heartbeat if you weren't watching at all times. The Hornet was honest, everyone said.

Not all pilots loved the Hornet. Some thought it was a bitch. They regarded it as a highly complex, computer-driven machine—a smart, demanding bitch of an airplane—that sometimes made pilots wonder who was in charge. It could be a mini-version of the malevolent rogue computer Hal in the movie *2001: A Space Odyssey*.

They called the new generation of computerized flight management systems "glass cockpits" because most of the traditional flight data instruments—the round, mechanical gyros and pitot/static airspeed and altitude gauges—were replaced with CRT screens (cathode ray tubes, as in computer monitors). They looked like Nintendo games. Glass cockpits changed the whole pilot-to-machine interface. Now the airplane, receiving information from its computers, was doing things and going places without the direct, hands-on participation of the pilots. Or so it seemed. Perplexed pilots would stare at their flight displays in total bewilderment.

It was a joke, but one containing truth: The single most common utterance heard in a glass cockpit was: *"What the fuck is it doing?"*

The FA-18 Hornet was designed as a single-pilot fighter/attack aircraft. That meant one guy—or girl—did everything, instead of the two that crewed the previous frontline fighter, the F-14 Tomcat, and its predecessor, the F-4 Phantom. Even the ancient A-6 Intruder, an all-weather, low-level attack airplane, was flown by a pilot and a bombardier/navigator. Those were the old days, when a pilot flew the airplane and somebody else handled the mission specifics.

Now the Hornet pilot did it all. He flew the airplane and attended to all the other details with the aid of the fighter's highly sophisticated mission control computer and an array of six DDIs (digital display indicators)—monitor screens with a keyboard by which he could select multiple data routes and subroutes for every phase of flight or weapon he carried.

But sometimes it just got to be too much. Someone (in the Pacific fleet, it was said) invented the expressions "helmet fires" and "finger fires." When a novitiate Hornet pilot would start flipping through the modes on the DDIs like a channel surfer looking for MTV, pulling up the wrong page, then another, taking a wrong route and then another wrong subroute, burying himself in a miasma of confusion with a figurative cloud of smoke billowing from his skull—the poor freaked-out bugger was said to be having a helmet fire.

A related problem was the finger fire. Almost all the Hornet's flight and fire control commands were issued through the HOTAS— hands on throttle and stick. The control stick in the pilot's right hand and the throttles in his left hand bristled with buttons and switches. There were sixty-some combinations of button and switch commands by which the Hornet pilot did everything—from transmitting on a radio to steering the nose wheel to firing a missile to engaging the autopilot. HOTAS was what allowed a single pilot in the Hornet to perform all the tasks that were once done by multiple-pilot crews.

But the multitude of HOTAS switch and button selections, in the heat of a tense moment, could congeal to a fuzzy blob in an over-loaded pilot's brain. A harried pilot would start punching wrong buttons, thumbs and fingers flying, deploying a speed brake when he meant to engage an autopilot, turning off his lights when he intended to designate a target, firing his guns instead of releasing a bomb. He was having a classic finger fire.

Flight surgeons had a clinical term for such brain paralyses: "cognitive saturation." It meant the superbly trained pilot in whose education the taxpayers had invested something over two million dollars now possessed the intellectual powers of an orangutan.

What it came down to was that the Hornet was a new kind of fighter plane. It was a vehicle of the cyberworld. To fly the FA-18 Hornet—to master this smart-ass airplane—required a certain new faculty, something in addition to the traditional stick-and-rudder skills of the fighter pilot. You had to think and speak computerese. All the presentation of cockpit data was digital. Gone were the days when you just jumped in the cockpit of a fighter and flew the thing by the seat of your pants. Now you were supposed to *interface* with the machine.

Oh, sure, certain fundamentals about flying hadn't changed. To be a good fighter pilot, you still had to be a good pilot. But these days it helped if you were also a techno-geek.

★

Before their first flight, the students received a briefing from Lieutenant Tom "Slab" Bacon. Slab was the familiarization phase training officer. He was blond, short, and muscular, with an unlined face that made him look, everyone guessed, about sixteen years old. He wore a shoulder patch on his flight suit that signified he had logged a thousand hours in the FA-18 Hornet.

Slab's job was to shepherd the class through the initial phase of their training, which included the ground school, where they would learn all the Hornet's high-tech systems and performance parameters, the simulator course they would fly prior to actually getting into an airplane, and then the real thing—their initial flights in the FA-18.

Slab talked to the nuggets about procedures, about emergencies, about landings. "After a couple normal landings, we'll do an engine-out approach and landing. It does just fine on one engine. In fact, students initially do better with one-engine approaches than with two because they don't overpower the jet, using too much throttle."

To help slow the jet on the landing rollout, the Hornet pilot was supposed to bring the control stick between his legs back toward him slightly. This action caused the big horizontal control surfaces on the tail, called stabilators, to tilt to a twenty-five-degree angle, which added aerodynamic drag and helped brake the jet to a stop on the runway.

There was a small hazard associated with this. "Don't bring the stick *all* the way back in your lap," Slab warned. "All you need is about an inch and a half. That will get you full deflection of the stabilator. Anything more than that, and you've got the stick uncomfortably close to the ejection seat handle."

The ejection seat handle was a lanyard attached to the seat between the pilot's thighs. With either or both hands, the pilot could grab the handle and pull, firing the rocket-motored ejection seat, blasting himself up and away from the jet. He could do this anywhere, even on the ground. The parachute would deploy in time to save him.

Slab told the wide-eyed students a true story. "This actually happened. On the landing roll the pilot yanked the stick all the way back to the stop. One of the buttons on the top of the stick got caught in the ejection seat handle. Then he shoved the stick forward again and—*pow*—there he went. Big surprise. He ejected himself right there on the runway."

The pilot was attached to the seat and the parachute by "Koch" fittings, which were four metal clip-buckles, one at each shoulder and hip that fastened the pilot's torso harness to the straps in the airplane. The Koch fittings were designed to be fastened and released by two fingers. The fittings were the pilot's anchor point to his life-saving parachute.

Slab told another eye-opener. "Check your Koch fittings. They *have* been forgotten. . . ."

One of those events was witnessed by everyone on an aircraft carrier. A Hornet was launched from the bow catapult, then experienced some sort of control failure. What happened next was a tableau that no one watching from the flight deck and bridge of the carrier would forget.

As the jet plummeted like a sick eagle toward the ocean, the pilot ejected. Back on the ship they saw the tiny dark shape of the pilot pop out of the fighter, soaring in an upward arc. They saw him separate from the seat, just like he was supposed to. And they waited for the long white plume of parachute to blossom above him, like it was supposed to.

And they waited.

And while they waited they watched the small dark shape of the pilot arc downward toward the ocean. Not until the last instant did it suddenly become clear to them what was happening.

No parachute.

Sploosh. And then nothing.

The image of that little splash on the ocean remained frozen in the memories of a hundred witnesses.

That one got to them. No one in the briefing room spoke for a moment. They sat there for a moment imagining what it would be like . . . grabbing the handles and punching out of the cockpit of your stricken fighter—*whoom!*—a successful ejection, and then feeling the seat separating from you just like it was supposed to . . . waiting for the parachute to open . . . tumbling through space, waiting, waiting . . . then the horrible realization . . .

Yeah, man. Great idea. Check those damn Koch fittings.

★

To no one's surprise, the first to finish the ground training course was Chip Van Doren, who was the undisputed champion computer whiz of class 2-95. He had zipped through the course—the CAI and the simulators—ahead of everyone else and was scheduled for FFAM-101—the first real airplane hop.

First flights in the Hornet were always in a two-seater—the FA-18B or FA-18D model. It was like driver's ed. The instructor rode in the backseat, where he could coach, observe, critique, and keep the neophyte fighter pilot out of serious trouble.

Chip Van Doren's instructor for his first Hornet flight was Slab Bacon, which pleased Van Doren. The nuggets liked Slab. He was an up-front guy who gave them no bullshit.

Flight instructors tended to fall into two categories: those who taught, and those who critiqued. Of the two roles, the easiest by far was critique: itemizing the bungling student's errors and dumping them on him like a litany of sins. The tougher and more useful task was to teach. Good instructors taught by example. And they allowed—with a watchful eye—a student to make his own mistakes, thereby enabling him to learn what not to do.

Most of all, good instructors had to be cool. Unflappable. They had to remain calm even when it seemed clear that a particular student had been sent from hell just to kill them. Maintaining coolness was a prerequisite when you were instructing nuggets.

Van Doren showed up two hours early. It was his duty to fill out the mission briefing board that covered most of one wall in the briefing room. The student was supposed to write in with grease pencil all the data for the upcoming flight: times, communications frequencies, weather, call signs, operating area, divert information, fuel required. On the bottom of the board he wrote the emergency of the day, the selected procedure that every student that day would be required to recite during his briefing.

Slab appeared precisely at brief time. He reviewed everything on the day's agenda. He had Van Doren recite all the required emergency memory items: ejection procedures, spin recovery, engine failure. Slab went through the entire flight from engine start to the final landing. He hit every detail, including how to adjust the seat and where to place your feet when climbing the boarding ladder. It was the longest and most thorough briefing Van Doren had ever endured.

When he was finished, Slab said, "Any questions?"

★

It was one of those crisp February afternoons in Florida, with high cumulus and a sky so clear and blue you could see forever. Chip Van Doren and Slab Bacon walked across the ramp toward their waiting FA-18D, number 307. Van Doren felt like a pack mule with all the gear strapped and fastened to him—the clunky flight boots, the G suit fastened around his legs and torso, the torso harness with the Koch fittings that would attach him to the seat straps in the cockpit, the SV-2 survival vest containing the inflatable life vest and about ten pounds of paraphernalia—flares, lights, radio, mirror, water—stuff intended to keep him alive wherever he might come down. They wore their helmets, complying with the air wing requirement that everyone—mechanics, fuelers, pilots—wear a hardhat on the flight line.

As pilots did for every flight, they made a walk-around inspection. Slab led the way, pointing out to Van Doren the myriad items that had to be checked—landing gear struts, tires, panel fasteners, weapons pylons. They squatted under the fuselage, peered into engine inlets, exhausts, looked for leaks and cracks and dents. The Hornet's engines were susceptible to FOD (foreign object damage)— nuts and screws and debris that the jet's intakes vacuumed up from the ramp like a Hoover gobbling dirt. A single one-inch bolt going through one of the Hornet's intakes would transform the GE-manufactured turbojet, low-bypass engine to a disintegrating, fire-spitting, blade-throwing creature from hell.

As he walked around the jet, bumping things, struggling with the fastener of an inspection panel, banging his head on a weapons pylon (so that was why they wore helmets!), Van Doren could feel the plane captain staring at him. "Plane captain" was the Navy's appellation for "crew chief," the sailor who was responsible for the cleaning and fueling and general airworthiness of that particular airplane. He was a youngish kid, all of nineteen or so. He was gawking at Van Doren like he'd just landed from Alpha Centauri.

"This is his first time," Slab explained unnecessarily.

"Yes, sir, I can tell," said the kid.

The two of them, Slab and the plane captain, got Van Doren strapped into the front seat, a chore akin to plumbing a patient for multiple surgery. The safety pin was pulled from the Martin Baker ejection seat, which has a separate handle on the side to arm and disarm the mechanism. After the engines were started and the jet was taxiing, the pilot armed the seat, enabling a ground-level ejection. Shoulder and waist straps were attached to the fittings on his torso harness. Four retention straps, one around each thigh and ankle, were attached to keep his legs from flailing during a high-speed ejection. An oxygen hose and radio coupling mated to a connector on the torso harness. The hose from the G suit plugged into a connector on the left console, which supplied the air that inflated the pilot's G suit.

G's were units of acceleration. One G was the force of the earth's gravity. When the jet pulled up steeply or pulled out of a dive, the Gs increased from the normal one G to four or five or more, increasing the pilot's effective weight by four or five times. The blood drained from his head to his lower body, causing "grayout" (a loss of vision and wooziness) and, ultimately, "blackout" (unconsciousness). With the onset of Gs, the G suit inflated around the pilot, squeezing his legs and abdomen, preventing some of the flow of blood downward from his brain and helping him maintain consciousness. Wearing an inflated G suit felt like having a boa constrictor wrapped around the lower half of your body.

Van Doren was finally installed in the front seat of the Hornet. When Slab had settled himself into the rear cockpit, they started the engines. On the plane captain's signal, they deployed the flaps and speed brakes, and actuated all the flight controls, while he checked them all from the outside. With the pretaxi checks completed, off they went.

"Cecil Tower, Roman one-oh-seven ready for takeoff," Van Doren said on the radio.

"Roger, Roman one-oh-seven," replied the tower controller. "Wind zero-seven-zero at eight, cleared for takeoff on runway niner left. Switch to departure control."

Then came the part that Van Doren had not experienced in the simulator. No matter how realistic the sights and sounds of a modern simulator, they didn't replicate the unique chemistry of flight: that rush of adrenaline when you release the brakes and push the throttles forward, past the detent into afterburner and—*babloom!*—you hear and feel the two torches of flame behind the jet nozzles and—holy shit!—you feel yourself shoved back in the seat as the beast goes hurtling down the runway like a drag racer out of the chute.

That was something else new to the nuggets: afterburners. The jets they learned to fly in the training command were equipped with basic jet engines. No afterburners. The afterburner of a jet engine was a thrust augmenter, like the passing gear of a car's automatic transmission. You selected afterburner by pushing the jet's throttles all the way to full power, then nudging them even further past a detent. The exhaust nozzles of the jet engines widened and a spray of raw fuel was injected into the exhaust blasts.

Chip Van Doren was making his first afterburner takeoff. It felt like popping a wheelie on a motorcycle. Lighting the afterburners produced a satisfying deep-throated roar and a blossom of flame like the tail of a comet from each exhaust. It instantly upped the thrust of each General Electric F404 turbofan engine from an impressive ten thousand pounds of thrust to a neck-wrenching six-teen thousand pounds. The afterburners on a jet fighter were used for short spurts of maximum energy.

It was another joke—and a standard condition—that the nugget fighter pilot was at least forty miles behind the jet on his first flight. His brain was still back there behind the airplane somewhere, trying to catch up.

So it was with Van Doren. They were already at flying speed, still barreling down the runway, when he heard Slab say gently on the intercom, "Rotate, Chip. Let's go flying."

Oh, yeah.

Van Doren was mesmerized, watching the concrete runway zip past like a video in fast forward. He "rotated"—nudged back on the stick—which lifted the nose of the fighter upward.

The Hornet leaped into the air. They were flying. *Really* flying, and accelerating like a fox in a forest fire.

"Gear up, Chip."

Oh, yeah.

Still mesmerized. The Hornet was accelerating so fast it was already close to the limiting speed for the landing gear. If you delayed retracting the landing gear on an afterburner takeoff, the jet's excessive speed would cause serious damage to the gear.

More gentle suggestions. "Anticipate the level-off, Chip. We're climbing ten thousand feet a minute."

Oh, yeah.

And so it went. Slab suggesting, reminding, coaching, Chip Van Doren going through his simulator-taught procedures, staying a good solid forty miles behind the Hornet.

Out in the operating area, off the Florida coastline east of St. Augustine, they leveled at twenty thousand feet. Van Doren put the Hornet through the basic aerobatics he had rehearsed in the simulator. He did barrel rolls—big, graceful corkscrew rolls through the sky. Then he did aileron rolls, which were quick, neck-snapping rolls around the fighter's center line. The Hornet was capable of a roll rate of 720 degrees per second, meaning it could perform two complete revolutions around its axis every second.

Van Doren did a loop—a great vertical circle in the sky. Then a split-S—rolling the jet inverted and pulling the nose straight down to complete the bottom of a loop. They practiced slow flight—*very* slow flight—which the Hornet could do in a way never seen before in a Navy fighter.

The Hornet could literally stand on its tail, almost in a hover, with its nose cocked fifty or more degrees above the horizon, indicating only a little over a hundred knots of airspeed. This was called "high alpha"—engineering lexicon for high angle of attack, the angle at which the airplane's wings cut (attacked) through the air. The Hornet possessed this unique ability to fly at very high alpha, screeching almost to a stop in the sky, maneuvering behind the tails of its supersonic opponents.

Then they flew supersonic. Van Doren dropped the fighter's nose, shoved the throttles into afterburner, and flew beyond the so-called sound barrier, something he had never done before in the subsonic T-2 and A-4 trainers he had previously flown. It was something the Hornet did with ease.

Van Doren watched the digital Mach indicator on the HUD (head-up display) in the windshield show .99 Mach (meaning ninety-nine percent the speed of sound), then 1.0 (one hundred percent). He let it build until he saw 1.2 Mach. One hundred twenty percent the speed of sound.

That's all there was to it. The only way he could see that they had shattered the once-unattainable "sound barrier" was by the little yellow digital indication. In the FA-18 Hornet the sound barrier was not a barrier at all. It was just another number.

When they had finished practicing in the operating area, they returned to the traffic pattern at Cecil Field for touch-and-go landings. Van Doren was gaining confidence with the new jet. He was catching up—almost. He had gone from forty miles behind the jet to about twenty.

Slab was prompting less now, letting Van Doren figure things out for himself. This was what familiarization flights were supposed to be about: letting the student get familiar with the beast he was riding. It was something akin to the contest of wills between a new rider and his horse.

Slab demonstrated the landing, using the Fresnel lens—the optical glide path indicator that was installed on every carrier and air station in the Navy. The Fresnel lens was a mirrorlike board at the edge of the runway, next to the landing area. The mirror had a row of green datum lights on each side and an amber "meatball" in the lens that moved up and down according to the pilot's position on the glide slope.

When the pilot saw that the ball was exactly between the green datum lights on the lens out there by the runway, it told him that he was on the correct descent path. If he scrupulously "flew" the ball, meaning that he kept it in the middle of the lens—between the green datum lights—his jet would plunk into the landing area exactly on target. If he let the ball go high, off the top of the lens, the jet was too high on its approach path. It would land beyond the touchdown zone, missing the arresting wires of the aircraft carrier and caroming off the deck back into the air. Worse, if the ball went low, settling off the bottom of the lens, meaning he had gone below the glide path, it meant he was toast. Literally. His fighter crashed into the unyielding blunt ramp of the aircraft carrier.

Navy fighter pilots flew the ball every time they landed, on land as well as sea, just to keep their skills up. It was this specialized ability that allowed them to bring their twenty-ton, swept-wing fighters down to the heaving, slickened, ludicrously minuscule decks of aircraft carriers—right on target. It was what made naval aviators different from their fighter pilot counterparts on the rest of the planet.

So they practiced incessantly. They practiced flying the ball even when they were landing on a thirteen-thousand-foot runway, as Chip Van Doren and Slab Bacon were doing today. To a Navy fighter pilot, it was the most important skill in aviation. Weapons delivery, air combat maneuvering, formation flying—those were all items of business necessary to carry out your mission. Flying the ball was something more vital. It meant getting home alive.

Chip Van Doren had the same trouble every new pilot had trying to fly the ball: He overcontrolled. The tendency, at first, was to jam on too much power to correct a descent, causing the ball to shoot off the top of the lens. Or yank the throttle back too much, causing the ball to sink off the bottom. The ball, centered between the datum lights, was the pilot's cue to a precise path to touchdown. The trick was to make tiny, precise corrections with the fighter's two throttles. Squeeze on a bit. The ball is moving ever so slightly up . . . squeeze off a tiny bit . . . that's enough, put a little back on . . .

"Like milking a mouse," old carrier pilots used to say. Tiny inputs. Anticipating the results of every movement of throttles and flight controls.

They made six touch-and-go landings—landing and then pushing the throttles up to take off again—before it was time to call it a day. They had been out for one hour and a half. To Van Doren, it seemed like ten minutes.

When he unstrapped and climbed out the front seat, he realized he was soaked with perspiration. It had been a very intense ninety minutes.

The two pilots climbed down the boarding ladder and pulled off their helmets.

"Well?" said Slab, the instructor.

"Awesome," said Chip Van Doren, the new fighter pilot.

★

By the end of March 1995, each of the nuggets of Class 2-95 had made at least his first fam flight in the Hornet. Broad grins covered the young faces. It was a rite of passage. They could hang out in the ready room, wearing their gray-green flight suits, and not feel like spectators at a soccer game. Now, by God, they were *in* the game. Real, bona fide, ass-kicking players. They were fighter pilots, at least to the extent that they were now flying real fighters and not simulators.

In addition to the Gladiators squadron patch stuck on the shoulder of his flight suit, each was now entitled to wear the bright red Hornet patch adorned with the silhouette of the FA-18, courtesy of the McDonnell Douglas Corporation.

They compared impressions. Angie Morales was the most coolly analytical: "I was surprised by the . . . *energy* of the airplane. In the landing pattern, I felt a little behind the airplane at first. The tremendous energy—that's something you don't get a feel for in the simulator."

One of the McCormacks—Heckle or Jeckle, no one could yet tell—sauntered into the ready room with a profound observation: "Wow! It flies just like the simulator."

Which got a laugh. Everyone understood that it was both a joke and the truth. They were still going through the head trip—a peculiar inversion of perception that went with "flying" a simulator. They had spent nearly a month flying the simulated version of the Hornet.

Now that they had gotten to the real thing, it just didn't seem . . . real. Reality and simulated reality—they were indistinguishable.

Burner Bunsen was last. He came marching—*swaggering*—into the ready room after his FFAM-101. Sweat stained the back and the armpits of his flight suit. He summed it up for all of them. "Unreal," the Marine announced. "Un-freaking-real."

CHAPTER NINE

SLAB

Sometimes Slab Bacon wondered what would have happened if he had stayed in law school. Looking back, it seemed such an unlikely career shift—the law office to the cockpit of a fighter. He knew one thing for sure, though: He liked being a fighter pilot a hell of a lot more than he would have liked being a lawyer.

Although he had grown up in an Air Force family, Slab hadn't been interested in a military career when he was in school. He hadn't applied for ROTC scholarships or academy appointments.

When he graduated from Northeast Louisiana State, he went on to law school at the University of Texas. But at the end of one season of clerking in a Dallas law office, a dismal truth was sinking in: *I hate this goddamn job. And what I hate about it most of all is . . . lawyers!*

It was possible in those days to go directly into aviation officer training at Pensacola, get a commission, and be a naval aviator. Right off the street. It was 1987 and the Cold War was still hot. The Reagan military buildup was in full gallop. The Fine Mesh was still coarse enough to admit even law school dropouts. It was the end of Slab Bacon's career in jurisprudence.

Watching Slab at work in the squadron offices, you could see vestiges of the law clerk. Slab was obsessively organized. He kept track of all his duties and projects on a grease board over his desk. He could be seen in the passageways of the squadron, always moving at warp speed, carrying pieces of paper on some urgent mission. Slab was *busy*. He was the busiest lieutenant anyone had ever seen.

A few of his colleagues thought that perhaps Slab was too busy. "Slab's anal, you know," observed another instructor, who made it a point *not* to be busy. "He's a compulsive doer. Doesn't matter what, he's gotta be *doing*. Drives us crazy, him running around like a god-damn dog in a meat locker."

But Slab was the kind of junior officer that senior officers loved. Slab would do all the gritty little jobs that everyone hated—the monthly reports and assessments and record keeping and bureaucratic bullshit that plagued every branch of the military. The Navy—*especially* the Navy—loved record keeping. Slab was known as a *doer*, and his career, because of it, was on a fast track.

Slab, of course, was more than a paperwork whiz. He was also a good instructor who could fly the hell out of a Hornet. Like all the instructors in the RAG, he had earned for himself a reputation as a strike fighter pilot.

It was no coincidence that his commanding officer in his fleet squadron, VFA-86, had been Commander Matt Moffit, the same officer who now commanded the RAG. Moffit had observed Slab Bacon in action. Both in peace and in war.

★

It was early in the Gulf War. They'd been bombing from high altitude, above ten thousand, because the CAG (commander, air group) didn't want to risk losing any airplanes to ground fire this early in the game. That would come later, when they went in to support the ground invasion.

Slab had come back from a mission over the desert. He was sitting in the ready room when Matt Moffit, his skipper, barged in.

"CAG wants to see you, Slab. Now."

For a fleeting minute, while Slab followed his skipper down the passageway, down the ladder to the second deck, it crossed his mind that he might be getting a medal. A Distinguished Flying

Cross? A Navy Commendation Medal? Of course! Why else would he be summoned to the CAG's office?

And then Slab saw the CAG's face. He was not smiling. The CAG looked like he had just digested a cinder block. Matt Moffit, a man who smiled a lot, was standing there wearing the face of an undertaker.

Forget the medal, Slab told himself. *This is not a medal day. Today you're dog meat.*

CAG was holding up a blurred black and white photograph, the kind they copied from cockpit videotapes. The photo was a close-up of a ship in the water. The ship was some kind of freighter. It had several holes in the hull, and smoke was pouring from the deck. The ship looked like someone had blown the living shit out of it.

★

His target—his *real* target—had been obscured beneath the clouds that day. His wingman had diverted back to the carrier with a mechanical problem. So there he was, all alone, bombs on board, ammo left in the guns, with nothing to shoot at. He would have to jettison the bombs before returning to his aircraft carrier, the *America.*

So far, thought Slab, it was a boring war.

Then he saw it, just offshore. It wasn't going anywhere, no wake, just sitting out there in the gulf. Even from fifteen thousand feet, Slab could see that the ship—it looked like a small freighter—had already been worked over.

He called Alpha Whiskey, the airborne tactical controller. He told them about the ship.

"Roger, Galeforce sixteen. The vessel you're looking at . . . ah, we confirm that it is definitely hostile. The same ship was targeted yesterday by some A-6s. Apparently they didn't sink it. Do you have weapons on board?"

"Affirmative."

"It's all yours."

The CAG had ruled that they must drop their bombs from an altitude above ten thousand feet. *Oookay*, thought Slab. *No problem.*

Slab rolled into a forty-degree dive on the target vessel. He "pickled"—pressed the weapons release button on his control stick—

off two Mark 83 one-thousand-pounders. These were so-called dumb bombs, meaning they had no guidance after they were dropped from the Hornet. It was the FA-18's own computerized bombing system that imparted "intelligence" to the bombs. The computer resolved all the factors of speed, dive angle, and wind, and released the bombs at a calculated point in time and space to deliver them precisely onto the target.

But it was a fallible system, particularly when you dropped from such a high altitude. Too many variables were introduced *after* the bombs went, particularly the wind direction and velocity below ten thousand feet, which could skew the bomb trajectory by a hundred feet or more.

Slab felt the *whump!* as his bombs kicked off the rack on his starboard wing. He pulled up, grunting under the G force, and looked back over his shoulder at the target. He saw two water-geysering explosions—a hundred feet behind the ship. Christ! If anyone was on board down there, they'd be laughing their asses off.

It was time to push the envelope. Just a little. He rolled in on the target again. This time he pickled at eight thousand feet. He felt the satisfying *whump!* again as his bombs kicked off the rack. He pulled up and looked for his hits.

Fifty feet. To the port side.

This is bullshit, thought Slab. With that thought, his own computer—his fighter pilot envelope-pushing logic machine—started going through a complex rationalization. The ten-thousand-foot floor was really meant for targets in the desert, right? That's where they have all the missiles and antiaircraft guns. This is over water, right? So the rule doesn't apply, does it? Not really. . . .

Down he went. Steep and low. Slab pressed his dive until the Iraqi ship swelled to the size of the *Bismarck* in his windshield. *Whump!* His bombs went, and Slab pulled up hard. He was low over the water. Grunting, he looked back over his shoulder.

He saw a large geysering bomb plume at the waterline, on the port side. And directly amidships—where the ship's superstructure used to be—a great, orange, metal-shrouding, oil-belching fireball. It was a horrific sight. And glorious.

Now what? Well, hell, he was down here anyway. The bombs were gone, but he still had guns. . . .

Slab rolled in again on the smoking ship. He could see no sign of life, no boats in the water, no one shooting back. The Iraqi crew had hauled ass as soon as the A-6s showed up yesterday.

At a range of a thousand yards he opened up with the rotary cannon mounted in the nose of the Hornet. *Brrrrrrrraaaaaaaaaaaap.*

The M-61 rotary cannon was a fearsome weapon. It fired at an incredible six thousand rounds a minute. He saw the tracers arcing into the ship. Pieces were flying off the hull, off the deck, ripping loose like debris in a hurricane. Sparks flashed. Holes opened in the rusty slab-sided hull.

He made another strafing pass. Six thousand rounds a minute— *brrraaaappppp . . . brrrraaaaaaaaaaaaaaaaap*—firing until the ammo was finished.

He took one last look as he climbed out over the gulf. The freighter was low in the water. Smoke billowed from the hatches, from the shattered superstructure, from the holes in the hull. The Iraqi ship was not in good shape.

Back on the deck of the *America*, Slab went to the intelligence office for the mission debriefing. He told them about spotting the ship and about being cleared on to it by Alpha Whiskey. Yes, he said, he thought he got some good hits. He decided not to be too specific on the matter of *altitudes*.

And then, almost as an afterthought, he turned over to the intelligence officer the HUD (head-up display) tape—the onboard cockpit video that recorded everything you did.

★

The CAG was holding the black and white photo of the smoking freighter. It was an enlargement taken from Slab's HUD video.

"Slab, what altitude was this?"

"Ah, sir, I might have gotten a little below the floor altitude—"

"Seven hundred feet."

"Sir, I don't think—"

"SEVEN . . . HUNDRED . . . FUCKING . . . FEET! That happens to be nine thousand three hundred feet below the minimum delivery altitude."

Now Slab knew. He *definitely* was not here to get a Distinguished Flying Cross.

"Yes, sir. I may have made a bad decision."

The CAG had a lot on his mind, being responsible for the activities of eighty-some warplanes and the fates of all their pilots. This was not his first war. As a fresh young nugget, he had been caught up in the last days of Vietnam. He was a man who understood the passions of young fighter pilots, and he wouldn't give a nickel for one who wasn't willing to pursue the enemy—even down to seven hundred feet.

"Slab, you get this through your head. I'm not gonna lose any airplanes because of stupid cowboy stunts like this. If I so much as suspect you of doing something like this again, I'll kick your ass all the way from here to Baghdad. You got it?"

"Yes, sir."

★

Slab Bacon survived the Gulf War. He even collected a few medals and then received a prize assignment: instructor in the Strike Fighter RAG. Slab had a textbook Navy career going. Slab Bacon, everyone figured, was on track to get command of a squadron, maybe an air group, maybe more.

But like many naval aviators his age, Slab Bacon had reached a crossroads in his life. He was thirty-three years old and had given eight years of his life to the Navy. And he had recently acquired three items of overwhelming importance in his life: Brenda, Brandon, and Hannah. Wife, stepson, baby daughter.

Stay in or get out? It was the kind of gut-wrenching decision every would-be career Navy pilot goes through. Stay in, hope your career advances without a major glitch, pray that your family has the stamina and understanding and resourcefulness to endure the years of separation while you're deployed aboard a succession of aircraft carriers. Raise your kids in absentia. Trust that your wife still keeps her poise and balance after enough casketless funerals of your friends.

Or you get out. Slab had old squadron mates who had resigned when their contracts were up, gone to the airlines, into business, back to school. Slab's best friend was a pilot with Federal Express. After his second year with the airline, he was making exactly twice Slab's Navy salary. The best part was no six-month deployments aboard carriers. No missing seeing your kids grow up. No casket-less funerals.

The problem was, Slab loved the Navy. And he especially loved flying strike fighters. Nothing, absolutely *nothing* would be sweeter or more fulfilling than taking command of his own seagoing fighter squadron. But to do that, he—and his little family—had to pay the price.

But in early 1995 something came to Slab's attention—a fighter pilot's job that was, for him, at least, made in heaven: *The Swiss Air Force was buying Hornets.*

Thirty-two of them—brand-new FA-18 strike fighters. And now the Swiss were requesting the *loan* from the U.S. Navy of a few qualified FA-18 instructor pilots to serve with the Swiss Air Force as liaison officers and advisers. A few good men.

Like Slab Bacon.

Switzerland! It would be an assignment made in heaven for their little family. Yodelers and cheese and ski slopes and mountain vil-lages . . . Brenda could just see them, ensconced in their alpine chalet, the kids in an international school, chatting in German and French, living the good life. . . .

In February 1995, Slab Bacon put in his formal request for the assignment. It received a positive endorsement from his com-manding officer, Captain Moffit. The letter was routed upward through the chain of command, formally requesting that Lieutenant Bacon be considered for an exchange posting with the Swiss Air Force. By late summer, Slab was told, a decision would be made.

In the meantime, Slab Bacon reached a private decision. If the Swiss job came through, he was in the Navy to stay. He would be a lifer, with all that it entailed—the long cruises, the sacrifices. If not, he was gone.

CHAPTER TEN

TAMING THE BEAST

Now that Class 2-95 had finally begun flying, they no longer saw much of each other. Their schedules were all different, with flights slated from predawn until late at night. In between actual hops in the FA-18, they still had a heavy simulator schedule. Almost everything they did in the Hornet—bombing, instrument flying, air combat maneuvering—first had to be rehearsed in the simulator.

It was a grueling schedule, beginning before dawn if they were on the first launch of the day. Briefing began an hour and a half before takeoff time. The actual flight lasted another hour and a half. After landing, they taxied their jets to the fuel pit, remaining in the cockpit until the fighter was refueled, a process that sometimes took another hour. Another student would be waiting to strap into the jet and take off on another training mission. VFA-106's stable of Hornet jets spent almost no idle time on the ground.

After securing the jet and shedding the layers of flight gear, it was time to swill down a couple of Cokes and cool off. In a single training flight in the Hornet, along with the preflighting and re-fueling sessions, a pilot could sweat off four or five pounds of body weight.

The instructor would debrief for at least an hour, going over the entire flight. If it was a weapons flight, they would view the cockpit videotape. A single flight, from briefing to debriefing, might take five to six hours.

They did this twice a day. Wedged in between the flights were simulator sessions, lectures, all-officers meetings (AOMs), and stints as squadron duty officer. Days at the squadron could stretch to twelve or fourteen hours.

The only time the class was together was during one of the lectures. An instructor would talk about some upcoming phase of training—formation flying or air-traffic-control procedures or the like. Sometimes it would be one of the "touchy-feely" square-fillers like "sensitivity" training—response to the newly mandated policy toward homosexuals in the service ("Don't ask—don't tell"). And there were lectures, of course, on the hot-potato subject of "gender integration," which, of course, produced hee-haws and wisecracks among Class 2-95.

By now the nuggets had fallen into routines of their own. Road Ammons was the top jock of the bunch. His typical day began at six in the morning, when he would suit up and go to the squadron. In between training events, he would put on shorts and T-shirt and jog for four or five miles around the perimeter of the base. In the evening, before heading for home, he'd stop at the gym to pump iron.

Road still had the thickly muscled build of a linebacker. It was back at Tennessee State that Road had wrestled with his first big career dilemma: play professional football, for which he already had a tantalizing offer, or take his commission in the Marines and pursue his dream of being a fighter pilot. Football was something he already knew. Something he was good at. Man, he was *good* at bashing heads with guys out there on the playing field. And besides, it was seriously good fun. On the other hand, the Marine Corps and the very long shot of getting into fighters—well, all that was a very iffy proposition.

Football lost, of course. Here he was, a first lieutenant in the U.S. Marine Corps, learning to fly fighters. And working his butt off doing it.

But sometimes in a private moment, Road would fantasize. When he let his imagination roam back, it would be a Sunday afternoon . . . the autumn of the year . . . the roar in the stadium swelling like thunder. His cleated shoes would dig into the artificial turf and he'd launch himself into the play—*Whap! Slam! Thunk!*

Yeah, football was neat, all right. Road loved the game. But in the final analysis, that's what it came down to: Football was a game. Flying the FA-18 Hornet was something more than a game. Flying a fighter put you way out there in a place that few other mortals knew about. You knew you were doing something that only a handful of other human beings on the planet would ever be allowed to do.

So here was good old Road, one time prospective pro football player, trudging along the Cecil Field perimeter road, grunting through a dozen reps of bench presses at the base gym, just to keep some semblance of his college jock condition. Someday, he told himself, when life steadied down a little, he might like to do something really jocklike: run a marathon, do a triathlon, something. Once a jock, always a jock.

★

That was just another of the ways in which they, the new kids, were different. *Jogging!* It was a mutation of fighter pilot character that would make the older generation of Right Stuffers puke in their hard hats.

Times had changed. Staying in shape was a high priority among the new generation of naval aviators. A fighter pilot who smoked these days was as rare as a rocket-boosted biplane. This new bunch didn't even *drink* like the pilots of yore, at least not in the same prodigious quantity and frequency as the previous generation, whose sacred duty it had been to belly up to the bar virtually every afternoon after flying.

These days a pedestrian could get trampled to death at any naval air station by the herd of joggers that hit the sidewalks every morning and evening. Physical fitness was prized by the nuggets nearly as much as brains and talent.

Like most of the other nuggets, Sally Hopkins, or "Shrike," as she was now being called at the squadron, was a jogger. She was also a weight lifter, and two or three times a week she could be seen there in the gym, right alongside Road and the others, sweating and grunting, hoisting barbells and pumping iron.

Outside of the squadron, Shrike didn't have much social contact with her classmates. She lived in a small rented house on a tree-shaded street in a Jacksonville suburb. On weekends she liked to "feed the right half of my brain," as she put it. This meant going to a concert, or the theater, or just listening to some good jazz at one of the beach clubs. And she loved ballroom dancing, when she could find it, and didn't mind the fact that her partners were usually over sixty. "They're the only ones who know how."

Shrike, technically, wasn't a nugget. Nuggets, by definition, were aviators fresh out of the training command with no previous operational experience. Shrike had already completed a tour flying jets in a utility squadron based in the Philippines. But her flying career had been suspended for two years while she was earning her master's at the naval postgraduate school in Monterey, California. The two years out of the cockpit were now causing her problems. Her stick and rudder skills were rusty. She was playing catch-up.

But that was only one of Shrike's problems. Her mouth was another. She could be heard saying, not too discreetly, that she thought the instructors were down on her. And they were down on her, in her opinion, for no other reason than who—and what—she was. "They don't want me here," she said. "I'm a threat to them because I'm a woman."

There it was, out in the open. Shrike was invoking the Gender Thing. The hot potato. These days, it was the one subject guaranteed to start a firefight.

Her classmates in 2-95, when they heard her talk like this, would sneak nervous glances at each other. One of the goals of being a nugget in the Fleet Replacement Squadron was to slide through the place as slickly as possible. Avoid friction. Offer no opinions, especially opinions on a subject as dangerous as the Gender Thing. Keep your mouth shut.

It just wasn't in Shrike's chemistry to keep her mouth shut. Another RP from a couple of classes ahead was a lieutenant commander who had been around the Navy for a while. He tried to explain it to her.

"Chill out, Shrike," he said. "The instructors are just macho guys who expect you to show them a little deference. Around here, you gotta be a little humble."

"Humble? Why should I—"

"Pretend. It's a game. *Play* like you're humble."

"I don't see why I should have to kowtow to someone who thinks they're so damned superior."

"Hell, they *are* superior, at least here in the RAG. It's their show. Live with it."

She was having trouble living with it. In Shrike's opinion, the instructors were talking down to her. "In a briefing, they talk to the *guys* in the class. They talk right through me, as if I weren't a real person."

She thought she was being shortchanged in the amount and quality of instruction. An instructor's postflight critique, to her, would come off sounding like personal criticism, without anything constructive. Every flight seemed to be a check flight. "Too much evaluation," she complained about her instructors. "Not enough instruction."

And so it happened that Shrike was the first in the class to get a SOD. "SOD" meant signal of difficulty, what they used to call a "down"—a flunking grade for that particular activity. SODs were like strikes in a baseball game. You could collect a few before you were out. Then you might get another chance at bat. Or you might not.

She was on her sixth fam flight, still doing the get-acquainted maneuvers out in the training area and then coming back to do bounces—touch-and-go landings—at Cecil. She entered the traffic pattern back at Cecil by coming into the "break," which meant flying over the landing runway, then "breaking" to the left or right to join the traffic pattern parallel to the runway and lower the jet's landing gear and flaps for landing.

All this she did correctly. After the break, on the downwind leg parallel to the runway, she identified herself on the radio for the benefit of the landing signal officer, who was stationed at the end of the runway. The LSO was out there to monitor the touch-and-goes of the new fam-stage students, just in case they did something stupid.

Shrike did something stupid. She made her approach turn to the runway, lining up nicely with the runway. The *wrong* runway. Cecil Field, being a Master Jet Base, was blessed with *dual* east-west runways, side by side, which were aptly named Two-Seven-*Left* and Two-Seven-*Right*. The left runway was the landing runway, and the right was used for taking off. It was important to know which was which.

Shrike was aimed at runway Two-Seven Right.

"Wave off, wave off!" said the LSO on the radio. Shrike pulled up and went around the pattern again. On the next pass she was careful to land on the *left* runway.

She might have gotten away with it. All she had to do was shut up.

"Not good headwork, Shrike, trying to land on the wrong runway," the LSO said in the debriefing.

"It wasn't a big deal. There wasn't anyone on the right runway."

"It's a very big deal anytime you land on a runway you're not cleared to land on."

"Well, sure, but there wasn't any harm done. You don't have to make a big fuss about—"

"It was more than bad headwork," said the LSO. "It was unsatisfactory. I'm writing it up as a SOD."

Shrike was stunned. And then furious. She sat through the rest of the debriefing red-faced and tight-lipped. A SOD! She *knew* it! They were setting her up. This was probably just the beginning. They weren't going to give her a chance.

★

They all made mistakes, of course. Nuggets, by definition, were prone to making boneheaded errors, which was why they were kept under protective scrutiny. Whatever they did, wherever they flew, it was under carefully controlled conditions. During the familiarization stage of training, the weather had to be forecast to remain VFR (visual flight rules), meaning the students weren't allowed to fly on days when the sunny Florida skies were likely to turn dark and violent. They weren't allowed to fly with less than substantial reserves of fuel, just in case they committed the error of getting temporarily lost, or in case they needed to buy time to sort out a mechanical problem with their jet.

Nor were they allowed to fly together, students out there gadding about on their own, without the watchful guardianship of an instructor. The instructors were like mother geese tending their flocks of inept goslings.

Only as the students moved into the tactical phases of training, with more Hornet time behind them and more experience getting themselves out of trouble, would the strict control start to relax.

Little by little, in carefully controlled increments, the nuggets would be treated less like hapless airborne incompetents and more like fighter pilots.

★

Chip Van Doren's first boneheaded mistake was of a lesser magnitude. He was supposed to do the flight planning for his fourth fam stage hop, an instrument training flight to another base and the return. He spent more than two hours planning the mission. He obtained the weather, both current and forecast. He pulled out the approach charts for the flight-planned destination, Moody Air Force Base, which was a couple hundred miles northwest of Cecil. He studied the route and memorized the en route air-traffic-control frequencies. Then he filled out all the briefing data on the big wall board in the briefing room.

Van Doren was pleased with his work. He had gone above and beyond what was required, down to drawing multicolored lines on the chart showing courses, distances, times for each leg of the flight. The chart looked like an abstract art piece. Van Doren sat there in the briefing room waiting for the instructor to show up, thinking about how impressed the instructor would be with his pre-flight preparations.

The instructor showed up. He was a taciturn lieutenant named Phil Cauley. "What the hell's this?" Cauley asked when he saw the briefing board. "Moody Air Force Base?"

"Our destination, sir," said Van Doren.

"Didn't you check the schedule?" said the instructor. "We're supposed to go to Patrick Air Force Base."

Patrick? Van Doren groaned. Patrick was another base, down south by Cape Canaveral. *Shit. I read the wrong damned schedule.*

"This flight," said the instructor, "has just been delayed for as long as it takes us to refile our flight plan. Training time is valuable here, Lieutenant, and you just wasted some of it. It's *your* responsibility to read the schedule and plan accordingly."

"Yes, sir." Van Doren scrambled to fill out the new flight plan while the instructor watched him dourly.

Despite the lousy start, the rest of the mission went without further calamity. For his blunder in flight planning to the wrong airport, Van Doren received a "below average" on his grade sheet. But at least it wasn't a SOD. SODs were handed out for blunders of a greater magnitude.

For Chip Van Doren, the blunder of greatest magnitude was yet to come.

★

The commitment kept going up for newly designated aviators. Back in the late eighties and early nineties, when most of the current RAG instructors were still nuggets, the service obligation was six years after receiving your wings. Then it went to seven years. Now, in the post–Cold War downsizing mid-nineties, it had been raised to a whopping *eight years* of service from the time they received their wings. That meant a fighter pilot would be well into his thirties before even being eligible to leave the service. He was obliged to spend, including Naval Academy or ROTC time and the two or so years in flight training before winning his wings, nearly a decade and a half in uniform.

The reason for the whopping commitment was the whopping cost of the training. Each of the Fine Meshers' college degrees had cost the taxpayers a hundred or so thousand dollars, followed by initial flight training with a total bill of something over a million. And then the newly winged nugget went to a RAG like VFA-106, running up a bill of several hundred thousand more dollars just to become qualified in a *real* fighter like the FA-18.

It was a hell of an investment—consuming nearly eight years and roughly two million dollars—to acquire the services of a single fighter pilot. And the services lasted, maybe, four years.

That was it. Four years in a squadron, and often less. After the pilot logged a thousand or so hours in his jet, landing two or three hundred times aboard an aircraft carrier, surviving at least two lengthy deployments at sea—he was replaced. Gone. Back to the beach.

Which didn't make sense, of course. It seemed an incredible waste because the fighter pilot was, by now, a valuable national resource. It was like a baseball coach yanking his players from the lineup as soon as they started hitting home runs.

But that was the Navy way: Keep 'em rotating. Three or four years in a squadron, another three or four in a shore billet, back to sea for another stint. You went from sea duty, which meant the combat squadrons out there on the aircraft carriers, back to shore duty, which meant a job as an instructor, or perhaps a cushy assignment to postgraduate school or test pilot school.

Sometime during that first shore duty period, when the fighter pilot's obligated service time was ending and he was faced with going back to sea duty, he confronted the Big Decision: Stay in, or get out?

It was too soon for the nuggets of Class 2-95 to make the Big Decision. They still had most of their commitment ahead of them. But it was in their thoughts, something they talked about late at night with their wives, a pending decision that each knew he would have to make: Stay in or get out? Be a lifer, with all that that entailed—long separations, hazardous duty, a modest, rather scrimpish life style on Navy pay. Or get out. Take a seniority number with an airline and live the good life, at about twice the compensation of a military career. Or take your advanced degree to the marketplace and work in one of the rarefied disciplines of aerospace engineering.

Some, like Road Ammons and Shrike Hopkins, were already sounding like lifers. They were talking about assignments they might have *in the next century.* And J. J. Quinn, of course, *was* a bona fide lifer, having already put in thirteen years in the Marine Corps. The others—the McCormacks, Angie Morales, Chip Van Doren—weren't so sure. They said they were keeping their options open.

Burner Bunsen was the only one to declare that he was definitely *not* a lifer. To Burner, flying fighters and shooting missiles and being a bristle-headed Marine were a hoot, just like any other team sport. Just like hockey or crewing or football were a hoot. But then you moved on. Burner said that when his obligation was finished, he was going to grow up and get a real job. "I can see it now on the résumé," he said. " 'Marine Corps fighter pilot.' Man, they're gonna love me on Wall Street!"

★

From familiarization flights they moved on to the tactical phases: formation flying, air-to-air refueling, and AWI (all-weather intercepts). The nuggets loved it. This was more like it! They were getting closer to the real thing.

Formation flying was a requisite skill that every naval aviator learned early in basic flight training. Everything in tactical aviation that involved more than one fighter was done in formation. The Hornet was a superb formation airplane. It was so superb, in fact, that it was the fighter of choice by the Blue Angels, who flew their entire performances with plane-to-plane separations of only three feet.

Formation flying was a specialized hand-eye skill, like musical ability or language fluency. For some pilots it came easily, naturally. For others, flying precise formation would always be a harrowing, sweaty-palmed ordeal.

Maintaining your position a few feet away from the lead jet was something akin to zooming down a freeway, staying three feet away from the fender of the car in the next lane. But in the jet you had the third dimension—the up-down axis. Tight formation flying was an internal mind game, a reflexive activity that occurred at a subliminal level of consciousness. It was like the thrust-and-parry of fencing, the fencer reacting to events with almost instantaneous response. His brain interpreted problems and issued solutions at a vastly swifter speed than he could *think* on a conscious level. It was as though his eyes and hands were being controlled by a different command center. And, in fact, they were.

An experienced formation pilot's hand would perform these mini-corrections, dozens per second, making tiny control inputs, while his eyes registered every tiny displacement of his jet from the leader's. But with his brain—his on-line conscious computer—he might be chatting with the leader about the weather. Or solving a navigation problem. Or thinking raunchy thoughts. It was this Zen-like ability to detach, to let the subconscious take over, that made precise formation flying possible.

Flying three feet apart wasn't the tough part, at least not after the pilot learned the basic skill. Jets rarely collided when flying formation. It was *getting* in formation that could be the hairiest of maneuvers. The join-up, in fighter parlance, was called a "rendezvous." In a jet like the Hornet you could come ripping up to the lead aircraft with a speed advantage of a couple hundred miles per hour. It was like rushing up to the edge of a cliff on skis—and trying to stop exactly three feet away.

It took practice. When you did it wrong, zinging in with so much closure speed that you couldn't stop, you performed an "underrun," meaning you leveled the wings and slid beneath the lead aircraft. As you did this, whizzing under him like a runaway bobsled, he winced and grunted a prayer that you would miss him.

Night formation flying was even more demanding. "The only difference between night and day formation flying," Navy flight instructors used to say, "is that at night you can't see anything."

That was all. Since you couldn't see, you relied on radio dialogue and the little white formation lights that looked like glowworms in a pasture and didn't tell you much about how fast or slowly you were joining on the lead until—*Cheeee-rist!*—suddenly there he was right in your face.

Formation flying was like other phases of fighter training. It seemed difficult and dangerous. But you kept doing it over and over—until one day it struck you: Hey! I can *do* this. No sweat.

CHAPTER ELEVEN

THE REAL THING

The nuggets soon learned about the instructors—who were the good guys and who to watch out for. Mongo was a good guy. So was Slab. Another was Zoomie—Lieutenant Commander Allen Baker—a former Air Force officer who had become disaffected because he hadn't been assigned to fighters and switched his commission to the Navy.

A favorite was Lieutenant Chris "Barney" Barnes. Barney was thirty-two. He had a crew cut, a beer belly, and a vocabulary like a boatswain's mate. He also had a reputation as being possibly the best bomber in the business. It was a reputation he wore proudly and didn't mind advertising. Barney had an eye and some kind of internal aiming device for putting bombs inside a tiny circle on the earth. He didn't even mind if people were shooting at him, which they had for a while in 1991 while he was dismantling large items of Iraqi infrastructure.

During her first briefing with Barney Barnes, Shrike nearly heaved her lunch. What got to her wasn't Barney's language, which was colorful and eloquently profane. And it wasn't the way he sometimes punctuated his narrative by pausing to scratch his crotch.

Being a woman in what was still mostly a man's Navy, she had gotten used to all that—the expletives and crotch-scratching and, worst of all, the noisome and mostly anonymous flatulence of her male colleagues. All that she could deal with.

But this—*yukkkk!* It was enough to make her barf.

It was the Styrofoam cup. They were already five minutes into the briefing before she began to wonder about the cup. It was always in Barney's hand. He would be going on about today's four-plane lineup, who would fly what position, radio procedures, where they were going to rendezvous, what their bingo fuel (minimum fuel quantity) would be—and without missing a beat he would spit something dark and evil into the cup.

During a break, she took a peek at the cup. And wished she hadn't.

Barney was a dipper, which explained the ever-present lump under his lower lip. The cup was for expectorating the black, evil-looking residue. The lump and the cup and the spitting were as much a part of Barney's style as his flight suit and boots. And colorful language. And scratching his crotch.

★

Later, no one could figure out how Barney had gotten the gig with Charlton Heston.

Barney, for God's sake! How had he gotten such a glitzy assignment? After all, it wasn't as if there were a shortage of glib, good-looking guys in the squadron. VFA-106 had a full roster of Tom Cruise look-alikes who cleaned up well and could grin their way through the most formal occasion.

The Navy was throwing a dinner party for movie star Charlton Heston at the Naval Air Training Command in Pensacola. The old actor was a longtime Navy booster and a Reagan Republican who had helped lead the chorus for the massive military buildup of the eighties. The bash was supposed to honor Heston for his long record of support for naval aviation. It would be covered by television and newspaper reporters and, in the wake of the Tailhook mess, was supposed to throw some favorable light on Navy pilots.

VFA-106 had a special relationship with the actor. Because the squadron had always been called the Gladiators, and because their emblem was a gladiator helmet, Heston had years ago donated to the squadron the helmet he wore in the movie *Ben Hur*. For two decades now the helmet had been enshrined like the Hope diamond in the VFA-106 ready room.

Now the squadron thought it would be a neat idea to send someone to the affair in Pensacola—with the helmet. They would have pictures taken with the helmet while Heston chatted with a pilot from the squadron. It would be great publicity. And for the pilot who got to go . . . well, it was a chance to be seen in the company of celebrities and perhaps get his own career nudged along.

But *Barney*? Barney was jovial and chatty, sure, but was he . . . *refined*? Barney Barnes, of ball-scratching and dip-spitting fame, was about as refined as a Shriner at a debutante ball.

Barney Barnes was chosen because he happened to be *from* Pensacola. The squadron executive officer decided that it would be fitting that Barney return to his hometown to represent VFA-106 at the Heston bash.

Later, considering the circumstances, it was agreed that Barney had comported himself with aplomb. He looked grand in his starched dress whites, high collar snapped up to his chin, gold-winged and bemedaled. He sat there on the dais with the heavies—a couple of flag officers and Pensacola city officials and, of course, Charlton Heston, who everyone said had portrayed so many biblical characters that he looked more like God than God Himself.

Barney couldn't help noticing that Heston, whom he vaguely remembered as a studly young warrior in *Ben Hur* and later as a flint-eyed Navy pilot in *The Battle of Midway*, was *old*. Jesus, he looked *ancient*. Even his clothes were old, patched at the crotch, as though they were his favorite togs, and now that he had reached a certain seniority he'd wear any damn thing that pleased him. His shoes looked like he'd been gardening in them and forgot to change when he came to dinner. Charlton Heston might still look like God—but a senescent, absentminded God.

It came time for the helmet. The cameras were blinking away.

Barney and Heston were standing there at the dais. Barney hauled out the helmet and started to say his thing about how grateful the squadron was that Heston had given it to them and how they kept it in a glass case in the ready room . . .

A flicker of recognition passed across the old actor's face. He stared at the artifact. *Helmet . . . oh, yeah, I remember that thing.* He grabbed the helmet and thanked Barney for the gift.

"Uh, sir, I'm just supposed to show it to you and then—"

The old actor had the script wrong. He thought the helmet was for him. Now he *wanted* the damn thing!

Heston had a firm grip on the helmet. So did Barney. They stood there tugging at the helmet while the cameras whirred.

Barney could see his life flashing before his eyes. And his career. "Mr. Heston," he muttered in a low voice, "my executive officer said if I don't come back with this goddamn helmet, he would kick my ass all the way to Cuba. I gotta have this thing back."

Heston gave him a perplexed look. *What the hell is this kid talking about?* Suddenly—*synapse!*—he got it. Heston laughed and released his death grip on the gladiator helmet. The crisis passed.

From then on, they got along famously. They went from dinner to a closed room where a local television reporter wanted to interview the two of them together.

The interviewer, a woman, said to Barney: "You must be honored to be in the company of someone like Charlton Heston."

"No, not really," said Barney.

"No?" she said. "Why not? Charlton Heston is a famous actor."

"Sure," said Barney. "But Mr. Heston got famous by *acting*. Pretending to be someone like me. I'm the real thing."

Heston cracked up. He thought this was very funny. The interviewer did not. The segment was cut from the final telecast.

But what Barney had said was captured there on videotape. It was what fighter pilots *really* thought of themselves. Movies like *Midway* and *Top Gun* were pure illusion. Actors like Tom Cruise and Charlton Heston were only wishful pretenders. Fighter pilots like Barney Barnes were the real thing.

★

Every Navy fighter pilot will tell you that one of the silliest aviation movies ever made was *Top Gun.* He would say the film was cartoonish, adolescent, sexist, technically erroneous, simplistic, farcical. He would also tell you he had seen the movie maybe, oh, eleven times.

That was the peculiar paradox about *Top Gun.* It had a story line that might have been constructed by Dr. Seuss. The Tom Cruise leading character was something out of MTV, a cocky, swaggering, motorcycle-riding bad boy named "Maverick" Mitchell, who broke all the rules. Maverick buzzed towers and ships and busted altitude limits and pursued women into the ladies' room, and he got away with it because everyone thought he was as cute as a cockatoo. Maverick's only problem was, he wasn't a team player, which caused him a few problems with his work.

During the intense competition for Top Gun honors in the fighter weapons course, Maverick and his back-seater, Goose, lose an engine in their F-14, go into a flat spin, and have to punch out (eject). Goose, who is also Maverick's best buddy, is killed in the ejection, which sends Maverick into a tizzy. He loses his cockiness and, thus, his combat edge. He walks away from the Top Gun school. At the end of the movie, in a dogfight with MiGs, Maverick experiences a personal epiphany, regains his confidence, and blows the enemy out of the sky.

It was all very silly, real fighter pilots would tell you. But the absolute silliest part about it, the plot twist that got the biggest hoo-haws in Navy ready rooms, was when Maverick lost his nerve. *He quit? The candy-ass copped out just because somebody got killed?*

Of all the errors of fighter pilot portrayal, that was considered the most serious. In the view of the real fighter jocks, the specter of death was just something you accepted—a fact of life, so to speak. *Hell, man, people get killed. You don't let it spook you.*

But *Top Gun,* for all its silliness, broke box-office records like Maverick Mitchell shattered windows. It was the top box-office grosser for 1986. Even the hard rock sound track from the movie shot to the top of the billboard.

Top Gun was a huge hit because it splashed all over the screen the thunder and glamour of Navy fighters in action. Sitting in a surround-sound theater, you could *feel* the afterburners of the F-14 Tomcats. You could get nauseous watching the *real*—not animated, made-in-Hollywood—dogfight scenes shot from real cockpits over the high desert of southern California. The spectacular aerial footage was real because the Navy, most uncharacteristically, had placed a squadron of F-14s at the disposal of the producer, Paramount studios (calculating the per-hour cost of an F-14 Tomcat fighter at seventy-six hundred dollars), and even allowed the studio to shoot part of the movie aboard the nuclear carrier USS *Enterprise.*

It turned out to be a salutary investment for the Navy. *Top Gun* became the Navy's top recruitment draw. After *Top Gun* hit the screen, enlistment offices were overrun with aspiring naval aviators and Tom Cruise stand-ins. And even though Navy public relations officers cringed when they first saw the movie, with the Maverick Mitchell antics and the bawdy language, it was clear that *nothing* had ever come along to glamorize naval aviators like *Top Gun.*

The movie also scored because it tapped into another perennial theme: the image of the single combat warrior, the lone fighter pilot who sallies forth at high noon to challenge a single warrior opponent. It was the ancient knightly sport of jousting, with updated equipment. Sir Galahad in a flight suit.

The movie endures. Somewhere in every Navy ready room, stuffed in a locker among the stacks of videos that pilots watch to kill time between flying duty, is a much-viewed copy of *Top Gun.* It still gets played a lot. The pilots all know the film is silly. Farcical. Cartoonish. They love it.

CHAPTER TWELVE

KARA

"Well, it finally happened. . . ."

That's how the news spread around the squadron ready rooms in the Navy. Everyone was saying it: *It finally happened. . . .*

What had finally happened was an event out on the West Coast, in the Pacific waters off California. It occurred about the time the Class 2-95 nuggets were beginning their training at Cecil Field, and it delivered a seismic shock through the Navy, all the way to Washington.

★

Lieutenant Matt Klemish, riding in the backseat of the Tomcat fighter, didn't like what he saw. They were in their approach turn to the aircraft carrier *Abraham Lincoln,* and they had just overshot the turn, veering to the right of the approach path.

Klemish was the RIO—radar intercept officer. The aviator sitting in the front seat was a newly qualified fighter pilot. And at this moment the new pilot was having a hard time getting the Tomcat lined up—slewing the nose to the left, skidding the airplane, trying to get back to the center line.

"You're five knots fast," Klemish warned on the intercom.

"Roger," the pilot acknowledged.

The Tomcat was still turning. About then, Klemish heard a barely audible *pop* from one of the engines. *What the hell was that?* But then his attention was drawn to the airspeed indication. It was decreasing.

"We're ten knots slow," he said in the intercom. "Let's get some power on the jet."

He didn't feel the power coming up. The jet was still slow.

Now Klemish *really* didn't like what he was seeing. They were much too slow. And low. Three hundred feet and settling. *What the hell was going on?* The Tomcat didn't seem to be responding to the throttle the way it should.

Through the front portion of the cockpit canopy, Klemish could see the blunt gray aft end of the aircraft carrier. From this angle it looked like an apparition jutting from the ocean.

Klemish thought this would be a good time to knock off this approach. Things were getting hairy out here. Go back up and try it all over again.

The LSO, standing on his platform at the port-deck edge of the aircraft carrier, had already reached the same conclusion. The two rows of red wave-off lights began flashing. The LSO called, "Wave off! Wave off!"

A wave-off signal was an order. It meant, *Go!* Abandon the approach and go try it all over again. Shove the throttles up and get the hell out of there.

The pilot shoved the throttles up. But the Tomcat wasn't answering like it should. Instead, it yawed left. They were still slow, cocked up at a dangerous attitude, slewing leftward.

"WAVE OFF! WAVE OFF! Level your wings and climb!" the LSO called.

Now Klemish *knew* they were in trouble. They were still settling.

He could see the deck of the carrier. He told himself that when they sank to deck level, he was going to eject.

"Raise your gear," the LSO was calling. His voice was emphatic now. "Raise your gear! Power!"

At that instant, they lost it. The big Tomcat fighter stopped flying.

Klemish felt the jet lurch to the left. The nose plunged downward toward the ocean.

"Eject! Eject!" yelled the LSO.

Klemish was already grabbing for the ejection handle between his legs. His hands found it, and he yanked.

Blam! Klemish's seat fired like a shell from a cannon. In a blur of motion he felt himself blasted into the windstream, arcing through the air . . . separating from the seat . . . felt the jolt of the chute deployment . . . waiting for the ocean to take him—

Splosh!

It felt like hitting concrete. Gagging on the gallon of seawater he had just ingested, he yanked downward at the toggles on his survival vest, then felt the sides of the vest inflate.

He thrashed at his Koch fittings to detach the parachute. Klemish was moving by instinct, by imprinted training, bobbing in the ocean swells, trying to recall the rules of water survival every naval aviator learns.

As he thrashed in the water, he became aware of the *whop-whop-whop* above him. He looked up, and there was the plane guard helicopter over his head, frothing the water like a goddamn Kansas tornado. A couple of seconds later, the rescue swimmer was out of the helicopter and there in the water with him, getting him stuffed into the padded sling dangling at the end of the hoisting cable.

As they were being hoisted back up to the helicopter, Klemish could see the other plane guard helo. It was hovering over the gray mass of the Tomcat fighter, which was quickly settling beneath the waves.

He didn't see a rescue swimmer or a sling being hoisted down to the water.

It had all happened so quickly. Fewer than five minutes had elapsed from the time they rolled into the groove, overshooting the centerline, to when Klemish stepped out of the rescue helicopter onto the deck of the *Lincoln*.

He was on his way to the dispensary to be checked out for injuries. On the way down the ladder, he paused to look back toward the flight deck. Maybe the pilot had gotten out okay.

No one was climbing out of the other helicopter.

No one had been pulled out of the ocean.

In the ejection sequence, which *he* had initiated when he pulled the ejection handle, the backseat in the Tomcat fighter fired first, leaving the cockpit at angle slightly to the right of vertical. Four-tenths of a second later the front seat fired, angling out slightly to the *left*.

The Tomcat was rolling hard to the left when the crew ejected, and Klemish's trajectory had been nearly parallel to the surface of the ocean. His chute opened an instant before he struck the water. Which meant that the pilot in the front seat, ejecting an instant later and more to the left, must have been fired directly into the water—before the parachute had a chance to deploy.

That's the way it looked on the videotape. In replay after replay, you could see the deadly sequence—the big fighter slewing and yawing out of control, then the moment of truth . . . snapping to the left and plunging toward the ocean. You could see the little dark shapes of the crew members hurtling from the cockpit as the jet entered its death dive.

From one of the shapes streams a white plume of parachute. From the other, nothing. The other little dark shape smacks the water like a stone.

She was killed instantly. Kara Hultgreen and her F-14 fighter sank to the floor of the Pacific.

★

The news traveled, literally, at the speed of light. The report was flashed from the *Abraham Lincoln* to the Naval Air Forces, Pacific command, at North Island, San Diego, whose public affairs department dispensed it to the media. They consumed it like hungry jackals.

The Navy's first woman fighter pilot was killed today in a training accident while . . .

Even before an official accident investigation could begin, the issue of gender, like a renascent plague that began with the Tailhook affair, was visiting the Navy again. Recriminations were flying like flat bursts:

"She shouldn't have been there . . ."

"The Navy was pushing her to do something she wasn't ready for . . ."

"It proves that women shouldn't be flying jets . . ."

"They gave her preferential treatment, and it got her killed . . ."

"Well, the damned liberals and feminists finally got what they've been wanting: They got someone killed . . ."

The repartee in the press was nasty. To the opponents of gender integration, the Hultgreen accident was proof positive that women didn't belong in the cockpits of jets. Letters to the editor flooded the pages of *Aviation Week, Navy Times,* and newspapers like the *San Diego Union* that had large military readerships. Most of the letters were from outraged males who were convinced that Kara Hultgreen had been allowed to kill herself in order to serve a political agenda of the Clinton administration.

The Navy found itself enmeshed in yet another media war. And in true Navy fashion, it waged this new media war just like it waged all the old media wars: It lost.

It wasn't that the Navy public affairs office actually *lied* about the circumstances of the accident. They just omitted some pertinent details. And obfuscated some others.

For example, the Navy declared that Lieutenant Hultgreen was a competent and qualified carrier aviator, one with "above average" grades for landing the F-14 board carriers. Furthermore, the accident in which she lost her life, they declared, had nothing to do with pilot error. She was the victim of an insidious failure of the Tomcat's left engine, from which virtually no one, experienced or not, could have recovered.

This information, the Navy said, was all corroborated in the MIR—the mishap investigation report—which, of course, was privileged information and not for scrutiny by parties outside the Navy.

Which might have put a lid on the controversy. But then someone from *inside* the establishment, presumably a disgruntled male aviator, put the entire MIR on the Internet, via the America On-Line service. Suddenly the facts were out there for everyone to see.

Yes, the accident board had concluded that the left engine probably *did* experience a compressor stall, causing it to fail. But the failure was exacerbated and probably *caused* by the pilot's yawing of the nose to the left, compensating for overshooting the approach to the carrier. Yawing the nose, in effect flying sideways through the air, blocked the flow of air through the left engine air intake and caused the engine to stall. The airplane also had a history of a sticking bleed valve, which in these circumstances would also have contributed to the stall. Whether or not she knew an engine had failed, she did not compensate with the necessary input of right rudder that would have kept the jet flying straight. She allowed the jet to slow to an unsafe airspeed. By the time the LSO radioed "Wave off!" and she responded with a burst of power, only the right engine responded.

What happened next was what fighter pilots called a "departure." It meant that the jet stalled and snap-rolled to the left.

What caused the accident? According to the mishap investigation report:

> *Aircrew factor*—Pilot attempt to salvage overshooting approach led to reduced engine stall margin, contributing to left eng comp stall. RAC II.
>
> *Aircrew factor*—Pilot failed to execute proper single eng wave off procedures. Aircrew factor—Pilot failed to inform Radar Intercept Officer (Lt. Klemish) of single eng emergency.
>
> *Material factor*—Left engine directional control valve stuck in bleeds closed position.
>
> *Aircrew factor*—MP (Mishap Pilot) failed to make timely decision to eject. MP lost situational awareness, failed to scan AOA (Angle of Attack), allowed pitch attitude to slowly increase and exceeded maximum controllable AOA of 20 units.
>
> The causal factors of this mishap and injury are a result of overcontrol, external distraction, cognitive saturation, channelized attention, wear debris, complacency and problem not foreseeable.

Hultgreen had already completed RAG training—the qualification program in the F-14—and had reported to her fleet squadron, VF-213, which was scheduled to deploy aboard the *Lincoln*. Despite the Navy's early bumbling attempts to categorize her as an "above average" aviator, she had, in fact, a record that put her in the lower middle. Although she had performed well in the tactical phases of training, she had failed on her first carrier qualification attempt, having a particularly difficult time landing aboard the carrier at night.

On her second shot at the carrier, Lieutenant Hultgreen passed, qualifying aboard the ship for day and night operations. At the time of her last flight, she had accrued over twelve hundred total flight hours and fifty-eight carrier landings.

Was Hultgreen "above average"? No.

Was she "qualified"? Indisputably.

Then why did she crash?

The grim truth about aviation accidents was that most were caused by *pilots*. Often the fatal sequence began with a subtle mistake, an oversight, a mishandled control input. And then another event, sometimes unrelated, compounded the mistake. If the pilot was unprepared, or inexperienced, or unlucky—he, or she, became a statistic.

Which is what happened to Kara Hultgreen. Her flawed landing attempt on the *Lincoln* deteriorated into a life-or-death scenario faster than she could have imagined.

During a lull in the Hultgreen controversy, someone had the sense to point out that the violent death of a fighter pilot, really, wasn't a rare event. Kara Hultgreen happened to be the *tenth* student fighter pilot to die in a Navy training accident since 1992. Furthermore, of all F-14 candidates training to land aboard aircraft carriers, fully *twenty-four percent* failed on their first qualifying attempt.

All in all, the circumstances of the accident were quite unremarkable. The only thing that made them remarkable was that Lieutenant Hultgreen was a woman.

★

Even Kara Hultgreen's funeral became a flashpoint for male anger. Why, some demanded, did the death of one aviator generate such a

wave of high-level mourning? If all the stuff about gender integration and equal treatment and mutual respect were really true, why
weren't deceased women pilots treated the same as their dead male
colleagues?

When a male fighter pilot bit the big one and immolated himself
in a smoking crater somewhere, who came to *his* casketless farewell?
If you were the deceased and a mere lieutenant—a *male* lieutenant—what you got was a handful of squadron buddies, your
folks, siblings, and wife or girlfriend, all of whom didn't fill the first
two rows of the chapel. The president definitely wouldn't show up.
Nor would the chief of naval operations. Probably not even one
lousy congressman.

A chaplain would be there to lead the crowd in a few verses of the
"Navy Hymn." Your commanding officer, of course, would be there.
He would be looking morose, mostly because you had screwed up
his squadron's safety record. Someone might recite John Gillespie
Magee's poem "High Flight."

And that was it. Afterward the squadron pilots would mumble
their condolences and head for the parking lot. They'd shuck their
uniforms and reassemble at some joint downtown like Hop's or the
Swinging Door and knock back a few in remembrance of ol'
Whatzisname.

That's the way it had always been. At least, that's the way it had
always been until the Navy had women pilots.

★

By early 1995, three months after the Hultgreen accident, the other
women naval aviators were feeling the heat of the controversy. The
most bellicose voices in the military were those decrying the
"double standard" that they believed was being applied to women in
naval aviation. Female aviators, they charged, were graded on a different—which was to say, *easier*—scale. In other words, women
were not squeezing through the same Fine Mesh that men candidates did. Was the military pursuing a gender-biased form of affirmative action?

Whether or not the charges were true, the controversy was making
life stickier for the two surviving members of the Terrific Trio. Word

was filtering down from the A-6 RAG in Oceana, Virginia, that Lieutenant Bonnie Detweiler was having her own share of trouble checking out in the A-6 Intruder. She had already received more than one SOD and was in danger of washing out.

And down at Cecil Field, Lieutenant Sally "Shrike" Hopkins, in the FA-18 RAG, was making herself even more controversial.

One of the questions fired at the Navy after the Hultgreen crash was, why didn't women aviators receive FNAEBs (Fleet Naval Aviator Evaluation Boards)? A FNAEB (pronounced *Feenab*) was a formal board of inquiry that was conducted when an aviator experienced difficulty in a phase of training. A FNAEB investigated the pilot's problems and then recommended whether he or she should be retained. It was pointed out that *men* candidates usually found themselves standing before a FNAEB for exactly the same transgressions that women seemed to be getting away with. Both Hultgreen and another woman aviator going through F-14 training had received low enough grades to merit a FNAEB.

FNAEBs? Was it true that women weren't getting them?

It became a moot question. In March 1995, another member of the Terrific Trio bit the dust, but not in the same spectacular manner. Bonnie Detweiler failed her carrier qualification training. She received a FNAEB and was removed from further A-6 training. She would not be going to a fleet squadron.

That left Shrike Hopkins. Of the brave and hopeful Terrific Trio, she was the only one still in the game. And things weren't looking so good for her. Shrike had just gotten *another* SOD.

PART TWO

METAMORPHOSIS

★ ★ ★

So the pilot kept it to himself, along with an even
more indescribable . . . an even more sinfully
inconfessable . . . feeling of superiority,
appropriate to him and to his kind, lone bearers
of the right stuff.

—TOM WOLFE
THE RIGHT STUFF

CHAPTER THIRTEEN

"A" IS FOR ATTACK

Bombardment is the sledge hammer of airpower.

—*Claire Lee Chennault*
AVG (Flying Tigers)

Attack.

In naval aviation parlance it always had a specific meaning. It designated that realm devoted to the obliteration of enemies *on the ground.* An attack pilot was a bomber. And a rocketer. And a strafer.

In the hierarchy of military flying, being an attack pilot was not at the apex of the ziggurat. Attack pilots were the mud-fighters, the guys who flew down in the weeds and delivered fire on the heads of the enemy. And who took fire in return.

Being an attack pilot had always implied a certain *expendability.* Losses were expected. It was like walking into a barroom brawl: You always hoped to land a lucky first punch and take the guy out, but you *knew* you'd probably take a few hits yourself. That's just the way it had always been for attack pilots. That's the way it was in World War II, in Korea, and in Vietnam, where the Navy's greatest aircraft losses by far were in the A-4 and A-7 attack squadrons.

Fighter pilots, by contrast, remained high above the mud-fighting. They dwelled in the high pure stratosphere, tracing their lovely contrails, awaiting the summons to go joust with an incoming MiG. Fighter pilots wouldn't think of spoiling the sleek lines of their jets with ugly bomb racks, nor would they burden their nimble fighters with crude tons of high explosives. After all, fighters were supposed to go *fast*, like thoroughbreds, not plod over the paddies like aerial pack mules.

For decades the fighter/attack enmity in naval aviation had festered like a congenital jungle itch. This new business of "attack"— the *A* in FA (*F* was "fighter")—still offended the fighter community. The new air-to-mud mission, meaning the strike function of the so-called FA-18 strike fighters, was somehow *undignified*. Bombing? Flinging ordnance (the Navy's label for a variety of munitions) at grunts on the ground? The old label, "fighter pilot," used to mean only one thing: You fought other airplanes. Air-to-air. Period. Like knights of old, you climbed onto your steed and went one-on-one against another guy on *his* steed. It was all a modernized evolution of the old single-combat warrior ethic.

Fighter pilots were the king of the hill. Everything else that flew, including the lowly strike pukes, were simply *targets* for real fighter pilots. Fighter pilots were the hunters and killers.

Well, times had changed. The aging F-14 Tomcat, which had reigned for over twenty years as the weapon of choice of any self-respecting Navy fighter pilot, was losing its potency. The Tomcat was getting old, and its technology was outdated. Just maintaining the complex fighter, with its variable-sweep wings and incredibly complicated systems, was a materiel officer's nightmare.

Sure, on a good day the Tomcat, in the hands of an aggressive pilot, could still mix it up with any of the hot new fighters, including the FA-18 Hornet. But the good days were getting rare. The Tomcat's glory days were over.

Which meant that the classic, king-of-the-hill, Top Gun fighter pilot stereotype was out. He was being replaced by a new breed: the strike fighter pilot. The pilot for all seasons. With a machine like the FA-18 Hornet, the strike fighter pilot could launch with a load of bombs, engage and kill an enemy fighter, then go on to destroy a surface target.

It was the "strike" in strike fighter. It was what the nuggets of 2-95 would learn next.

★

Except for the fam phase, all the other phases of training—strike, fighter weapons, CQ (carrier qualification)—were done on "dets"— detachments—away from home base. Married pilots—students and instructors alike—had homes and families in Jacksonville, close to Cecil Field. Depending on your marital status and social proclivity, dets were either great fun or worse than being deployed aboard a carrier. In places like Key West or Fallon, you lived in a BOQ (bachelor officers' quarters) and ate Navy chow, at least breakfast and lunch. Most evenings you socialized with your squadron mates at the officers' club bar, rolling dice for rounds of beer and swapping tales of old adventures. On CQ dets you lived aboard the carrier for perhaps a week or more.

Going off on det was like going to summer camp. You got away from the day-to-day tedium of the squadron, with its paperwork and mandatory meetings and command scrutiny. You also got away from *home*, which for some was an occasion to loosen up and sow a few wild oats. Being on det was the equivalent of a businessman's convention in another city. It was a time for attitude adjustment.

Best of all, going on det was *fun*. You went to places like Key West, the laid-back party island down at the tip of Florida, or out to the high desert in Fallon, Nevada, with its tumbleweeds, rattlesnakes, and nearby Reno casinos. Being off on det also dissolved some of the caste distinction of the training environment. Instructors and students could drop the instructor/student uptightness and kid each other a bit. They convened every evening at the BOQ bar to knock back a few—sometimes more than a few—and rehash the day's adventures out there on the weapons range.

Everyone loved strike phase because it was conducted way out in Nevada, far from the rank-heavy atmosphere of the strike fighter command. Fallon was the spiritual home of the attack community. It was also the site of the Naval Strike Warfare Center, called "Strike U."

Fallon was the place where you could get your Hornet down in the weeds, ripping across the sagebrush like a roadrunner in high blower. Out there you learned to fly at four hundred or so knots, a hundred feet above the dirt, avoiding enemy fighters and missiles, penetrating the defenses of a hostile country.

You got to shoot guns, fire rockets, drop *real*—not just practice—bombs. All this you did on *real* targets—tanks, trucks, buildings. And with thousands of square miles of open space, you could practice low-level navigation at weed-top altitude. The Fallon range was the world's greatest amusement park for strike fighter pilots.

★

Before going to Fallon, the nuggets flew three low-level navigation sorties from Cecil Field. The first was with an instructor in the backseat. Then they flew a solo hop, with the instructor flying behind them in a chase plane, like an airborne baby-sitter. Each student also flew a radar navigation training mission, riding in the backseat of one of the squadron's tandem-seat Hornets, with his head buried in the jet's APG-65 radar display.

They traveled to Fallon one of two ways: in the cockpit of an FA-18, or in the back of a Navy C-9 transport, which was a military version of the McDonnell Douglas DC-9 jetliner. Two nuggets— Chip Van Doren and Burner Bunsen—still needed the squares filled for radar navigation training flights, so they got to fly out in Hornets. The others—J.J., Angie, Shrike, Road, and the McCormacks—flew out West in the C-9. The rest of the detachment's jets would be ferried out by instructors.

"Wow!" said Angie Morales when she stepped off the jetliner onto the ramp at Fallon. She stood there on the concrete staring at the scenery. The Sierra range swelled in the west like a mural against the afternoon sky. You could see spring snow on all the high crests. The transition from the Florida flatlands to this—the high Sierras—was like changing planets.

★

The bombing target complex was about twenty miles square and featured an assortment of targets with concentric rings that looked like giant dartboards laid on the ground.

This was where the strike fighter students got their first exposure to dive-bombing, dropping the twenty-five-pound Mark 76 practice bombs. The Hornet's MER (multiple-ejection rack) carried twelve Mark 76s.

Barney Barnes was the instructor and flight leader. Bombing was Barney's special passion, and he loved teaching the subject. Students got a kick out of bombing with Barney, because he made a game of it. He got them to compete with each other, betting beers on their hits. He debriefed his flights at the Rocket Bar, where they settled all the beer bets.

Barney Barnes gave the nuggets a briefing. "Here is where we separate the men from the boys," said Barney. Then he caught himself. "Excuse me, ladies," he said, pretending to suddenly notice that Sally Hopkins and Angie Morales were in the class. "I mean, here is where we separate the *strike* fighter pilots from the interceptor pukes."

Shrike and Angie knew what he meant. They didn't mind. Barney was one of those guys they *knew* wasn't down on them because they were women. As an instructor, Barney Barnes was egalitarian: He picked on *everyone*.

Barney was part instructor and part entertainer. His mannerisms and his language—he had a masterful range of arcane obscenities—seldom offended anyone, even the women. Most women pilots, in fact, would tell you they *preferred* working with Barney. Barney never condescended to them, playing that hyper-sensitive post-Tailhook gender game that they ran into everywhere these days. There was no bullshit about Barney.

Barney's students for the first flight were J. J. Quinn, Shrike Hopkins, and a student from the German Navy, Lieutenant Commander Dirk Henschel. Henschel was there to qualify in the FA-18, then to remain as an instructor pilot in the RAG. He had served an exchange tour with a U.S. Navy A-6 squadron and already knew as much about carrier aviation as any pilot in the RAG. He was a tall, blondish guy with a bushy mustache. Everyone liked Henschel for his wit and laid-back style.

Barney believed in aggressive bombing. "If you don't act like a steely-eyed, hard-ball killer," he told his students, "then you oughta be flying helos or S-3s."

Aggressive bombing meant rolling in on target abruptly, hard, and steep. "On the roll in, you gotta 'squat' the jet," Barney said. "Honk the nose around hard, put some Gs on the sucker, then pull the nose down to the target. That way you lose hardly any altitude while you're getting the nose around to the run in. If anybody down there's pissed off at you, you won't be giving them an easy target to shoot at."

In its purest uncomputerized form, dive-bombing was a skill roughly akin to dart throwing. It was a hand-eye exercise, performed while hurtling toward the earth at over five hundred miles per hour. You aimed your jet at a target that was marked like a giant bullseye on the ground. You tried to put your illuminated aiming pipper smack on the bullseye, strived to maintain a precise airspeed, dive angle, and wind correction, and at a predetermined height you released your bomb. The big blunt weapon, now devoid of intelligence either human or electronic, soared downward, guided solely by the forces of gravity, wind, velocity, and, most nuggets would tell you, pure blind-assed luck.

That, at least, was the way dive-bombing had been executed for the first fifty or sixty years of aerial warfare. But toward the end of the Vietnam War came weapons called "smart bombs," and then came smart jets like the Hornet that possessed their own onboard intelligence. You still dove your airplane at the target, and you still tried to keep the pipper on the bullseye, but the many variables—wind, speed, dive angle—were taken into account by the jet's mission computer.

A modern fighter like the Hornet employed a system called auto-bombing. The heart of the system was the jet's mission computer, into which was fed data from the fighter's inertial navigation platform—dive angle, velocity, drift, all the factors that determined the bomb's impact point on the ground.

During his bomb run, the pilot superimposed an illuminated pipper in his windscreen display over the bullseye, then designated the target by thumbing a button on his stick. A vertical line, called the DIL (displayed impact line), appeared on the HUD (head-up display). The pilot pulled up from the target, keeping his wings level, using the DIL for guidance. The computer figured out the release point and—*whump!*—kicked the bomb off the jet at the precise moment.

"Be on the line," said Barney, stuffing a fresh wad of dip under his lip. "That's how you get hits. At this point, anything inside of fifty feet is awesome. In a few weeks, you'll be pissed about anything over thirty."

It was still possible, of course, to make gross errors. The computer's logic could be severely skewed by ham-handed control inputs from the pilot or by sloppy and imprecise target designation.

Auto-bombing was used to drop what they called "iron" bombs. These were "dumb" weapons like the five-hundred-pound Mark 82s, one-thousand-pound Mark 83s, and two-thousand-pound Mark 84s. Dumb bombs were nothing more than streamlined containers for raw high explosives, no different in principle from the conventional bombs used in World War II. Any intelligence imparted to dumb bombs came from the fighter's onboard computer *prior* to weapon release. Once released, the dumb iron bomb soared off on its mindless way like a thrown dart.

The Hornet also carried modern "smart" weapons, like the Maverick and Walleye, which were video-guided bombs equipped with control vanes that allowed the bomb to be "flown" to its target while the attacking aircraft made its escape. These were among the spectacularly successful weapons the world watched on CNN during the Gulf War—bombs and missiles that could be threaded through the ventilator shafts and half-opened windows of Iraqi buildings.

But for a nugget fighter pilot, all that would come later. Fallon was where you came to learn the basics. That meant you learned dive-bombing the old-fashioned way—dropping dumb bombs with the assistance of the Hornet's computers.

That's what they would do, day after day on the weapons ranges at Fallon. The nuggets would practice diving at high-angle and low-angle, from all altitudes. At first they would practice on the giant circular dartboard targets marked on the ground; then they moved on to real targets—tanks, trucks, fabricated buildings. They practiced low-altitude "lay-down" delivery, releasing simulated napalm and cluster bombs from as low as three hundred feet.

On the wall of the briefing room was a blown-up aerial photograph of the target complex. "See this nice big tempting bullseye?" Barney said, pointing to a target with concentric rings. "Don't even think about it. That ain't your target. That's the nuke target. It's only used for dropping those big two-thousand-pound simulated nuclear bombs." He pointed to a smaller, less distinguishable target about a mile away. "This is the one you're looking for."

He rapped on the photograph. "I'll say it again, just for effect: Don't fuck up and go for the wrong target. Once a month some dumb shit bombs the wrong target, and it's an automatic SOD."

The students all nodded. *Wrong target? Yeah, we know that.* It was pretty obvious. What kind of dumb shit would make a mistake like that?

★

They took off in ten-second intervals. Barney first, then Dirk Henschel, who was the left wingman—Dash Two (number two in the formation). J. J. Quinn, being junior in rank to Henschel, was assigned to the Dash Three position, off Barney's right wing. At the far right side of the formation, in the Dash Four spot, was Shrike.

They flew over the southern boundary of the target complex at fifteen thousand feet. Barney checked in with Range Control on the tactical frequency.

"Roger, Roman five-nine. With positive target identification, you're cleared in hot. The range is hot." "Hot" meant the jets were cleared to arm their systems and release weapons on the target.

Barney signaled Henschel by radio to slide over to the right side, into the gap between the leader and J. J. Quinn in the number three jet. In a loose right echelon—the jets stacked on the right side— Barney led the flight into the target area. One by one, at seven-second intervals, they broke off to the left, setting up a racetrack pattern around the bombing target on the ground.

Barney rolled in. Seven seconds later, Henschel.

Eight more seconds. J. J. Quinn was next.

J.J. was suddenly very busy. It was an abrupt switch from flying formation, with *all* your attention focused on the airplane directly next to you, then coming back inside the cockpit, punching up all the buttons and switches for bombing, and getting the jet in the right place to dive on the target.

J.J.'s gloved fingers were darting across the digital display indicators like nervous ferrets.

Select the right program, the one that will drop only *one* bomb at a time.

Select auto-bombing mode.

Select the master armament switch on.

Where was the damned target? There. Right under the left wing.

Okay, start your roll-in. *Be aggressive.* That's what Barney told them. *Squat the jet.* Honk the sucker around, snap the nose down on the bull . . . there it is . . . get the pipper over there where it belongs . . . designate the thing . . . hit the pickle button . . . check your altitude . . . fifty-five hundred, start your pull up . . . follow the DIL . . . stay on the line, keep the wings level . . .

Plink. The bomb released.

"Dash Three," came the voice of the range spotter. "What target are you aiming at?"

What target? Quinn was confused. Why would the spotter be asking a question like . . .

J.J. had four G's on his jet, pulling up from his dive. He craned his neck to look backward and down, down there at the big inviting target, just in time to see the white plume of smoke erupt from his bomb.

The nuke target. Just like Barney said. *Once a month some dumb shit bombs the wrong target. . . .*

CHAPTER FOURTEEN

FALLON

The days at Fallon were long. By the time the nuggets finished with debriefing, viewing their cockpit tapes, and putting in some mission planning, it was well after dark. Usually no one felt like going into town, which was five miles away and required cleaning up and changing clothes. They just slouched over to the officers' club bar, where it was okay to wear their stained and evil-smelling flight suits, and slammed down a few cold beers.

For decades the officers' club bar had been called Ruthie's, after the bartender and proprietress. Ruthie was a Navy icon. She had been running the officers' club bar at Fallon, everyone figured, since Nimitz was a midshipman. It was *her* bar, and in it Ruthie was the final authority on everything—dice rolls, bombing bets, career decisions, marital problems.

She was fifty-something, short and roundish, tough as a Nevada muleskinner. She dispensed justice Old West–style—by heaving troublemakers out on their tails. Rank was irrelevant. Ruthie threw out commanders, captains, colonels—offenders of all stripes. Usually they came slinking back the next day bearing flowers and apologies.

The place was a shrine to naval aviation. The walls were covered with squadron plaques, patches, decals, memorabilia from long-ago wars and campaigns, yellowed photographs of airplanes and aviators long extinct. Ruthie had known them all.

On a rare evening, the nuggets would change out of their grungy flight suits, clean up, and head into town.

Fallon was like something from a Clint Eastwood movie. It had a Wild West flavor that appealed to young fighter pilots: the snow-crested Sierra range, the windblown, sagebrush-and-rattlesnake feel of the high desert, the gambling houses, and the rude cow town flavor of the community. You got the feeling that this was a very good place for gunslingers.

Fallon had no visible industry other than a few casinos and the stockyards at the edge of town, which, with an east wind, gave the place a rich, moist manure smell. Visiting aviators favored a joint called the Bird Farm, a dumpy-looking bar with a hand-painted sign that read FIFTY CENT CRAPS. The Bird Farm had a jukebox and a few blackjack and craps tables and cheerful, go-to-hell ambiance. Like Ruthie's, it had Navy memorabilia all over the walls—plaques and posters and photographs of old and dead warriors. It was run by a grizzled old retired Navy chief petty officer. The chief didn't mind if his young fighter jocks got a little shit-faced and rowdy as long as they paid for their beer and left some change on the blackjack tables.

After a session of drinking and gambling, you could go next door to La Cantina, a Mexican restaurant, just as dumpy as the Bird Farm, with the right kind of atmosphere for a gaggle of pilots with a load on. At the front door was a miniature golf putting lane where you could gamble for your dinner.

A night on the town in Fallon was a rare treat for the nuggets. Even then, they went home early. Training days at Fallon *always* began before dawn.

★

It was even more intense than the tough grind back at Cecil. Briefings for the first flights on the weapons range began at 0530 (five-thirty A.M.). Each student flew twice a day. Briefing, flying the mission, debriefing, repeating the cycle in the afternoon consumed twelve, fourteen, sixteen hours of each day. In between training flights and in the evenings the students were required to plan low-altitude navigation flights and coordinated deep air strikes.

It was a bone-numbing, wearying schedule. "There's too much to learn," Road grumbled one night over a beer. "We should have done some of this mission planning and map studying back at Cecil."

No one disagreed. Each of the nuggets was looking hollow-eyed and drained. Burner was not his wisecracking self. He was slouched against the bar, nursing a beer. Neither of the McCormacks felt like Heckling and Jeckling. J.J. was not only feeling like the old man of the bunch, he *looked* it. His thirty-five-year-old face looked like it was sixty. The flecks of gray hair were turning to streaks. Shrike Hopkins and Angie Morales stopped in to say hello to the guys, then headed for their rooms.

But it was worth it. For the first time they were *doing* something with the jet, not just taking off and flying around, then trying to get the thing back on the ground in one piece. All the years of training—college, flight training, graduate school—were finally coming down to this: They were performing a *mission*.

Sure, it was still training, but in another part of the world those *could* be enemy tanks and trucks down there, and those winding desert roads *could* just as well be your ingress route to Libya or Bosnia. Those adversary fighters lurking out there to intercept you were every bit as adept and clever as the MiGs over the Iraqi desert.

★

A pecking order had begun to emerge among the nuggets of 2-95. Each weapons delivery mission—high-angle bombing, low-angle, strafing—was scored. And as the scores accumulated, day after day, some were consistently higher than others. The best bomber of the bunch was turning out to be Burner Bunsen.

Burner's CEP (circle of error probability) during the second week of weapons training was twenty-six feet—the average distance from the bullseye for each of his bombs. It was an impressive score for a nugget. Even for seasoned fleet pilots, anything inside thirty feet was considered superior marksmanship.

The other nuggets were having mixed results. One day Road Ammons managed to put his first two bombs directly on the bullseye. "Hooeeee!" he crowed on the radio. "Beat that, you plumbers."

Then he proceeded to put each of his next four bombs somewhere between the one-hundred- and two-hundred-foot rings. It was the worst CEP of the day for anyone. It cost him the obligatory round of beers at the club.

Shrike was having accuracy problems. She was managing to keep most of her bombs inside the hundred-foot circle, which was considered the outer limit of acceptability. But seldom could she cluster her bomb hits *really* close to the bullseye. When marked on a chart, Shrike's hit pattern looked like a test pattern for a wide-bore scattergun.

Two students' scores, to no one's surprise, were nearly identical. The McCormack twins, as if to authenticate their identicalness, turned in bombing results that were nearly mirror images. Each had a CEP of forty feet. But Russ's hits were clustered in a neat pattern at nine o'clock—the left side of the target. Rick's were at three o'clock—on the right side. "We like to maintain a balance," they explained.

In number of bullseyes, Chip Van Doren was the close rival of Burner. But Chip was beset with streaks of unpredictability. On any particular day he could put at least three bombs inside the twenty-foot ring. The next day he couldn't find the hundred-foot circle. He would come back from such a flight, stalking across the tarmac tight-lipped and frustrated.

Angie Morales was doing well, particularly with forty-five-degree bombing. On each sortie she was scoring at least one bullseye. Her CEP was in the thirties, just behind Chip Van Doren.

The greatest frustration was being felt by the ex-helicopter pilot, J. J. Quinn. He had more experience flying close to the ground than any of them. But all J.J.'s experience had been accumulated at a leisurely hundred miles an hour, whop-whopping along at the pace of a fast minivan. In his new life as a fighter pilot, J. J. Quinn's view of the world had compressed to a sagebrush-and-earth-colored blur. His brain was still synchronized to helicopter speed—about four hundred miles per hour slower than his FA-18 fighter.

The truth was, J.J. was slow. He took longer to do everything—plan his flight, preflight his jet, taxi out to the marshaling area, rendezvous with the other jets in his flight. In the bombing pattern, his intervals were too long. His dive angles were too shallow. Sometimes J.J. would roll in on the target—and then pull off again—*without* releasing his bomb.

"Why didn't you drop?" Barney wanted to know.

"I wasn't ready," the Marine explained.

The instructors were beginning to wonder about this guy Quinn. They were wondering if he would *ever* be ready.

★

Angie Morales didn't have a call sign yet. "Who ever heard of a fighter pilot named *Angie*?" said Burner one day in the ready room. "That's really embarrassing. We gotta fix that."

So her classmates tried to come up with a call sign. The problem was, Morales just hadn't distinguished herself by doing anything legendary—bombing the wrong target, getting lost, forgetting her landing gear. She went about her business, completing each phase of the training syllabus without fanfare. She was never the best, nor the worst. In a room full of noisy male fighter pilots, she *still* blended into the backdrop like a bird in a forest.

One day at happy hour Burner announced that he had a new call sign for Angie Morales: Rambo.

Rambo? At first, no one could figure it out. What kind of a name was that for a girl? Then they got it: She, of course, was so *un*-Rambo-like, with her quiet unobtrusiveness, it was funny. Rambo Morales? Why not? It sounded good on the radio. Anything was a better name for a fighter pilot than *Angie*.

Angie Morales fought it at first. But she had been around long enough to know that was futile. The more you resisted a new call sign, the more it stuck, like Super Glue.

So Rambo it was. *What the hell?* she figured. *It could be worse.* At least she hadn't *earned* her call sign the way most nuggets did: by doing something stupid.

★

One day the Phantom Flathatter came to Fallon.

The Phantom was famous. No one knew who he was, except that he *had* to be a Hornet pilot. For a couple of years now the Phantom had been leaving photographs of his handiwork stuck on the walls and bulletin boards of the various strike fighter bases.

This visit had the usual result: one of those rolling Navy inquisitions that nearly equaled the Tailhook investigation.

It started one day when a photo appeared on the wall in the Fallon BOQ bar. No one knew who put it up. Certainly no one knew *anything* about who took the photograph. Everyone who walked past it the first time had the same reaction: "Holy shit, that's an . . . FA-18 . . ."

That's what it was—on an eleven-by-fourteen-inch blowup, not of great quality, but pretty good considering the cloud of dust through which it was taken. You could see the photographer's feet. He appeared to be sitting in the bed of a pickup truck. At the bottom of the blown-up photograph you could see the truck's tailgate, which looked dented and rusty. You knew that from so little detail it was probably impossible to identify what kind of truck it was and, more importantly, *whose* pickup had been used for the photo shoot.

About fifty yards behind the pickup, nose-on through the trail of desert dust, hauling ass up the dirt road toward the truck at what appeared to be about ten feet above the road, was a thirty-eight-million-dollar U.S. Navy fighter.

It was just so *blatantly* illegal—you had to admire the perpetrator for his sheer ballsiness. Flathatting!

Flathatting was the Navy's term for unauthorized buzzing. If an aviator yielded to the temptation to go screeching over his girlfriend's house, or the old man's farm, or a section of Nevada dirt road, he was guilty of flathatting. And it would cost him his wings.

Unless he was the Phantom Flathatter. The Phantom had been getting away with it for long enough now that he had achieved almost mythical status. The Phantom not only did it—he stuck up photos *proving* it! Pilots at bars around the country speculated about his identity. Some thought there had to be more than one Phantom, based on the sheer volume of his work.

He, they—whoever—had obviously gone to a great deal of trouble to coordinate the stunt, getting someone to drive the pickup, someone to shoot the picture, then flying his jet at weed-top level down a dirt road, up the back end of the pickup truck.

The photograph didn't stay on the wall long. By the next morning it had come down and was on its way to the office of the deputy chief of naval operations for air, who, of course, wanted a full investigation into who the hell was flathatting out there over the desert in *his* goddamn FA-18s.

It quickly became clear to everyone that they were wasting their time. No one knew anything. No one knew anyone who knew anything. No one *wanted* to know anything. Photo? Pickup truck?

The Phantom could have been any of a hundred or so pilots who visited Fallon for strike training. The fleet squadrons from both the Pacific and Atlantic fighter wings all paid annual visits to Strike U. And it was an old tradition for pilots to chip in and buy beat-up old pickups just for knocking around the desert roads.

So the Phantom went unpunished. Again. And that was fine with most of the pilots who passed through Fallon. The caper had a sort of Robin Hoodish theme to it. He made them laugh. It was nice to think that in today's uptight, shrinking, Fine Mesh Navy, there might still be *outlaws*.

★

They finally got a break. Two whole days, over a weekend. "Go," the instructors all told them. "Get the hell out of town. Go to Reno or Tahoe, and unwind, gamble, get drunk, see a show, go skiing. Do something that's fun. Do whatever gets your mind off strike training."

The nuggets needed no urging. By now they were hollow-eyed zombies, having spent every day out there on the desert skimming the sagebrush, every night poring over tables and charts and manuals in the mission planning room. Each had lost at least five pounds. They had seen enough of the sagebrush and the rattlesnakes and the hard dry desert of the Fallon weapons range.

By nine o'clock Saturday morning, in a convoy of Hertz compacts, they were on the road to Tahoe. The whole detachment from Cecil—instructors and students—had pooled funds and reserved a big condo at a place called Lakeland Village in Tahoe that served as their administrative headquarters and crash pad. The nuggets stashed their bags and hit the main strip in town like kids let loose from detention.

Burner, Road, and Chip Van Doren headed straight for the casinos to play some blackjack and craps, knock back a few beers, ogle some showgirls. Shrike, Angie Morales, and the twins found a place that rented ski gear. They heard that Heavenly Valley, the big ski complex that towered over Lake Tahoe, had spring snow, and you still could get in a half day of decent skiing.

J. J. Quinn, as usual, felt like a senior citizen at a kindergarten party. Even among the instructors, who were closer to his age, he was out of place. Between instructors and students—even graying students like J. J. Quinn—there was still that invisible thin curtain.

So J.J. hung out with his classmates, adolescents though they were. He trailed along with Burner and Chip and Road, poking into the casinos, having a beer at every place they stopped, pretending to care what the odds were against beating the house at craps. What J.J. *really* cared about was getting home. He missed his wife, Dorothy, and his kids, who were back in Jacksonville. He wished he was home, his feet propped up in front of his fireplace. He'd be sipping a brandy, listening to some Brubeck and maybe reading a little detective fiction, something from Wambaugh or Elmore Leonard. That was more to his taste than prowling these neon sidewalks with a bunch of kids on a weekend binge.

Sunday came. With the sun descending on the western rim of the Sierras, the Hertz rental convoy headed back to Fallon. There were some bruises among the skiers. The slopes had turned out to be downright dangerous this late in the season. The soft spring snow had transformed to mean summer slush. They'd taken some lumps and spills and, in Russ McCormack's case, one spectacular cartwheeling bone-rattling crash. No one broke anything, due mainly to the inherent toughness of young bones.

There were some mountain-sized hangovers. The casino-hoppers, including tag-along J. J. Quinn, had worked the tables and ogled the showgirls and slammed down beers until nearly four A.M. J.J., who *hated* hangovers, looked like a cadaver. His head throbbed and his stomach roiled and he swore he would never drink again. At least never with these goddamn kids.

★

They had reason to be glad they'd had a break. It was time for LAT—low-altitude training—the *real* adrenaline-pumper of strike phase. LAT meant getting your jet down low to the weeds, navigating across vast expanses of unfriendly terrain.

Things happened fast at four hundred twenty knots. Especially at only a hundred feet above the craggy surface of the Sierras. Any distraction, mistake, lapse of attention, and—*bloom!*—you became one with the earth.

It was an exhilarating, nerve-wracking exercise. LAT was fundamental to the strike fighter business. It was also the most dangerous activity in tactical aviation, and thus had to be practiced until it became second nature. Down at weed-top level was one of the strike fighter pilot's principal places of business. It was where he lived—and fought—while making his way to a target.

They entered the dangerous new world carefully, like a bather settling into a hot tub. The first hop was flown at five hundred feet, which afforded a comfortable margin of safety. At five hundred feet you could *see* what was coming—towers, buildings, wires. You could see them in time to turn or climb and miss them.

Down at a hundred feet, it was like peering into a cone. What you saw was immediately ahead and beneath your nose. The view on either side was a greenish brown blur. At that speed and altitude, with only a two-degree nose-downward nudge, you were three and one half seconds from becoming molten protoplasm.

Your only real defense from unseen objects like towers and power lines was by being *exactly* where you intended, which meant following the course line you had plotted on your navigation chart. The Hornet was equipped with an inertial reference platform—a space-age navigation device run with laser gyros that, when programmed with accurate information, *knew* where it was on the surface of the planet. The FA-18's instrument display included a moving map that was continually updated with information from the inertial reference platform. The map display showed the pilot his course line—the "yellow brick road"—and his actual progress along the road.

The hazards of low-altitude navigation were many. There were manmade objects like microwave towers and power lines. There were birds of all kinds, especially *big* birds like hawks, eagles, and buzzards, who by their own arrogant nature weren't inclined to yield right-of-way to other airborne creatures. A bird the size of a buzzard, when rammed at over four hundred knots, could bring down your twenty-ton strike fighter as surely as a radar-guided missile.

The most insidious danger of low-level navigation, however, was the pilot's own fallible perceptions. Sometimes, for no obvious reason, pilots just flew into the ground. The reason was usually the same: In the high-speed environment close to the surface, the human neural system could be fooled. Gently rising terrain could go unnoticed for a critical few seconds. Depth perception became useless over snow, slick water, shadowed ground. Two feet looked like twenty feet. Or two hundred feet.

Thus another course rule at Fallon: No low-level nav hops until two hours after sunrise. None during the two hours before sunset. Those were rules like so many others in strike fighter training: They were written in blood.

To nuggets on their first trip to Fallon, the danger of low-altitude tactics was largely academic. They all knew the numbers. They had been required to study the tables that showed TTIs (time to impact) from each hundred feet of altitude. They knew that a zero-G nudge—a gentle pushover—from a hundred feet had a TTI of 2.5 seconds. In less than three seconds you were one with the earth. They knew that a descent angle of five degrees meant you *had* to pull up no closer than 250 feet above the ground. They knew the rule of three seconds maximum to have your eyes inside the cockpit, then you *had* to go back out. Three in, then out. Check your chart, check the ground. Keep checking.

They knew all that. It was simple. Chart to ground. Keep checking. It was academic. Don't become one with the earth.

Then one day during their second week at Fallon, it stopped being academic.

★

Burner had downed a couple of beers with him at the club the night before. Standing there at the bar, still wearing their flight suits, Burner and the guy had talked about the Marine Corps, about flying Hornets out there in the high desert, about not hitting the ground.

And then he did it. His name was Blowser. He was a pilot in an El Toro–based Marine squadron, VMFA-251. They were there at Fallon's Strike Warfare Center for refresher training.

The next day he went out to the high desert and hit the ground.

The circumstances were classic, right out of the LAT manual: the eastern slope of the Sierras in the late afternoon, snow-covered terrain, flat light, depth perception nil. The FA-18 was on a low-altitude training flight, using radar and inertial nav, following one of the canned training routes that began down in the desert flats at Fallon and climbing up the Sierra divide, heading southward along the ridgeline, then back down over the desert. As required by the course rules, a second F-18 was flying chase, above and behind the low-flying Hornet.

It was early spring. A bright sheen of snow still covered the upper slopes. The high overcast filtered the afternoon sun, lending a dull, dimensionless cast to the terrain. The pilot was down low, skimming the ground, following the winding course up a mountain slope, moving at 420 knots. As he rolled the jet into a steep bank to turn the corner, he clipped a ridge.

The sleek FA-18 strike fighter disintegrated into a fireball. The flaming wreckage caromed on up the snow-covered slope, scattering its pieces for over a mile.

The mood that night at Ruthie's was subdued. The nuggets drank their beer and exchanged chatter about nothing in particular, avoiding the subject that was on all their minds. They were all working hard at not noticing the cluster of Marines at the far end of the bar, the pilots from the squadron that had just lost the jet. And a squadron mate.

The same question preyed on each nugget's mind: What did that guy *do* out there? What was he thinking about? What mistake caused him to plant his jet up on that ridge?

Sure, they knew, at least in a academic sense, the reason for all the rules and dictums about low-altitude tactics. But until today, that's what it had been—*academic*. Now the hard truth was sinking in. This job really *was* dangerous. Hell, man, this stuff could get you killed!

CHAPTER FIFTEEN

SHRIKE

Shrike Hopkins didn't like the way the day was shaping up. On her way to the squadron that morning she could see the wind sock out by the runway. It was snapping around like a pennant on a speed-boat. This was going to be one hell of a windy day.

That was Fallon's biggest limitation: the wind. The Fallon air station had only one long strip, Runway 31-13, running northwest-southeast. Most of the time the single runway was perfectly suitable for the tactical jets that used the base. But sometimes a gale-force wind would kick up out there on the desert and come howling across Fallon's single runway.

Which always meant trouble. Fighters like the FA-18 Hornet and the F-14 Tomcat had crosswind limitations. They couldn't take off or land in a crosswind—a wind blowing perpendicular to the runway—greater than thirty knots. If they were already airborne and a crosswind came up that exceeded their limit, the procedure was to lower the jet's arresting hook—the same one used for carrier landings—and make an arrested landing.

Every naval air station, including Fallon, was equipped with an arresting wire. It was a cable stretched across the runway and con-nected to an apparatus called a "water squeeze," which acted like a giant brake. In an emergency, jets could land with their hooks down and come to a quick stop, just like on an aircraft carrier. The landing jet's tailhook engaged the cable, which dragged it to a halt in less than a thousand feet.

Shrike made her way across the parking lot toward the squadron ready room. The wind was gusting. It snatched loose strands of her long blond hair, stinging her face. *Yes*, thought Shrike, *this is shaping up to be an interesting day.*

★

The damned landing gear!

Shrike had just taken off from Fallon, headed for the weapons range. Now she was staring at the red light in her landing gear handle. She had tried to raise the landing gear handle to retract the wheels of the jet—and something wasn't right. The goddamned gear hadn't come up or, at least, it wasn't *indicating* that it had come up.

Great, she thought. Here she was with bombs on her jet, and she was supposed to join her flight and go bombing. And her gear was not safe. It might be up, down, or hung up somewhere in between. What to do?

What she did, she realized several seconds later, was precisely the *wrong* thing to do. She cycled the landing gear. She put the gear handle down. All three wheels locked into the down position.

But she wanted to fly the bombing hop, didn't she?

She raised the gear handle again.

Unsafe again! The red light was glowing in the clear plastic landing gear handle.

Something was definitely not right. And now another nagging thought had already entered into her brain: *I shouldn't have done that. I shouldn't have cycled the gear.*

It was an axiom in jets: You didn't mess with landing gear problems. If the gear showed an irregularity, like an unsafe indication when you raise it, you never cycled the thing in order to get the wheels up. That was because if the landing gear had a broken actuator or linkage mechanism, cycling the gear could jam it irretrievably. You might never get all the wheels down. In the FA-18 Hornet, that meant you had to eject. Once you got the wheels down, indicating safe, you *left them down*.

It was too late. Shrike had jumped the gun. Now she had to confess.

She called Fallon tower and told them that she had a problem and needed to go into a "Delta" pattern—a holding pattern over the airfield. Then she did what she wished she had done after the first indication of a problem: She called the operations duty officer.

"You did what?" the duty officer asked on the radio.

"I cycled the gear," she said. "It didn't fix the problem."

She could almost hear the ODO groaning. In her mind's eye she could see his face reddening, the brow furrowing. "Stand by," he said. "Let's get the book out."

While Shrike orbited overhead Fallon, the ODO plunged into the FA-18 operating handbook, called the NATOPS (Naval Air Training and Operating Procedures Standardization) manual.

The "Landing Gear Unsafe/Fails to Extend" procedure contained sixteen separate items. At the top of the procedure was a big warning box. It said, "Do not cycle the landing gear."

So much for that step. The ODO read the rest of the procedure to Shrike over the radio. They came to the item about the landing gear circuit breaker.

"Okay," said the ODO, "it says here to check it in. Go ahead and make sure the sucker is pushed in."

She did. It was.

"Swell. Fantastic. Now let's finish the rest of the procedure. And leave the handle where it is now, understand? Don't screw around with it anymore."

"Okay." The ODO sounded sarcastic. Shrike made herself keep her mouth shut.

"And then we're gonna have Comet join up on you so he can make a visual inspection of the gear. After that you're gonna take the arresting gear. You have to catch a wire because that's the procedure with the gear problem, but the fact is, everybody's gonna be doing it anyway because the crosswind at Fallon is blowing over thirty knots now. Understand?"

"Yes, *sir*, I understand."

★

Shrike landed back at Fallon and caught the arresting wire with her tailhook. No problem. The gear episode was over. No damage done. That should have been the end of the matter, she figured.

She figured wrong.

She knew she had screwed up the procedure for dealing with an unsafe gear. Now she had to hear about it from everybody else—from the duty officer, from Comet Haley, who was supposed to have been her flight leader for the bombing mission, and even from the other students.

One of the other students, a Navy commander who was going through FA-18 qualification before becoming executive officer of his own Hornet squadron, was in the ready room. "I can't wait to hear her story about *that*," he said. Or words to that effect.

Someone reported the commander's remark to Shrike, who was already on edge from the gear incident. She stormed into the ready room and confronted the commander. What the hell did he mean by a crack like that? She didn't have to take that kind of crap from another student! Talking down to her, pulling that commander-lieutenant stuff, implying that she, being a woman, was going to offer some kind of a *story* . . .

Things got out of hand. Shrike said the commander had no right to badmouth her. He said he was doing no such thing. Shrike said it sounded like verbal assault to her.

Verbal assault? Wait a minute . . . did she really mean that? Wasn't that dangerously close to sexual harassment?

It was. And she meant it. At least in the heat of the moment.

A silence descended on the ready room. Uh-oh. There it was: the *Gender Thing*—loose again, jumping out of its dark hiding place like a red-eyed, saliva-dripping junkyard dog.

Comet Haley tried to get the combatants to back off from their firing positions. Eventually Shrike and the commander cooled down. Already they were regretting most of the things that had been said. But of course the things *had* been said. Now they were out there on the floor, like somebody's dirty socks. Neither was willing to take them back.

A report of the whole messy business—the gear problem and the accusation of harassment—got back to Cecil Field.

Captain Moffit, commanding officer of the FA-18 RAG, knew better than to ignore the Gender Thing. As a senior officer, he had already seen many of his colleagues caught in the jaws of that junkyard dog. So he did the only prudent thing a commanding officer could do in these post-Tailhook days: He ordered a JAG (judge advocate general) investigation of the verbal assault allegation.

A JAG investigation was a standard military legal tool. It was a miniversion of a grand jury inquiry into an alleged wrongdoing. The officer appointed to conduct the JAG investigation was a woman, a lieutenant commander. After she interviewed all the officers who had been present in the ready room that day in Fallon, she issued a five-page summation of her findings. The whole matter, she concluded, had been overblown. Nothing had been said that could be construed as sexual harassment. Lieutenant Hopkins, in an emotional state after a harrowing flight, had overreacted to an innocuous ready room remark.

Which suited everyone, including Shrike, who was already regretting the hornet's nest that had been stirred. But in all the brouhaha about sexual harassment, the original issue—Shrike's mishandling of her landing gear emergency—had been somehow obscured. And *that,* most of the instructors were becoming convinced, had been the real motivation for the verbal assault charge: to deflect attention from her grade sheet for that flight.

With the harassment issue put to rest, the commanding officer redirected everyone's attention: "She had a gear malfunction. She violated standard operating procedure. She should have gotten an unsatisfactory grade."

And so she did. For that day's flight she received a grade of "unsatisfactory."

Shrike was stunned. Another SOD! That made two. Three SODs, sometimes four—that was the limit. Then you faced a FNAEB.

It was so goddamned unfair! Now she no longer had any doubt. They really *were* out to get her.

CHAPTER SIXTEEN

SNIPER

Shrike wasn't the only one having a bad day in the weapons phase at Fallon. It seemed to be a rule: Everyone had to have at least one unbelievably bad day out there on the range. You'd have a sortie when your bombs seemed guided by a computer from hell. The bombs would hit long, short, or so wide of the bullseye that the target spotters a mile away would be diving for cover whenever they heard your call sign.

But the bad days would pass, like a transient virus. And so it was with the nuggets of 2-95. By the end of the first week at Fallon, they were having mostly good days. They had one more week on the range. Now more bombs were falling on the bullseye. More low-level nav hops were staying on course, checkpoints hit on time, minimum safe altitudes observed. The nugget fighter pilots were feeling good about themselves.

Except for J. J. Quinn. J.J.'s bad days still outnumbered his good ones. He hadn't gotten a CEP for bomb hits inside a hundred feet. The consensus of the instructors was that J.J. was going to be all right, but it would take a while. J.J. was a plodder. His helicopter pilot's brain was still plodding at a velocity, everyone figured, somewhere between hover and autorotation speed.

Part of J.J.'s problem was confidence. He had none. Or when he *did* have it, something would happen to knock it out of him. He couldn't escape the recurring notion that he just didn't belong here. After all, he *was* from the wrong community, the dog-soldiering, helicopter-flying branch of the Marine Corps. And the wrong generation. Age thirty-five was a hell of a time in life to take up fighter piloting. What was he doing here?

Sometimes J.J. would stand off by himself at the bar in Ruthie's, observing his youngish classmates. They were kids, cutting up, ribbing each other, making bets on bomb hits and strafing scores. He felt so goddamned *old*! They were like his kid brothers and sisters—fun to have around, but damn, it would be nice for a change to have some adult company.

Out there on the range, J.J. dreaded hearing the bomb spotter's report after each run. Of the twelve bombs they normally carried on each sortie, he might get two or three inside a hundred feet. He could hear just a *hint* of a sneer in the spotter's voice: "Hundred-fifty feet, six o'clock. . . ."

Hits were called out by their direction from the center of the target, as on the face of a clock. Six o'clock meant the bomb had fallen short, at the bottom of the bullseye. "Off target, nine o'clock," called the spotter, meaning J.J.'s bomb had hit so far left of the bullseye it wasn't even in the same congressional district.

J.J.'s bad days were coming one after the other. And then one afternoon near the end of his training at Fallon, he had a *very* bad day. His worst day ever.

★

It was midmorning—the perfect time to be on the weapons range at Fallon. The spring sunshine was washing the desert in a golden hue.

It was a multiweapons period. Each Hornet was carrying twelve Mark 76 practice bombs as well as a full load of ammo for strafing. Today was their first time on the strafing targets, their chance to fire the awesome M-61 cannon mounted in the nose of the Hornet.

Slab Bacon was the instructor and the flight leader. Slab's wingman would be Road Ammons. As usual, J.J., being the senior student, was assigned to lead the second section of two fighters. His wingman was Burner Bunsen.

The four Hornets taxied out to the long runway at Fallon and, as briefed, took off in ten-second intervals. They rendezvoused in a wide left turn, sliding into a cruise formation, with Road positioned on the leader's left wing, and the other section—J.J. and Burner— off his right wing. Joined up, the flight banked to the right and headed for the target complex called Bravo Nineteen.

"Low-Safe up and ready," called a voice on the range frequency. The "Low-Safe" was a propeller-driven T-34C trainer, usually flown by an instructor pilot, who orbited the target at two thousand feet. The Low-Safe's job was to monitor the bombing pattern— watching for too-low pull-outs, too-steep dive angles, possible collision courses.

The Low-Safe pilot today was a lieutenant commander from the Air Wing staff. It was his first time on the range.

"Roger, Low-Safe, we have you in sight," said Slab.

"Roman flight, the range is clear," called the spotter in the range control tower. "You're cleared in hot."

In they went, Slab first, then J.J., Road, and Burner, at eight-second intervals, diving at forty-five degrees on the giant dartboard.

Slab dropped his first bomb.

"Fifteen feet, four o'clock," called the spotter.

Then J.J.

"Two hundred forty-nine feet, six o'clock," the spotter said.

J.J. groaned. Two hundred forty-nine feet! It wasn't even in the ball park. It was like throwing at a dartboard and hitting the floor.

Slab offered instruction: "You're too shallow, J.J. You're only about thirty degrees. You gotta steepen up."

Dive-bombing amounted to an exercise in applied physics. If you dropped your bomb from too shallow a dive angle, it tended to fall short of the target. The steeper you dived at the target, the less error you would experience in the twelve to six o'clock axis.

"Roger," said J.J. On his next run he steepened up. But only a little. His bomb hit at 114 feet. Again at six o'clock.

And so it went. More big misses. Meanwhile Road and Burner

were getting hits inside fifty feet. Burner's last two bombs were bullseyes. Road planted one at ten feet. J.J. finished with a seventy-foot hit at nine o'clock.

For J.J., it was turning out to be just another bad day. Then it got worse. It was time to go strafing.

★

Gunfighting was always a dangerous business. Whether practiced on the streets of Tombstone or low over the Nevada desert, the basics remained the same: You still had to get close to your enemy, get a fix on him over the barrel of your gun, squeeze a trigger.

It was face-to-face warfare, and you could see at deadly proximity the results of your work. The strafing fighter had to get down close to the ground, in his enemy's home turf, close enough to see the whites of his eyes. The danger was twofold: The fighter doing the shooting was, of course, subject to being shot himself. And while he was shooting it was easy—insidiously easy—to become fixated . . . obsessed with the intoxicating lovely havoc he was causing there on the ground until—*oh, shit!*—there it was right in his face: the earth rising to meet him.

The M-61 rotary cannon mounted in the nose of the Hornet was a weapon straight out of a video arcade game. It was a Gatling gun, equipped with six barrels. Six thousand rounds a minute the thing fired, spewing fire and destruction like the wrath of Vulcan. It was mesmerizing, watching the earth erupt and the target banners shred and scrub brush dissolve like mown grass. You could feel the staccato thrum of the gun through the airframe of the jet. You could even *smell* the sweet cordite smell of the expended ammunition.

The strafing targets at Fallon were nylon banners ten feet high and twenty feet wide, erected vertically out on the weapons range. The banners were rigged with acoustic sensors to record each round of ammunition that penetrated the nylon. You dove on the targets at an angle of fifteen degrees downward. At about a thousand feet altitude, as the tiny banners swelled to the size of billboards in your windscreen, with the gunsight symbol in your HUD superimposed over the middle of the target, you squeezed the trigger on the control stick.

Brrrraaap! Just once, a short burst to see where you were hitting, checking out the accuracy of the sight and the bore sighting of the cannon. The gun only carried 568 rounds of twenty-millimeter shells. You could switch the rate of fire from 4,000 to 6,000 rounds per minute. At the maximum rate, you could get carried away and blow all your ammunition in one run.

So in the Hornet you learned to shoot in short bursts—*brraap! brraap!*—working the cannon like an artist dabbing paint. As in most forms of weapons delivery, aggressiveness paid off. The closer you flew to the target—the harder you pressed—the more hits you were likely to score. An unintended consequence of too much aggressiveness, of course, was becoming one with the target, a feat that had been accomplished more than once during strafing practice out there in the high desert at Fallon.

The course rules were supposed to prevent things like becoming one with the target. The strafing parameters required the attacking aircraft to roll in at three thousand feet above the ground, diving at *precisely* fifteen degrees. Five degrees more or less was reason to abort the run. You accelerated from about 350 knots to 480 knots in the dive, and you were allowed to fire the gun in the dive from twelve hundred feet to nine hundred feet. No lower. The restrictions were intended to prevent anyone from pressing too hard.

Still, fighter pilots being what they are, sometimes they pressed. And sometimes that had unintended consequences.

It occurred both in training and in combat. You pressed the strafing attack in close, disregarding the one-hundred-foot minimum altitude rule, notching up the speed, pressing it right up to whites-of-their-eyes closeness, squeezing off a burst—*brrraaap!*— and just as you pull off the target you feel it: a dreadful impact in the vital organs of your jet: *thunk, thunk, thunk.*

Your own bullets. They had ricocheted off the flat hard desert, right back into the belly of your jet. You had just shot yourself down.

★

The strafing targets were about five miles north. In the briefing back in the ready room, Slab had gone over the course rules, how you *had* to positively identify the correct banner before you opened fire with the nose-mounted cannon, how you *had* to call in "hot" when you armed your master armament switch, with your nose pointed at the ground. This was a no-fooling, real-time exercise with live ammunition. The cannon wouldn't care who it was shooting at, friend or foe.

Slab and his students had reviewed the map of the Bravo Nineteen complex, paying particular notice to the correct run-in line to the target banner. "The long, straight one," Slab said, pointing to the mile-long dirt road leading right up to the banner. "That's the correct run-in line. Not the zigzag line over there. That's another road, and it goes toward the spotting tower, where people work."

Straight lines. Zigzag lines. Roads in the desert. There in the briefing room, looking at the colored, unmoving map, it seemed so simple. Flying out there over the target complex, peering down at the moonscape of furrows and gullies and roads—it was confusing. What run-in line?

J.J. was having trouble finding the damned target. Where the hell was it? It was supposed to be squarish, about thirty feet high, broadside to the run-in line.

Was that it, over there? A big flat surface. That was it.

J.J. cradled his finger over the trigger, fixing the gunsight reticle squarely on the target. Two thousand feet . . . fifteen hundred . . . *Shoot!*

Brrrrraaaaaaaappp! He was getting hits. It was a glorious sight, J.J. thought, seeing the dirt kick up like that, the pieces flying off the target . . .

"Abort! Abort! Stop firing!"

"Stop, stop, pull up!"

"Don't fucking shoot!"

Everyone was yelling on the radio. Thirty seconds earlier, when J.J. was making his run-in along the *wrong* line, zigzagging toward the *wrong* target, no one took notice. Now that he had fired on the wrong target, which happened to be not a target at all but one of the *range spotting towers*, used by the range controllers to score weapons hits, everybody suddenly noticed. The radio frequency sounded like a tree full of chimpanzees.

Later, when the hysteria abated and the jets had returned to Fallon, several facts emerged. One—the happiest fact—was that no one was hurt. The spotting tower had been unmanned. And after J.J.'s zigzagging sneak attack, it seemed unlikely that they'd *ever* find volunteers to go back up there.

A contributing factor was the Low-Safe pilot: He hadn't been monitoring the range as he was supposed to. Or, as Slab put it: "The guy had his head up his ass."

Another interesting fact emerged when they got around to assessing the damage to the spotting tower: J.J. Quinn was a hell of a lot better strafer than he was a bomber. He had gotten eight solid hits on the tower.

★

In the list of major screwups, shooting the wrong target scored high on the roster. Death by friendly fire was one of the most ignominious events in warfare—something akin to a cop shooting another cop. It didn't look good on your record.

For the misdirected attack on the spotting tower, J.J. received another SOD. It was his second, and for a similar reason as before: he'd gone after the wrong target.

J.J. was on thin ice now. One more SOD and he would surely face an evaluation board. His career as a fighter pilot could come to a premature end. In fact his career as an officer in the Marine Corps could come to end.

All this was on J.J.'s mind that night in the bar at Ruthie's. His classmates—the unruly kids—were giving him a rough time, going on about mad-dog Marines who shot everything in sight. The McCormack twins were hiding behind the bar, pointing their fingers at people, going *Brrrrrp*, making machine gun noises.

J.J. was being a sport about it, taking it all in good humor. And then someone rang the gong at the bar to get everyone's attention. It was Burner. "I have a presentation to make," Burner said, "to Captain J.J. Quinn, United States Marine Corps."

He was holding up a newly embossed leather name patch, the

kind fighter pilots wore on their flight suits and jackets, with their gold wings, name, and rank. And their call sign.

J.J. groaned. He knew what was coming. He had just gotten a new call sign, one that he knew, no matter how much he fought it, would stick with him forever: SNIPER.

CHAPTER SEVENTEEN

SOD

It was the end of March 1995 and they were back at Cecil Field. The two-week Fallon det was behind them and with all the empty boxes checked on the strike phase syllabus sheet, the nuggets settled back into their workaday routine. Up at five, suit up and head for the squadron, brief and fly and debrief and brief for the next flight. In between hops you attend more AIDS and sensitivity and community relations lectures. It was all very much the same.

But it was different. In the time they had been out there on the high desert at Fallon, something had happened: They'd made the transition from neophytes to fighter pilots. Almost. They knew how to deliver high explosives on the heads—reasonably close, anyway— of a ground-dwelling enemy. They even knew how to *get* to the enemy's ground-dwelling place by skimming the floor of the high desert at no more than a hundred feet or so.

So it wasn't too hard to understand why some of them were walking now with just the slightest hint of a swagger. Hell, man, they were *fighter pilots*!

The RAG too was recognizing this new level of competence by— oh, so slightly—loosening the leash they kept on the nugget fighter pilots. It meant there was less direct supervision now of what they did in the air. Nuggets were even allowed to launch into the blue *all on their own,* off to complete a mission outside the watchful scrutiny of an instructor pilot.

It was a heady new experience. It opened up new opportunities for expanding their confidence. And, of course, it presented new opportunities for getting in trouble.

★

All the way across the parking lot to the great steel-doored hangar, up the long ladder to the upper deck, down the waxed passageway to the commodore's office, Van Doren replayed in his head the details of that morning's flight.

Why the hell did he do it?

Chip Van Doren didn't know. Some mutant cell gone amok in his brain stem? Maybe it was the scene in *Top Gun* where Maverick Mitchell comes ripping supersonic back to Miramar and dusts off the tower and rattles all the windows. But in the movie Maverick Mitchell had gotten away with it.

Chip Van Doren had not gotten away with it. Here he was, suited up in his khakis, shoes spit-shined, wings gleaming on his uniform left breast, on his way to do a rug dance in the commodore's office. He didn't know whether the wings would still be in place when he came out.

It had been an unbelievably cockeyed stupid idea. If he had just allowed his computerlike brain to process the idea for a few additional seconds, he would have rejected it. But he hadn't done that. Van Doren had seized on the idea and run with it like a monkey with a football.

He had been coming back solo from a touch-and-go session over at Whitehouse auxiliary field. He was solo. No leader, no wingman, no instructor observing like a mother hen. No one to keep him from doing something unbelievably cockeyed stupid.

He was only five miles from home. All he had to do was skim over the piney woods back to Cecil, enter the traffic pattern by flying directly overhead the active runway, then "break"—bank sharply to the left—to enter the downwind leg of the pattern, and land.

The only thing was, *real* fighter pilots liked to add a little pizzazz to the break. They might ask the tower for a "carrier" break, which meant a six-hundred-foot traffic pattern instead of the normal fifteen hundred feet. And they might notch the speed up a bit hotter than the normal two hundred fifty or three hundred knots. The hotter and lower you came into the break, the more awesome it looked on the ground. Looking awesome, as everyone in naval aviation knew, was everything.

Van Doren radioed the tower: "Cecil Tower, Roman three-eighty-six on a three-mile initial for runway three-six left." And then, after half a second's pause, added, "Request carrier break."

"Roger, Roman three-eighty-six. Carrier break approved."

Approved? Cool!

It was then that Van Doren's cognitive power reverted to that of a monkey on a moped. Zooming toward the break at six hundred feet, ripping over the woods like a fire-tailed comet, Chip Van Doren had one objective in mind: Look awesome!

He nudged up the throttles. At the Hornet's very light weight, with nothing hanging on the external racks and with only minimum fuel on board, the fighter accelerated like a scalded banshee. In his HUD on the windscreen, he might have noticed the digital airspeed indication ticking upward toward supersonic range. But he wasn't noticing. Van Doren was fixated on the great expanse of Cecil Field up ahead.

Five hundred knots . . .

Five-fifty . . .

The speed was increasing.

It all came down to applied physics. Somewhere around six hundred knots, varying with ambient temperature and altitude, lurked the mystical "sound barrier." At Mach 1.0, the exact speed of sound, a sonic boom was generated that reverberated over the landscape like the hammers of hell, shattering nerves and cracking windows.

Later it would be debated whether Chip Van Doren was actually doing Mach 1.0 or some fraction of a decimal point under. To the officer sitting there on the second floor of the building at the confluence of Cecil Field's runways, this fine distinction didn't make a bit of difference.

WhaaaaRoooooom!

It *was* a bit like the scene from *Top Gun*, when Maverick Mitchell buzzed the tower in his Tomcat fighter, causing the operations officer's coffee to spew like a geyser from his cup.

Except in this case it was the commanding officer of Cecil Field Naval Air Station, who was a Navy captain. The captain not only spilled his coffee, his pulse rate spiked to near-seizure level. Within seconds he was on the phone, demanding to talk to someone, *anyone* over there at the goddamned Strike Fighter Wing.

★

The commodore of the Strike Fighter Wing was also a Navy captain, but he held the honorific rank of one-star admiral. He had responsibility for *all* the Atlantic-based FA-18 squadrons, including the RAG. It was the commodore's job to dispense praise, promotion, and punishment.

Today was a day for punishment.

Van Doren didn't have to wait long. He was summoned right into the commodore's office. The commanding officer of the RAG was also there, looking grim.

The commodore had Chip Van Doren's personnel and training file in front of him. "You had a good record all the way through flight training, Mr. Van Doren. Top of your class."

"Yes, sir."

"What the hell were you thinking about this morning?"

Van Doren told him the truth: He hadn't been thinking at all. Certainly he hadn't thought about the outcome of his actions. He had no excuse for having rattled every window and jangled every nerve at Cecil Field.

"Was it worth losing your wings?"

Van Doren's heart sank. *Lose his wings?* His boyhood dream was slipping away like sand through his fingers. "No, sir," he said.

The commodore was an old attack and fighter pilot. In his time he had commanded his own squadron and a Carrier Air Wing. He knew all about fighter pilots—the thin distinction between envelope-pushing and professional discipline. He knew you *had* to cull out the bad weeds, the immature cowboys who flaunted orders

and disregarded rules. Guys like that would take your squadron
down with them. You had to get rid of them.

"In cases like this, I usually order an evaluation board," said the
commodore. "The board almost always recommends that the aviator
be terminated in the program. He's finished as a naval aviator."

Van Doren stood there, his pale Scot's complexion paler than
ever before. He kept his mouth shut, waiting for the commodore to
deliver the coup de grace.

The commodore took his time. He sat behind his desk, gazing at
Van Doren like he was a specimen in a lab. He seemed to be considering the matter: Was this kid worth keeping? The commodore
knew that you sometimes had to allow for misjudgments. An aviator
could learn from such an experience—if he was smart. Was this kid
smart? Or was he dumb as a dog turd?

"Mr. Van Doren, for making a stupid decision like you just did
this morning, you'll receive a SOD. An unsatisfactory grade."

"Yes, sir."

"I want your record to show that you've displayed a tendency
toward irresponsibility and immaturity."

"Yes, sir."

"Barring any recurrences of this behavior, you'll be retained in
the program."

Van Doren felt his life being returned to him. He did his best to
keep a straight face.

"But get this," said the commodore. "If you show any traits—the
slightest inclination—toward this kind of flying again, you *will* get an
evaluation board. And I assure you any such board is going to yank
your wings for good. Is that message loud and clear, Lieutenant?"

"Yes, sir."

"One more thing. You're going to write a letter."

"To whom, sir?"

"The commanding officer of this air station. You're going to
apologize for cracking his goddamned window."

★

Burner Bunsen's classmates had begun worrying about him. He was
behaving strangely. For one thing, he had stopped showing up at

Hop's, the hangout down in Orange Park where the single guys went to make hits on the local secretaries and nurses and groupies ("Oh, you're one of those *fighter pilots*!"). And on the weekends, which was the only time the nuggets could get together for some waterskiing, or golf, or to do some serious partying—Burner was nowhere to be found. He had disappeared. It was very peculiar because Burner Bunsen, of all the nuggets of Class 2-95, was the king of the party animals.

And then one Friday evening in mid-April, it all made sense. It was a squadron social at the Cecil Field Officers' Club. Everyone was supposed to be there—instructors, students, all the squadron officers. Burner walked in—and everyone got a good look at the reason he had been acting funny.

Her name was Greta. She was a graduate student in economics at the University of Florida, in Gainesville. She was tall, with flowing blond hair, dressed in a long red and white cocktail dress. In the opinion of every gawking young aviator in the room, Greta was a knockout.

Burner was in love. "My sister introduced us," he explained. "She works at a bank in New York, and Greta was doing an internship there. My sis calls up one day and says, 'You've gotta meet this girl I know who's going to grad school down in Florida.' So I did. And I've been spending a lot of time lately in Gainesville."

It was amazing, seeing Burner like this. Gone was the steely-eyed Marine, the bristle-headed, snake-eating, belly-crawling philosopher-killer. Here was a guy none of them had seen before, suited up in his Brooks Brothers houndstooth, falling all over himself fetching things for his date, introducing her around. Burner Bunsen was grinning like a sophomore at his first dance.

From then on the nuggets didn't see much of Burner outside the squadron. A few speculated that the new romance might be a distraction. Ol' Burner might, you know, lose his edge. Going through strike fighter training was something that took all your concentration.

They needn't have worried. Burner wasn't losing any of his edge. He finished strike phase with the best weapons scores of the class.

Even Barney, who seldom passed out compliments, was impressed. "The kid's good," he said. "For a Marine, he's unbelievable."

★

There was a side to Shrike that few ever saw. In fact, few of the instructors in the FA-18 RAG even wanted to acknowledge that beneath the plain-faced, flight-suited, quarrelsome exterior was a *woman*.

Sometimes they got a surprise.

Shrike would show up at a squadron party, or drop by the officers' club, wearing a dress. A *real* dress of the cocktail variety, and high heels.

Heads would turn. *Hey, look at . . . Is that who I think it is?*

It was. Shrike, in a cocktail dress, displayed a figure no one at the squadron suspected, having only seen her in a shapeless gray-green flight suit. The heels made her look taller, almost *lithe*, an attribute that had been hidden by the standard clunky black flying boots. Her long blond hair, unfettered by the bands and pins she used to keep it bundled inside her helmet, flowed naturally over her bare shoulders.

Shrike was, if not a knockout, at least an eye-catcher.

A silence would fall over the bar.

She loved it. What she loved most was that these were the same guys who, in the ready room, glowered at her like she was an alien on their front porch. Now they were gaping like spaniels at a cat show.

She never stayed long. Cocktail parties bored her. When she had gone, the men at the party—instructors and nuggets alike—would still be talking.

"I'll be damned," said an instructor. "Who would have guessed?"

"Guessed what?"

"Who would have guessed that Shrike was really a fox in disguise?"

★

What they had glimpsed, of course, was the *other* Sally Hopkins, the one that Shrike, the naval officer and woman fighter pilot, seldom turned loose in public.

Only on weekends, when she was free from training duties, did the other, softer Sally Hopkins come out of her shell. Then she could let her hair down, literally. She could unpin the long blond hair, put on sandals and cotton shorts and a halter, and climb into her Jeep. She liked to put the top down and head for the beaches, or for the riverwalk downtown where they had outdoor concerts and she could rollerblade along the water. It was the only time Shrike could feel like a girl.

A real date for Shrike was, actually, a rare event. For one thing, there just wasn't time enough to keep up the tedious training schedule and also have a social life. For another, the only men she was likely to meet during this time in her life were other pilots at Cecil Field. And *that*, thank you, was the last thing she needed: hearing more macho guy talk from the same Neanderthal fighter jocks she worked with every day.

Sometimes Shrike wished she were finished with this whole business of being a pioneer. Trailblazing for future generations of women just wasn't fun, with the resentment, the rancor, the pass-or-fail pressure of the strike fighter curriculum.

Sometimes she thought it would be *so* nice just to be . . . a girl. That was all. Just be a girl and wear pretty clothes and go dancing and have men open doors for her. She would take long bubble baths and have her hair permed and go to the theater. She would meet men who did not feel threatened by her and who respected her for what she was. She might even find the right one, and if she did, she might even consider starting a family.

It was all fantasy, of course.

When she caught herself indulging in wishful thinking, Shrike yanked herself back to reality. After all, she was too disciplined for such daydreaming. She had worked too hard, been focused on her goal for too many years to give it up now. She was almost there. Almost a fighter pilot. Almost on her way to the stars.

But, still, sometimes she dreamed. It would be nice, for a while, just to be a girl. . . .

CHAPTER EIGHTEEN

RICOCHET

Whenever the nuggets wanted to feel better about how they were doing, all they had to do was think about Lieutenant Junior Grade Rodney Shea. In his very brief career as a naval aviator, Shea had achieved legendary status in the RAG.

His official call, inevitably, was "Rico," but that soon gave way to the more convenient appellation "Ricochet." Shea had been in Class 6-94, several months ahead of the 2-95 nuggets. He had finished strike fighter training and gone to a fleet squadron already. But had not gotten through the RAG without leaving a legacy. Things happened to Shea.

"Did you hear about Ricochet?"

"Christ, what now?"

"He's getting a FNAEB at his fleet squadron. Word is, he's toast. The skipper is so pissed, he wants him gone instantly. Outa here, like now."

His troubles began back in the RAG. There was the famous occasion, for example, when he sauntered out to the flight line, preflighted his jet in a hurry, manned up, and launched. On the way down to Pinecastle target, where his flight was scheduled for a bombing exercise, Dash Four—the number four pilot in flight—

noticed Ricochet's jet had no bombs on the weapons rack. He was about to suggest to Ricochet that it might be awkward, bombing without bombs.

But then the squadron duty officer came up on the tactical frequency. "Ricochet, this is base. I want you to push the data-link button on the up-front control panel and check your aircraft number."

"Roger. It says number three-three-four."

"Terrific. Now check your briefing card. What aircraft does it say you are *supposed* to be in?"

Ricochet checked. *Hmmm.* Aircraft number 331. Wrong jet.

Taking the wrong jet was an error that could have disastrous consequences, especially if the jet had a maintenance problem, the wrong fuel load, the wrong weapons load.

That had been SOD number one for Ricochet.

★

A couple of weeks later Ricochet was with his class out at Fallon for strike phase. The final event in strike phase was an exercise wherein the entire class of students jointly planned a coordinated deep air strike on one of the target complexes at Fallon. The targets looked real, with derelict tanks and trucks and fabricated buildings.

The flight of eight Hornets set out for the target area. According to plan, they took different approaches to the target. The FA-18s converged on the complex. Some were assigned strafing missions, some to drop their weapons in a "lay-down" delivery from low altitude. Two, including Ricochet, were supposed to fly over a designated initial point, pull up steeply, then dive-bomb their assigned target. Ricochet's target was a prefab building, a plywood structure the size of a small hangar.

Things were going okay—until Ricochet was supposed to reach his pull-up point, an intersection of two roads. He missed it. So he kept on ripping across the floor of the desert, looking . . . looking for the damned intersection. . . .

Eventually he saw a couple of roads that intersected. Sort of.

Up he went. He rolled inverted. He looked for his target, pulling his nose downward, ready to aim his bombs.

Where the hell was the target?

Well, there *was* a structure down there that looked more or less like his target. Ricochet went for it.

Later, everyone agreed that it was indeed a blessing that Ricochet's bombs that day were only Mark 76 twenty-five pounders. Practice bombs. All a Mark 76 did was make a nice smoke plume so it could be spotted. Nonetheless, having *twelve* such twenty-five-pound projectiles come raining down on your pasture, through your barn, scaring the living shit out of your cows, was enough to make one old Nevada rancher *very* pissed off at the U.S. Navy.

★

They convened a FNAEB for Ricochet after the bombing incident at Fallon. The board carefully reviewed his records, all the way back to primary training. Ricochet, it turned out, had above-average flight training grades. His problem wasn't flying airplanes. It was *headwork*, an old aviation label for mental activity—good or bad—in the cockpit. So far, Ricochet's headwork had been appallingly bad.

But the board decided that Ricochet *must* be intelligent or he would never have gotten through all the layers of the Fine Mesh, all the way to strike fighter training. They decided in his favor. Ricochet's problems were just isolated aberrations. His headwork was *bound* to improve.

They were wrong.

★

Ricochet graduated from the RAG and reported to his fleet squadron, based there at Cecil Field. Within a month, he had ensured for himself a place in Navy legend.

It happened on a multiple-weapons flight—a bombing hop followed by an air intercept exercise.

They were carrying AIM-9 Sidewinder missiles on the wingtip stations. They had finished the bombing portion of the mission, and now Ricochet Shea was making intercepts on a section of two other Hornets, led by the squadron commanding officer.

Ricochet was supposed to be "sorting" the bogeys, meaning separating and identifying the potential targets using his air-to-air radar and the heat-seeking head of his Sidewinder missile.

He sorted out a target—the Hornet being flown by the skipper. Ricochet pressed the attack, obtaining a "lock" with the Sidewinder. All he needed was a "tone"—the squalling noise in his earphones that told him the Sidewinder's guidance system was tracking the target and was ready to be launched.

Suddenly Ricochet felt a *whoosh!* To his everlasting horror, he saw his Sidewinder missile *leave its rack on the wingtip!* The thing had fired! The missile took off like a greyhound out of the chute, its smoke-less motor leaving no trail as it whooshed off in the atmosphere.

It was whooshing toward the commanding officer's jet. There was no way to recall a launched Sidewinder missile. It carried its guidance system in the head of the missile. Once fired, the Sidewinder was off on its own seek-and-destroy mission.

Ricochet waited an eternity. Ten seconds. Twenty. Half a minute.

"Ah, Skipper?" he said on the radio.

"Go ahead."

"Uh, I had a TFOA." TFOA was shorthand for "things falling off aircraft."

"What's missing?"

"A Sidewinder."

"Did you lose it?"

"Sort of, yes, sir."

"How?"

"Well, it might have . . . uh, gotten itself launched—"

"Launched? When?"

"Just now."

Silence. The commanding officer sat in the cockpit of his fighter, looking around, waiting to see if he was going to die. As the sec-onds ticked past, a single well-defined objective swelled in his consciousness like a thundercloud: *If* he lived through this, he was going to *kill* that dumb sonofabitch who had just shot a missile at him.

He lived through it. The missile vanished. Back on the ground, the skipper wanted to see Ricochet's cockpit videotape. It was all there on the tape: Ricochet had turned *on* the master armament switch during the bombing exercise, then *forgot* to return the switch to the safe position. With the switch still on, Ricochet's Sidewinder missile was fireable and lethal.

Then he had done the last thing necessary—he squeezed the trigger. The only thing that had saved the skipper was that the missile had been fired before the acquisition tone had come on. The Sidewinder's guidance system needed about three more seconds' tracking time to home in on him.

It was the end of Ricochet. The commanding officer ordered another FNAEB convened. And he made it clear that he was in no mood to hear any bullshit from the board about how smart the guy was, about "isolated aberrations," about what a peachy training record he had. What he wanted to hear was that Ricochet Shea was *gone*. Out of there. History. Toast.

And so he was.

CHAPTER NINETEEN

"F" IS FOR FIGHTER

Only the spirit of attack borne in a brave heart will bring
success to any fighter aircraft, no matter how highly
developed it may be.

—*Luftwaffe General Adolph Galland*
Berlin, Germany

Anything is fair in knife fights and air-to-air combat.

—*Anonymous*
Tijuana, Mexico

The best part of strike fighter training, everyone said, was the
fighter part. The nuggets loved it. What they loved most about it
was where they did it.

Fighter weapons phase, like strike phase, was done on detachment—away from home. But instead of the sagebrush-and-rattlesnake
remoteness of Fallon, Nevada, fighter weapons phase was in Key West.

Everyone, it seemed, loved Key West. "It's awesome! The flying,
the base, the weather, the beach."

Not to mention the topless bars and the cheap drinks and the
hordes of groupie girls down there on spring vacation.

Key West was to Navy fighter pilots what the old Muroc Field (later Edwards Air Force Base) had been to Chuck Yeager and his comrades of *The Right Stuff*. It was a place nearly forgotten by the brass hats of the Navy, a little atoll so far out of the mainstream that you could get lost there.

Key West was the site of Boca Chica Naval Air Station, the Mecca of raw, unfettered, envelope-punching fighter jockeying. It was freedom! No commodores, no ill-humored brass watching you like cops at a school crossing. If you ripped into the break at Key West just a little hot, rattled a few windows . . . well, hell, hadn't the windows at Boca Chica *always* rattled? They were *supposed* to rattle, maybe even shatter once in a while, like cheap china. This was Key West! You could push your airplane and yourself right up to the limits, maybe even a little beyond.

Fighter pilots loved everything about the place—the glorious weather, the uncrowded air space, the ramshackle, go-to-hell ambience of the old air station. The flying was all daytime, clear-weather, air-to-air combat training. Key West possessed the sort of Margaritaville decadence that matched some maverick chromosome in the fighter pilot chemistry.

The best part was at the end of the day. Every evening, with a day's hard air combat training behind them, and before the Caribbean sun had slipped into the gulf, they were out the gate, barreling toward the old town of Key West and the pier-side honky-tonks and the splendid sinfulness of Duval Street.

Key West had developed a culture all its own. The island was a lively colony of Hemingwayesque drinkers, artists, brawlers, prostitutes, gays, fishermen, druggies, smugglers, treasure hunters, groupies of every persuasion—and fighter pilots. The most famous bar in the old town was Sloppy Joe's, where Hemingway used to hold court and where his picture now adorned every wall and was even on the T-shirts they peddled to tourists.

It didn't take long for young Navy pilots to slip into the mode of Key West living. In the uniform de rigueur—shorts, sandals, reasonably clean T-shirt—they hit Duval Street. It didn't matter that they were instantly recognizable to the locals as a G.I. The Key Westers had been seeing short-haired Navy jocks on their premises for half a century. Anyway, the natives were friendly, especially the girls in the bars, who, when you bought them a drink or two, would demonstrate that they just *loved* Navy pilots. . . .

★

Not everyone in the military felt the same way about Key West. To the *real* Navy, which was to say the hard-shelled surface sailors who valued thinks like shipshapeness and glistening decks and gray-painted edifices, Boca Chica was an embarrassment. A black-shoe naval officer's first glimpse of the ramshackle hangars, decrepit outbuildings, crumbling stairwells, sagging, rain-stained ceilings, and grass-thatched huts at the water's edge that served as off-duty drinking and fishing shelters would leave him gagging. It was the kind of place only the flyboys could love.

The Boca Chica air station had a collection of gale-battered hangars and a sprawling, sun-scorched ramp. Land crabs scuttled like minia-ture tanks between the buildings. A steady offshore wind blew in from the straits of Florida, rattling the ancient doors of the World War II–era hangars. Tropical showers meandered through the leaking roofs, puddling in the ceilings of the ready rooms, staining walls and mildewing the furniture. Pilots soon learned to avoid those chairs in the briefing room that lay under the cracks in the ceiling tiles.

One autumn afternoon an Air Force F-16 squadron arrived for temporary duty at Boca Chica. They were there to take advantage of the glorious weather and to utilize the Navy's high-tech weapons range facilities. The Air Force unit was assigned to occupy Hangar 17, the same one favored by the Navy detachments from Cecil Field.

A blue-suited colonel with spit-shined shoes came to inspect his squadron's new quarters. For a long while the colonel studied a hangar door, which would not close. The door had been rusted in place, he guessed, since about 1942. Then the colonel inspected the stairwells to the office spaces. He noted that they seemed to be shored up by timber pilings. He sniffed the dank, mildewed air. The colonel thought the ancient hangar was disgusting.

Then he entered a dark and mold-encrusted maintenance shop. He opened a metal locker. He found himself eyeball-to-eyeball with a Florida land crab the size of a cocker spaniel.

"Yaaarrrggghh!" The colonel bolted from the hangar. The inspection was finished. No way was any flying unit of the U.S. Air Force going to be billeted in a place so unhealthy, unsafe, and disgusting as Boca Chica's Hangar 17.

The story, of course, got back to the Navy pilots at Cecil, who *loved* it. It confirmed everything they had believed about the Air Force: The poor uptight blue suits didn't know paradise when they saw it!

★

Who are those guys?

That was the nuggets' standard reaction when they landed at Boca Chica. Parked there on the ramp were neat rows of fighters. But these fighters weren't marked in the sea-gray paint and distinctive U.S. stars-and-bars insignia of the Navy or Marines or Air Force. They had foreign-looking camouflage paint schemes and— *my God!*—East Bloc red stars on the tails.

They looked like *enemy* fighters.

Which they were, sort of. They belonged to the Navy's most peculiar fighter squadron, VF-45, whose mission was to provide bogeys—adversaries—for the Hornet and Tomcat squadrons that came to Key West for training. The adversary pilots flew an assortment of Navy and Air Force fighters—FA-18s, F-5Es, F-16s—all painted with the ominous mottled sky-blue camouflage paint schemes and the even more ominous red stars.

Being an adversary pilot was, in the opinion of most fighter jocks, the closest you could come to fighter pilot heaven. The bogeys were all experienced fighter pilots and each had been handpicked from a fleet squadron. Duty in the adversary squadron meant that you got to fly the world's hottest fighters. And it meant you spent your days flying air-to-air combat missions, from a nice long runway and *not* a floating steel slab of a carrier's flight deck, and you almost always flew in daytime and in good weather.

Briefings for the fighter weapons missions were held in a large room in one wing of the dilapidated adversary squadron hangar. The briefing room was divided down the middle. On one side sat the students and their instructors. On the other side sat the bogeys—the pilots of the adversary squadron. Good guys on the left, bad guys on the right.

A giant greaseboard covered the front wall. On the board were times, call signs, aircraft numbers, names of the pilots, designated operating area, radio frequencies—all the data for the coming mission.

Almost all the data. There were a few details missing, like how many bad guys you were up against.

On the side of the greaseboard marked BOGEYS was one call sign—"Bouncer." Beneath it was "And Friends." It meant that Bouncer, the adversary pilot, would be opposing the flight of students, and with him would be an unknown number of other adversaries. The mission was a four v. unknown—four friendlies versus an unknown number and type of bogeys.

It was all supposed to be very realistic, the red-star-marked adversary fighters, the unknown number of the opposition, the tactics they employed. The adversary pilots, with the different types of fighters in their inventory, mimicked the performance of specific enemy fighters. They could accurately imitate a MiG-21, or MiG-25, or the powerful MiG-29, and their tactics even matched the kill parameters of the various Russian-built air-to-air missiles. The adversaries were schooled in the tactics favored by fighter pilots of Libya, Iraq, Iran, Serbia—all the hostile air forces the Navy pilots might someday encounter.

The adversary pilots loved their jobs. They had so gotten into their roles that they even *talked* like pseudo-Iraqi bogeys on the radio:

"Akhmed, we have enemy Hornets twelve o'clock!"

"Rahjah that, Abdul. I have a lock."

The adversaries didn't always win. Since their job was to provide realistic opposition—and targets—for the fledgling Hornet pilots, they were frequently "shot down."

"Akhmed, we are lit up. The Yankee swine are launching missiles."

"Yeah, too bad about that, Abdul. Today we visit Allah."

★

Like the other nuggets, Road Ammons loved this phase of the syllabus. Air-to-air was turning out to be his strongest subject. He loved the one-on-one, best-jock-wins gamesmanship of the contest.

It reminded him of college sports, going up against an opponent and trying to beat his socks off.

Until he got to Key West, Road Ammons had believed he was *untouchable*. He had gotten this far in his flying career without any major mishap. No SODs. No life-threatening screwups. He had done well in fam phase, gotten better-than-average scores in strike phase. In fighter weapons phase, out here in the empty blue spaces over the Florida Keys, going one-on-one with the other nuggets and up against the adversary squadron guys—well, hell, man, he was kicking ass!

Sure, he had gotten *schwacked* a couple of times, getting too aggressive against a bogey and letting the guy's wingman sneak in a shot at him. That sort of thing—getting *schwacked*—was to be expected if you were trying out new tactics, learning what worked and what didn't. But in plain BFM—basic fighter maneuvering— good ol' Road Ammons was turning out to be one ass-kicking, mean-eyed, hard-ball fighter pilot.

Until this afternoon. This afternoon he fell out of the sky like a manhole cover.

★

Road's eyes looked like halogen lamps. "Shit, man, I thought we were gonna punch out!" he said in the Key West ready room. Gone for the moment was the trademark Yamaha grin and the aw-shucks shuffle. "That was the scaredest I've *ever* been in an airplane."

Road ripped the pop-top off a Coke can and downed it in two long swallows. He had been on the ground for an hour and a half now and he was still sweating.

It had been a one-vee-one, mea[...] fighter. The exercise was called basi[...] was the essence of air combat. High [...] nets, one-on-one.

Road had been flying with an ins[...] backseat. The mission was to go ou[...] against another student, who also ha[...] The instructors were there not just t[...] nuggets from imminent calamity. Th[...] Once in a while a nugget got in over[...]

They were being steered by GCI (ground-controlled intercept) radar to intercept the bogey, who in this instance was his classmate, Rick McCormack. In McCormack's backseat was another instructor, Comet Halley.

Road locked up the bogey on his own APG-65 radar. Then, about ten miles out, he obtained a VID—visual identification. The other Hornet looked like a sinister gray predator coming directly at him. Road could just make out the fighter's distinctive frontal silhouette—the angular vertical stabilizers that identified it as an FA-18. Road knew that the bogey pilot, the Heckle of the Heckle-and-Jeckle McCormacks, would at this moment be going through the same drill—locking *him* up with his own radar.

They were merging. Rapidly. Two specks in the Caribbean sky, coming at each other head on with a Vc—closing velocity—of eleven hundred miles an hour.

It was a classic opener for a one v. one. *Whoooooom!* Eyeball to eyeball, five hundred feet apart they passed, same altitude, twenty-nine thousand feet.

"Fight's on," called out Comet Halley.

And so it was. The idea now was to get behind your opponent, to maneuver into that thirty-degree cone, from one to four miles behind his tailpipe, which was the killing zone for the AIM-7 Sparrow and the AIM-9 Sidewinder air-to-air missiles carried on the Hornet. If you got closer, inside a mile from the bogey's tail, you switched to guns and tried to pop him Red Baron–style with the big Gatling gun in your nose.

With a level, head-on engagement like this one, at equal speeds, neither fighter had an advantage. The combatants either commenced a turning duel, each trying to turn harder than the other, cutting ⸺ross the radius of the turning circle to bring his nose toward the ⸺'s tail, or it became a scissors duel, as the fighters turned back ⸺ach other, crossing noses in another head-on pass, then ⸺ections to *again* cross nose to nose, and so on. They con-⸺—scissoring—until one managed to turn more tightly ⸺get *inside* the other's turn. In small increments he ⸺antage and got behind his opponent's tail.

With high-performance fighters like the Hornet, the scissors could go vertical instead of horizontal. As the fighters passed each other head-on, they pulled straight up, each trying to sustain the climb longer than the other, until one was forced to bring his nose down again, exposing his tail to a shot from his opponent. With evenly matched fighters, the vertical scissors might go on for several up-and-down cycles, which was called a "roller."

Road and McCormack flashed past each other. Road saw the other Hornet's nose start up. *He was going vertical!* Road matched him, hauling back on the stick, grunting under the six Gs he was applying to the jet. Up, up, up went the nose. The horizon dropped away. He could see only blue, blue sky directly ahead through the windscreen, getting bluer as the nose pointed straight to heaven. Through the top of his clear plastic cockpit canopy he could see the other Hornet. It was close, maybe only a hundred yards away.

They were both vertical. On parallel tracks. Straight up. Each staring at the other through his own canopy.

This was *very* damn close, Road thought. He was peering straight into the cockpit of Rick McCormack's Hornet. He could see McCormack and his backseater, Comet Halley, peering back at him. On this line, thought Road, it was going to be hard to pull the nose back down without hitting them.

They were getting slow, running out of upward velocity. It was time to pull the nose downward into the back half of a loop.

Road started to bring his nose downward, toward the horizon. Toward the other fighter.

Then he saw the other Hornet's nose move. *Toward him!* Damn! They were about to merge, going straight up! And running out of airspeed.

Road reacting instinctively. He "bunted"—pushed the nose away from the oncoming opponent—back toward the vertical.

Which was the wrong thing to do. With its dangerously low airspeed and the abrupt control reversal, the jet fell out of the sky.

Road Ammons's Hornet fighter did what they call a "departure," meaning it left the realm of controlled flight. The graceful FA-18

Hornet fighter became a free-falling body, gyrating, tumbling, flopping out of control like a dropped garbage can cover.

It happened so suddenly. *Hey, whoa, now . . . what's happening here? . . . Oh, shit . . . come on, airplane, stop doing this to me . . .*

Road was vaguely aware of Barney in the backseat. Barney was yelling in the intercom: "Road, what the fuck are you doing? Road, goddamn it, turn loose of the frigging stick! Road . . ."

The horizon was oscillating up and down. Blue sky was swapping places with blue ocean. Sky, ocean, sky. Road snatched the throttles to idle. He grappled with the stick, toggled the spin recovery switch, tried to remember the emergency procedure. He uttered the standard fighter pilot's emergency invective: *"Oh, shit. Oh, shit. Oh, shit . . ."*

"I've got it, Road," said a voice on the intercom. "Road, goddamn it, *I've got it!* Turn loose, Road. Lemme see your hands on the canopy."

Turn loose? Oh, yeah. Barney in the backseat. Barney the instructor knew how to stop this goddamn wild thing. Road turned loose. He put his hands up on the canopy rail, the metal support around the top of the windscreen.

The Hornet was doing a "falling leaf," swooping down from side to side in violent lurching movements, still falling out of the sky at twenty thousand feet per minute. The airspeed was indicating zero. It meant the jet had no forward velocity. No flying speed.

Gradually the oscillations dampened. The airspeed was creeping up. One-fifty. One-seventy. "It's coming out," Road said. "I think we're flying— *Oh, shit—*"

The jet was tumbling again. It wasn't coming out. Not yet. Once again the airspeed indicated zero. The Hornet was *again* flopping out of control like a dropped garbage can cover. Road clamped his hands on the canopy rail.

They fell through eighteen thousand feet. Still flopping.

Fifteen thousand.

The Hornet was doing another falling leaf. The airspeed was still zero.

The unthinkable was entering Road's thoughts: *We're gonna have to punch out of this thing. At ten thousand feet, we're gonna eject.*

Thirteen thousand. Still falling. The wild swinging of the nose was dampening. The airspeed was creeping back up.

One hundred knots.

One hundred fifty. One hundred eighty.

At ten thousand feet the Hornet was flying straight and level. Back under control.

Road allowed himself to resume breathing.

"You guys okay?" Comet Halley radioed from the other Hornet.

"Sure, we're okay," said Barney. "What's your position?"

"Your six o'clock, of course. By the way, thanks for the shot. You just got *schwacked*."

★

With other, earlier fighters such as the F-4 and the F-8, there was one standard spin recovery: You ejected from the beast. The FA-18 Hornet was considered a more benign jet. Sure, in basic fighter maneuvering, you *could* make it spin, or depart, as Road had done. And it *could* be violent. The Hornet would tumble, spin, perhaps enter a "falling leaf." It was almost always recoverable from such departures, though it usually consumed vast parcels of altitude to do so.

One feature of the FA-18's computerized flight control system was the spin recovery mode. Following a "departure" the pilot was automatically presented with a message on the DDIs (digital display indicators—or video screens): "Stick Left," or "Stick Right," telling them which way to deflect the control stick to counter the jet's wild oscillations. A large arrow also appeared on the screen *pointing* the direction the stick should be deflected (Navy pilots liked to say that the arrows were there for the Marines). If the spin recovery logic was slow to appear, the pilot could select it with a switch on his panel.

It was supposed to be a no-brainer. Obey the command. Follow the arrow, stupid. Sit there and wait for the jet to recover. The problem was that pilots were not inclined to sit there in a wildly gyrating fighter and wait for the thing to make up its mind whether it was going to kill them. They were programmed to *do something*. Try "A." Try "B." If that didn't work, try "C." Try every damn thing in the book.

And when nothing you tried worked, you yanked the handle between your legs—*ploom!*—and punched out of the thing.

This was the closest Road had ever come to yanking the handle. And he wasn't even sure how close it had been.

Back in the ready room, Barney was his usual cup-spitting, ball-scratching self, grinning around a fresh glob of dip. "It was good experience," he said. "Now you know the worst thing that happens when you screw up a vertical scissors."

"The jet departs?"

"Naw. That's nothin'. The worst thing is that while you're trying to recover, that other asshole gets a free shot at you."

★

An odd thing was happening. The class ranking of 2-95 seemed to belie the Navy's strong emphasis on an engineering or science background as a qualification for flying fighters.

In nearly every class at strike fighter training, one particular student would excel in one phase of training. But seldom would that same student be the best in other phases. A student with a natural flair for air combat maneuvering, for example, might be abysmally bad at carrier landings. Sometimes the best bomber would be a consistent loser in air-to-air fighting. Rare was the superstar who excelled at *every* phase of strike fighter training.

But here was Burner—the top student in the class, with the highest grade-point average and the most apparent natural aptitude in everything. No one could figure it out. Burner the philosophy major! Pointy-headed liberal arts types weren't supposed to make good fighter pilots. Here was an Ivy League poetry-reading philosopher, who didn't know a logarithm from a luggage rack, *beating* all the techies in the class.

What did it mean? Presumably, the Navy's preference for engineering and technical educations for fighter pilot candidates was because of the complexity of fighters like the FA-18. The thinking was, you *needed* a rocket science education to understand the high-tech nuances of advanced fighter aircraft.

The facts didn't always support such thinking. There were plenty of examples in the fighter business—technically challenged klutzes who

Headquarters of the Strike Fighter Wing Atlantic at NAS Cecil Field, Florida

Road Ammons flashing the Yamaha grin

Instructor pilot Barney Barnes in a typical pose, with a wad of dip under his lip

Landing Signal Officer shack at Whitehouse Field

Heckle and Jeckle, the McCormack twins

A bogey, captured in the head-up display of a Hornet *(John Wood)*

Rolling in on bombing target at Pinecastle Range

FA-18 Hornets with AIM-9 Sidewinder air-to-air missiles on their wingtips
(Official U.S. Navy photo by CWO2 Tony Alleyne)

Hornet on the catapult, being readied for launch *(Official U.S. Navy photo)*

Lieutenant Tom "Slab" Bacon, instructor pilot

Landing Signal Officer Lieutenant Chris "Pearly" Gates, during a break in the action aboard the U.S.S. *Nimitz*

Positioning an FA-18 Hornet, using every inch of space on *Nimitz*'s deck

"Shooter" gives the signal to launch a Hornet from the catapult. *(Official U.S. Navy photo by PH2 R. R. Knepp)*

A Hornet catches the number-three wire, under the watchful eye of the landing signal officer. *(Official U.S. Navy photo by PH2 R. R. Knepp)*

A Hornet goes supersonic. *(U.S. Navy Photo)*

couldn't start a lawn mower or program a VCR—who could fly the hell out of a pointy-nosed jet. It was enough to make everyone wonder: Did it *really* take a rocket scientist to be good in fighters? Or was there something else, some indefinable substance like Tom Wolfe's "right stuff," that certain fighter pilots, with or without techno-degrees, possessed in abundance and others would never have?

Burner, for his part, couldn't care less. Since coming to Key West, he had other things on his mind. He was spending all his time outside the cockpit with a telephone clamped to his ear. Already he had shoved countless rolls of quarters into the pay phone talking to Greta.

★

The only class member who *was* a bona fide rocket scientist, Shrike Hopkins, was having great difficulty. Shrike, who possessed the most advanced education with her graduate degree in astronautical engineering, also had the most experience in jet cockpits. But Shrike was paying a heavy penalty for the time she had spent in grad school—and away from the cockpit. Now she was playing catch-up.

Close behind Burner in grade-point average was Chip Van Doren, who *was* a card-carrying techie. Van Doren, the techno-freak, stored information about the FA-18 and its various missions like a computer data bank. And like his nontechie comrade Burner, he was a "natural" in the cockpit, seeming to be blessed with a built-in situational awareness. Flying an airplane was something he was simply good at.

★

To no one's surprise, the McCormack twins were only micro-points apart in grade-point average. In class ranking, they were somewhere in the middle of the register.

Lately the McCormacks had been doing something that drove everyone crazy. Rick had grown a mustache. For a while that pleased everyone—their classmates, their instructors—because for once they didn't have to guess which of the two grinning redheads, Heckle or Jeckle, they were talking to. "That's Rick, the one with the mustache. . . ."

And then one day, Rick shaved off the mustache. And Russ

began growing one. And then Rick began growing his back. And then *one* of them—by now no one knew *which* one—shaved his off again.

And so on. It was even driving their wives crazy, which they were beginning to think was the *real* reason the twins did such things.

Instructors gave up trying to debrief the grinning twins separately. It was just too frustrating, critiquing a mistake one of them made while the other sat there grinning like a Cheshire cat. *Why is he grinning like that? Am I talking to the wrong guy?*

"All right, Rick, you were really out to lunch in the pattern out there today. High and fast all the way—"

"Must of been my brother."

"The hell it was," said Russ. "It had to be you. I was right on speed—"

"Naw, it was you."

"I don't give a shit who it was!" said the exasperated instructor. "As far as I'm concerned, you were *both* dicked up. From now on, when either one of you screws up, I'm gonna nail you both."

★

Road Ammons was rarely the top student in any event. Nor was he ever the worst. Good ol' Road stayed where he had always been since the beginning of training: slightly above average.

Road was methodical in his approach to training. The goal was simple: Get through. Don't push envelopes. Don't show off. Don't run your mouth. Keep it between the lines.

So far this method had worked splendidly for him. Never had he received a SOD in his naval aviation career. He had completed every phase of training right on schedule. He was known as a solid, unflamboyant, nugget fighter pilot. And that was just fine with Road Ammons.

★

J. J. Quinn kept having these recurring nightmares. He dreamed he was the oldest guy in a contest, a decade more ancient than any of the sharp-witted kids against whom he was competing. The worst part of the dream was that the kids were winning.

Of course, it wasn't just a dream. He *was* older than all his classmates in strike fighter training. And for the most part, they *were* beating his socks off.

But J. J. Quinn was a plugger. Nothing, it seemed, had ever come naturally or easily for him. But he had persevered over every obstacle placed in his way since he entered the Marine Corps thirteen years ago. Inside his locker door at the squadron, he had taped a sign: CUN-NING AND TREACHERY WILL TRIUMPH OVER YOUTH AND SKILL.

Well, so far cunning and treachery weren't helping a hell of a lot. J.J. had already collected the two SODs, the second nearly costing him the ball game. Despite the predictions of some of his old helicopter cronies, J. J. Quinn was still flying FA-18s and, more incredibly, he was still alive. He was even doing reasonably *well* in the air-to-air phase of training. J.J. had surprised everyone, including himself, functioning like a real fighter pilot in the 3-D, dynamic air-to-air environment. Perhaps, just perhaps, he was thinking, all those years of experience, even in lowly helicopters, still counted for something.

★

There was a test every female aviator went through whenever she broke into a new peer group, a new squadron, a ship. The woman pilot would be sitting there minding her own business in the ready room, and a guy would toss out something like: ". . . there I was, falling out of the sky, and I knew this time I was really *fucked* . . ."

It was just to check for reaction. Every male eye would be looking sideways to see if the woman aviator got huffy about it, if she growled or complained. Then they would know: *Be careful around this one!* If she appeared not to be offended, or better, if she listened with some sort of interest in the story, she was probably okay.

With Angie Morales, it was hard to figure at first. She would put on her inscrutable expression, neither laughing nor wincing at the ready room raunchiness. Zero response. But now it was April, three months into the training syllabus, and the guys were beginning to understand Rambo Morales: She didn't care a hoot in hell *what* they said. The simple truth about Morales was that she was there to fly fighters, not to clean up anyone's language.

They didn't bother testing anymore. Rambo was one of the guys.

★

Shrike Hopkins, on the other hand, was definitely *not* one of the guys.

Road Ammons was worried about Shrike. He worried that she was playing the gender card—pushing everyone's crazy button with all that they-don't-like-me-because-I'm-a-woman stuff.

Road could feel a kinship with Shrike. They were both minority members in the business of naval aviation. Road was one of the few African-Americans in the strike fighter training program. Shrike Hopkins and Rambo Morales were the only two women in the program. They all knew what it was like to be different.

But it was Shrike who was brandishing her minority status like a loaded shotgun. Shrike Hopkins seemed to be *looking* for a fight, and she didn't care with whom. And it was making Road Ammons nervous as hell.

Shrike was a loner. She shunned most external support groups, including the "old girls" network of women naval aviators. Shrike wanted to prove she was there *not* because of gender but purely due to her ability. But these days, more than ever, she was feeling alone. She was the only one of the Terrific Trio still in fighters.

Road Ammons, of course, was different. Road *knew* he had the backing of a support group—his grandfather, his godfather, the tightly knit band of Tuskegee Airmen. And unlike Shrike, Road was *most* at home in the locker room camaraderie of the ready room. He could be good ol' Road, trading jibes, flashing the big grin, bonding with his squadron mates. Instead of using his minority status, Road made people forget it.

Shrike didn't give a flying fig about bonding or camaraderie or being a teammate. Shrike had never had someone like Road's grandfather or godfather to coach or counsel her, to provide a foundation of self-esteem. She had done it on her own—without a support system.

One night at the BOQ bar, Road said, "Hey, Shrike, I hear you've got the instructors so pissed off they'd like to use you for strafing practice."

"They're caught in a time warp. All white, all male Navy fighter squadrons. Those guys think it's 1960 and this is a John Wayne movie."

"Yeah, maybe. But I'd hate to see you bust out of here because you're so busy trying to change the world. Why don't you just, you know, sort of back off and keep a low profile? At least until training is finished and you're in a fleet squadron."

"Like be a wimp?" she said.

"Like back off. Keep your eye on the ball."

Keep your eye on the ball. Shrike hated those sports metaphors they used so much in the Navy. Like aviation was some kind of schoolboys' intramural sport.

Road was right, she knew. It was just that, *damn,* she hadn't come this far in her career to be talked down to by guys who thought women were some kind of subspecies. But she knew that she had to stay focused. Keep remembering what she was here for. She wanted to finish, didn't she? To do that, she had to play their game.

"Yeah, I hear you. I'll try. I really will."

★

It worked both ways. Road talked to Shrike about keeping her eye on the ball. And she talked to him about outer space.

That was something else they had in common: They both had secret aspirations.

Except that with Shrike, it wasn't so secret. She couldn't help letting it be known around the RAG that FA-18 training, for her, was just a stepping stone. Sure, she would do a tour in a fleet FA-18 squadron, but then she would, *of course,* be selected for test pilot school. Then NASA and space shuttle pilot training. Everyone knew that NASA wanted women candidates for the space program.

She was just, you know . . . passing through the RAG. On her way to being an astronaut.

Which was just one more thing that was making Shrike Hopkins unpopular. Most instructors thought that nuggets, male or female, ought to keep their impertinent mouths shut while learning the fundamentals of staying alive in a Hornet strike fighter. *The nerve of this broad! Just "doing" the FA-18, because it will look good on her astronaut résumé.*

Road, for his part, was keeping his mouth shut. Around the ready room, good ol' Road Ammons just flashed his Yamaha grin and joked with the guys and kept his profile low. Just the way he had been counseled. *Shucks, man, I'm nothin' special, here to learn, you know, just another Marine.*

Becoming an astronaut, of course, was a long shot for any naval aviator, minority or not. You needed an exotic background: a degree, preferably a graduate degree, in aeronautical or astronautical engineering. You had to be selected for test pilot school, the pool from which almost all pilot candidates for astronaut training were chosen. And to get into test pilot school, you first had to distinguish yourself as an aviator in the fleet, preferably in a fighter squadron.

But Road and Shrike were right about one thing: It wasn't written down anywhere, but it was undeniably true—being a minority member, whether black, brown, or female—*was* an advantage.

Shrike had a considerable head start over Road. She already had the academic credentials. On paper, Shrike looked like a prime candidate for NASA.

Road, with his degree in computer science, was a so-so scholar. He was a football player, not an honor student. He had graduated somewhere in the upper third of his class at Tennessee State. To be a serious contender for a space suit, Road knew he would have to finagle a master's degree in a techno-science. And he had to gain entry to test pilot school. And before any of those things happened, he had to finish the RAG. He had to become a fighter pilot.

CHAPTER TWENTY

BLUE ON BLUE

MiGs were born to die.

—*Sign on the wall in Key West*
fighter squadron ready room

"It's a *dynamic* environment out there. . . ."

You heard that word a lot in the air-to-air phase. *Dynamic.* What it meant was, things happened eyeball-poppingly fast in air-to-air combat—fighters merging with closing speeds of sixteen hundred miles an hour. It was like a knife fight in a darkened room. You never knew for sure where the enemy was coming from. Or how many you faced. But you had to get them before they got you. *How many bogeys do we have? Two? Shit, there are three . . . no, four!* It was a game of thrust and parry. Shoot and get the hell out.

One afternoon Shrike came back to the ready room looking shaken. "Jesus, that's scary," she said. "There were four bogeys out there. And during the whole fight, I only saw one of them."

VIDs—visual identifications of bogeys—were tough when you were peering through the stratosphere for specks approaching you at supersonic velocities. Some bogeys were easier than others. Easiest of all were the big fighters like the F-14 Tomcat, with its variable-sweep wings, which when folded back gave the Tomcat its distinctive delta-shaped plan view. And in a head-on view, you could clearly see that the Tomcat's two big vertical fins were parallel, not angular like the FA-18's V-shaped pair of fins or single-tailed like the F-16 or F-5E.

The toughest of all to spot, everyone agreed, were the F-5Es, which the adversary squadron bogeys also flew in the Key West operations. The Northrop-built F-5Es were souped-up fighter versions of the slick little T-38 trainer used by the U.S. Air Force. The F-5Es were the no-seeums of the fighter community—tiny, slim-lined, fast, and agile. Trying to VID an F-5E from twenty miles out was like spotting gnats. Once your eyes locked on to one, you didn't dare look away.

That happened a lot in air-to-air. Air-to-air was a different game than air-to-ground. Every nugget said the same thing: Strike phase—air-to-ground—was the most difficult to plan, but the easiest to execute. During strike training out at Fallon they had spent hours of every evening poring over low-altitude charts, planning missions, studying techniques, working out weapons loads. When it finally came time to execute the mission, it seemed easy, they thought. You just followed your plan, and it usually worked out.

Air-to-air was the opposite. There wasn't much planning involved. You were briefed on the tactics that would be employed that day, then you went out there to see what happened. But what happened was always different from the scenario on which you had been briefed. The air-to-air "furball" (so called because the flight paths of the engaged fighters, when traced on a plotting chart, looked like a tangle of hair) invariably evolved into something unexpected—a fast-paced, problem-solving environment, with a thousand opportunities for making mistakes. Everyone made them, but the pilots who made the fewest had the edge. They were the winners—those who possessed what the fighter community was now calling *situational awareness*.

It was a term that entered aviation lexicon back in the eighties. In its original context, situational awareness—SA—translated roughly to the "big picture," and was coined to describe a fighter pilot's perception of his three-dimensional environment. Pilots with *high* SA could enter a swirling multiplane furball and maintain a mental picture of their own position, the whereabouts of the involved aircraft both friendly and hostile, and their changing relationships. Pilots with high SA knew where they were—and where their enemy was. Conversely, pilots with *low* SA became disoriented and confused in the dynamic, vertical-horizontal environment. They had lost the big picture.

The term found its way into other disciplines of aviation. You heard it in civilian flight schools, in flight simulators, in air-traffic control centers. If an airline pilot became disoriented in a holding pattern or deviated from a glide slope or committed some sort of cognitive error, an evaluator would render the inevitable verdict: "Subject airman suffered loss of *situational awareness.*"

SA was an aptitude that fighter pilots acquired, if they were lucky, with experience. A few pilots seemed to come by it naturally and thus excelled in air-to-air combat. In others it was an inert substance. They found themselves always on the losing end of air combat maneuvering.

Or worse. Sometimes they even shot down the wrong airplane.

★

Getting shot down by his own wingman—or wingperson, in this instance—was getting damned tiresome, thought Slab Bacon.

True, it was only training, and students were *expected* to make mistakes. But not the same stupid mistake twice in a row. For the second consecutive exercise, Slab and his wingman had engaged the bogeys in the op area, sorted them out on radar, maneuvered into firing position, and then taken their simulated missile shots. Slab, as the instructor and section lead, had taken a shot at *his* bogey. And his wingman, the student and Dash Two member of the two-plane section stationed out there in a combat formation off his right wing, had also taken a shot. But not at the bogey fighter. At *him*!

It was a classic screwup: a BOB—Blue on Blue—engagement. "Blue" designated the good guys. The home team. "Red" was the enemy. The bogeys. The way the game was *supposed* to be played, Blue fighters opposed Red, and the acronym was BOR—Blue on Red. It was like shirts and skins in a pickup basketball game, a clear delineation of sides. In the real world, which was to say the *un*simulated hardball world of friendly fighters versus hostiles, a BOB had the consequence of death by friendly fire. Shooting your comrades in arms was the ultimate screwup.

Which was why the instructors were beginning to say that Shrike Hopkins might be a little short in the situational awareness department. She was having trouble sorting out good guys from bad guys. Recognizing who was on first. With Shrike flying on your wing, you were as likely to get hosed as the enemy.

★

It was a two v. one, meaning two friendly fighters versus one adversary. Slab and Shrike, as a two-plane section, were intercepting a single bogey. Slab had maneuvered the section so that he was merging nearly head-on with the incoming bogey. Shrike, stationed high on the right side, then had an angular, nearly broadside shot at the fighter. It was an ideal firing situation. She was supposed to "lock up" the target with her own radar and take the shot with the AMRAAM missile.

The AMRAAM (an acronym for the convoluted Advanced Medium-Range Anti Aircraft Missile) was a radar-guided weapon. A nasty peculiarity of the AMRAAM was that once it was launched it could lock on to *any* target that happened to be in front of it. When you *thought* you had a bogey locked up (acquired by the missile's target seeker), you had to be sure there were no other unintended targets *also* in the firing zone. Like your flight leader.

The AMRAAM was an undiscriminating attacker. It might home in on *anything* it saw, friend or foe, that was unlucky enough to be in its sights. The missile was like a chained Rottweiler. You didn't want to be in the same yard when someone turned the thing loose.

She took her shot. She had the bogey identified in her HUD. "Fox Three!" she called, signaling that she had pulled the trigger and simulated firing a radar-guided missile. The bogey should have been dead.

Someone *was* dead, but it wasn't the bogey.

Back in the debriefing room, Slab and Shrike watched the cockpit videotape of her shot on the bogey. In slow, agonizing detail, you could see what happened. The video replay of Shrike's HUD view showed the bogey fighter in the middle of the display. But in the bottom of the display was another, *closer* object. Another fighter.

Shrike hadn't noticed. She was fixated on the bogey fighter. She "fired" the AMRAAM (not a real missile, but a training device fixed to the airplane) and the omnivorous Rottweiler missile went for the closest, most convenient hunk of meat.

Which turned out to be Slab Bacon. Her flight leader.

"Aw, damn!" groaned Slab when he saw the shot on the video. "Why'd you do that?"

"It wasn't my fault," she said.

"Really? Whose fault do you think it is when you take a shot on your own wingman?"

"I didn't know you were there."

"It's your job to know." He reversed the video back to the point just before the shot. "Look. There I am, in the bottom of your HUD. The AMRAAM switched locks from the bogey to me. That's what it does. That's why you *never* take an AMRAAM shot with a friendly in your HUD view."

"Well, that wasn't emphasized in our briefing, that business about the missile switching locks. Anyway, I didn't see any other fighter way down in the bottom of the HUD."

Slab's exasperation level was peaking out. "Listen, Lieutenant, this is not an argument. It's not even a discussion. This is a debriefing, so please pay attention and try to be receptive to—"

"I *am* being receptive. I just think that you should understand that I didn't *see* the other fighter in the HUD. I didn't notice it, so how could I have known the missile would lock on to another target?"

So went the debriefing.

Slab Bacon was known as a cool, even-tempered instructor. Few people had ever heard him even raise his voice. Like most instructors in the RAG, Slab prided himself on maintaining a professional detachment from his students. You tried to keep emotions out of the training process. It just went with the job: You *never* let a problem student push your crazy button.

Now Slab's face was the color of erupted lava. He was struggling with the urge to choke the living shit out of this disputations, meat-headed, hamfisted nugget. Shrike Hopkins had found his crazy button.

★

It wasn't her last Blue on Blue during the Key West detachment. It happened again. And once again the unintended target was . . . who else? Slab Bacon. It was making Slab wonder: What was it about him? Why was Shrike taking shots at *him*?

After Shrike's second BOB, someone tried to assign her a new call sign. One morning when the pilots came into the ready room for the first briefings of the day, they noticed a change on the big wall-mounted schedule board. Each pilot's call sign was there, with checked spaces for each completed item in the curriculum. Someone had erased the call sign "Shrike." In its place they had written "BOB."

★

For Shrike, the air-to-air training at Key West was turning into the phase from hell. The harder she tried, the more mistakes she made.

On a training flight against bogeys from the adversary squadron, Shrike was assigned as the shooter. She was the one designated to "kill" the intercepted enemy jets. She was supposed to fly the wingman's slot, to the right of the leader in what was called a "combat spread," close enough to maneuver with him when the formation intercepted the enemy fighter. As they closed on the incoming enemy fighter, her job was to turn into the bogey and take a forward quarter shot at him with her radar-guided missile.

But Shrike was having trouble maintaining her position as wingman in the combat formation. She was never in the correct position, instead flying her jet high and wide of the formation, getting "acute" in relation to the other friendly fighters, meaning she was high and too far forward of her assigned place. When the leader turned to intercept the incoming bogey fighter, Shrike—the designated missile shooter—was floundering out there high and wide, out of firing position. She couldn't launch her missile.

The mission instructor was a lieutenant named Douglas "Coop" Cooper. On the next intercept Coop tried coaching her on the radio "Don't get acute, Shrike. Move it in."

She moved it in. But not enough.

"Idle power and speedbrake! Start your pull. Start your pull."

She started to pull toward the bogey. She was too far out, too late for the shot. Again the bogey escaped.

"Shrike, you gotta keep it in closer. Don't get acute, okay?"

"Roger."

They broke off and flew back to the CAP (Combat Air Patrol) station to start another run. Again they flew an intercept course toward the incoming bogey fighter.

It was the same story: Shrike was too wide. Too acute.

"Roll ninety degrees, Shrike! Roll *now*! Roll left and pull. Pull, pull—aw, damn!"

She missed the shot. Again.

This went on for four separate intercept exercises. Shrike missed three of her four shots on the bogey. Back in the ready room, Coop, the frustrated flight leader and instructor, put a check on her student grade sheet in the "Unsatisfactory" column. That meant SOD.

Another SOD. That made *three* for Shrike since she began FA-18 training. Three SODs were usually the limit. Any more unsatisfactory grades and a student could expect a FNAEB.

Shrike was still only about two-thirds through the Hornet syllabus, and she had used up all her allowable SODs. She still had to get through fighter weapons phase. And the most demanding stage of all, carrier qualification, still lay ahead.

Lately Shrike was getting this feeling of being a tightrope walker. She could see the end of the rope, but she still had a long way to go. And she was aware of all the ghouls out there watching, waiting, wondering whether she would make it. Sometimes she felt like just saying to hell with it and stepping off.

★

Chip Van Doren had a hangover. The pain he suffered on this Sunday morning was particularly excruciating because Chip was a lousy drinker. Booze had never suited him, and hangovers were as rare for him as toe fungus. At happy hour over at the BOQ bar, where nuggets were expected to belly up to the bar like two-fisted drinkers and slam down beers with their squadron mates, Chip would fake it, nursing his Miller Lites like they were cod liver oil.

"Chip, that's embarrassing," Burner told him. "I mean, hell, man, you gotta learn to drink like a fighter pilot!"

They were in Key West, after all. And in Key West, on a Saturday night midway through fighter weapons training, you were *supposed* to rip a swath down Duval Street. For nuggets in the strike fighter RAG, it was practically a sacred obligation.

Chip didn't have the only hangover. Most of the nuggets of Class 2-95 were nursing headaches of varying magnitudes. Only the women were relatively clearheaded. Shrike had excused herself early, complaining of a stomachache. Rambo Morales attended the opening ceremonies at the BOQ bar, but dropped out before the party got wild.

It turned out to be one of those rolling bashes, with no particular itinerary or motive. They warmed up at the BOQ bar, playing Crud (a two-ball team game on the pool table) and rolling dice for rounds of beers. From there they progressed downtown to observe the sunset from one of the westward-facing pier bars. Then to Fat Tuesday's, where they turned on to Kool-Aid Slushes, a brain-mangling concoction made mostly of grain alcohol. Onward to Sloppy Joe's, for Rum Goodies. It was there that Road Ammons, almost as unaccomplished a drinker as Chip Van Doren, disgraced himself by puking in a potted plant.

Someone declared that they *had* to eat something or the booze might go to their heads. So they stopped at the Pizza Hut to slam dunk several large-sized pizza supremes. Then they proceeded down the street to the Hog's Breath Saloon, the most popular watering hole for Key West–based fighter jocks.

And that was where Chip Van Doren was nearly killed.

He was leaning at the bar, carrying on a rambling conversation with a bearded, tattooed biker. The biker wore an earring and a ponytail. He stood, by various estimates, at least six and a half feet tall.

In midsentence, Chip lost it. *Baaarrrrroooouuugh!* Beer, Kool-Aid, rum, pizza—all in one amorphous wet projectile. It happened so suddenly. The biker couldn't believe it. He looked down in shock at his black, studded, knee-length leather boots. They were glistening in a dark red slime of tomato paste, mushrooms, pepperoni, olives, globs of undigested sausage.

And then the biker started to go crazy. He rose to his full height, red-faced and pop-eyed, looking like a tyrannosaurus about to rip the guts out of a platypus. He was pissed! He wanted to kill! This fuzz-nutted yuppie sumbitch had just hurled on his goddamn two-hunnerd-fuckin'-dollar boots!

And that's when Chip Van Doren *would* have been killed. Except that in the next instant the bar erupted in cheers, whistles, applause. A dozen grinning pilots from visiting Navy and Marine Corps squadrons were in the joint, taking their own libations. They'd seen the whole thing.

"Bravo!"

"Awesome!"

"A power barf!"

"Hey, do you Hornet guys fly like you drink?"

The biker caught himself. He glanced around the place, making a quick head count. He was outnumbered by twenty to one.

Despite his tattoos and immense size, the biker was a pragmatist at heart. If there was ever an occasion for nonviolence, this was surely it. The bike looked again at his puke-covered boots and shrugged. "Hell of a shot, buddy," he said. "I think you owe me a beer."

★

The rift between Shrike Hopkins and the instructor pilots was becoming as wide as the Gulf Stream.

One of the things that rankled them was Shrike's attitude: She just wasn't showing enough humility. They figured she ought to be showing a certain level of chagrin about the Blue-on-Blue missile shots. She could at least have looked remorseful and apologetic and gone through some requisite groveling. But it was becoming apparent to everyone that that wasn't Shrike's style. Instead of being remorseful, she actually seemed to think it was *funny*! She laughed about it, acting like she had been caught doing nothing more consequential than parking in a handicapped space.

It was making the instructors furious. Here was a nugget, mind

you, who seemed to think shooting down your wingman was
goddamn joke, right up there with Groucho Marx and Mont
Python!

"You're lucky," growled Marine captain Pat "Roller" Rin
"They've changed the grading criteria. It used to be, a Blue-on-Blu
was an automatic SOD."

"That's history," she responded. "Why don't you guys lighte
up? This is supposed to be training, isn't it? It isn't life-and-deat
stuff. Aren't we supposed to have fun?"

Another thing that rankled the instructors was the way Shrik
persisted in calling everyone by their first names. In ready roo
protocol, nuggets were *never* supposed to call seniors, particularl
instructors, by anything but their rank and last name or by the
radio call signs. Shrike affected an easy familiarity with senior
calling lieutenant commanders and commanders "Mike" an
"Joe," chatting with instructors like they were her kid brothers.
rasped on their nerves like fingernails on a blackboard.

And then there was the matter of the diary. One day during th
Key West detachment someone noticed Shrike sitting in a corner
the ready room pounding away on a laptop computer. "What're yo
writing?" he asked. "A book?"

"Maybe," she said. "I'm keeping a diary. Making notes abou
everything that happens here. So you guys better be careful wha
you say. It's all in here."

Then she laughed, just to let them know it was a joke. Nothin
serious, you know. It was supposed to be funny.

They didn't laugh. They went crazy. *Notes! A freaking diary . .
she's writing down everything we're saying ... we're gonna b
quoted in some kind of goddamn feminist manifesto!*

When she realized she had once again pushed some crazy but
tons, she tried to reassure everybody that, hey, back off, guys, it'
just a *diary!* She had been keeping a diary since she was nine year
old. The fact that people now wrote this stuff on laptop computer
that they hauled around with them didn't make them reporters fror
60 Minutes. Jeez! It was harmless.

It didn't matter. By now the paranoia had reached a level a

which the instructors distrusted *anything* they saw Shrike Hopkins doing. And Shrike, no stranger to paranoia, was more than ever convinced of a sexist conspiracy to have her dewinged and evicted from the strike fighter community.

★

Oddly, the instructor pilot who got along best with Shrike was Barney Barnes. Barney had no problem with Shrike's attitude. He didn't care about attitudes, just results. Shrike's problems he took as a personal challenge.

Shrike understood this and respected Barney for it. She liked the fact that he never talked down to her, and he couldn't be bothered by all those gender-correct distinctions in his briefings. Everyone got the same treatment from Barney, which suited Shrike just fine.

"We're gonna try something different on those assholes today," Barney said in a briefing. He went to the chalkboard and drew lines indicating the directions he and Shrike would fly versus the bogey fighters. "Those bogeys are so cocky," he said, "they're expecting us to do the same canned setup time after time. But this time we're gonna fake 'em."

He and Shrike would begin the engagement with the bogeys, as usual, from about forty miles out. As they converged, each side would be sorting out the other on their respective radars, determining the opponents' speed, altitude, aspect angle, trying to set up a missile-firing solution.

But what Barney had in mind was different. As the two groups of fighters, friendly and adversary, converged, Barney would abruptly pull his nose straight down, diving his fighter several thousand feet *below* the developing dogfight. Shrike, his wingman, would continue toward the approaching bogeys. On their radars she would look like a sitting duck. But as they turned in to her, setting up their own firing situation, they would be suddenly ambushed from far below. In full afterburner, roaring straight upward toward their bellies would come Barney—locked on and shooting.

Shrike was looking at the chalk lines on the board. "I think I get the picture now," she said thoughtfully. "You're using me as bait. You're gonna use a *woman* as bait."

"Of course," said Barney, unloading a glob of dip. "The sucker always fall for it."

So off they went, flying the mission just like Barney briefed. The encountered the bogeys in the op area, right on schedule. As the converged, she continued alone while Barney dove toward th ocean. Then he came roaring back up in a vertical climb at bette than six hundred knots. As the bogeys were still maneuvering to tak their shots at Shrike, Barney called "Fox Two." It was the signal tha he had launched a simulated AIM-9 Sidewinder heat-seeking mis sile. "Fox Two," he called again.

Two shots. Two dead bogeys. The suckers fell for it.

Back in the debriefing room, Shrike was on a high. Now, *here* wa something that was seriously good fun. She and Barney slappe hands in a high five. "Wow! It really worked."

"Sure it worked. What did I tell ya?"

★

By the second week of the Key West detachment, two more stu dents had committed BOBs—taking shots at their leader.

They were disgusted with themselves. One was an experience fighter pilot going through Hornet transition training. He kep saying, "What a stupid trick. I *knew* better. What a stupid trick."

Another was Burner, who had been having great success in ai to-air, winning most of his engagements. He was mortified. "Shit. thought I had the guy locked up . . . and then I blew it."

They wanted to put the matter behind them. Swallow their med cine and get on with the program. But Shrike wouldn't let them. Sh loved the fact that she wasn't the only one who screwed up. See The guys did it too!

She wouldn't shut up. The guys wanted nothing so much as throttle her and make the whole sordid mess go away.

The next morning someone had written on the wall board next t Shrike's name, "Misery loves company."

★

Shrike almost made it through fighter weapons phase. She flew mos of the remaining training flights without any serious problems.

The last flight of the Key West syllabus was the class strike. Thi was supposed to be a classic furball, a multiaircraft engagement in which every friendly fighter, eight FA-18s altogether, flew against an unknown number of adversaries, which would be a mix of red-starred FA-18s and F-5Es pretending to be Soviet-built MiGs. Shrike was assigned as the Dash Three fighter in a four-plane formation. As Dash Three, she was the leader of a two-plane section and was responsible for Dash Four, flying as her wingman. Her job would be to keep her two-plane section in combat formation with the lead two-plane section.

The elements of the friendly force were supposed to be "stacked" in holding patterns, vertically separated by two thousand feet each, while they assembled. When all the elements of the strike force had rendezvoused at the holding point, then the strikers would commence the ingress into enemy airspace.

Things started going to hell early.

Shrike saw her lead section up ahead, waiting for her in the holding pattern at thirty-two thousand feet. Below, at thirty thousand, was another section of friendlies. And another at twenty-eight thousand, all going around the holding pattern waiting to begin the strike.

With her wingman close to her own jet, Shrike was closing fast on the lead section. Up ahead she could see the two tiny dots of the leader and his wingman, waiting for her in the left-handed holding pattern. She slid slightly to the left, to rendezvous on them from the inside of the turn.

The two little dots were swelling rapidly in her windscreen. They were no longer dots. Now they were getting *big*. Real, identifiable, full-sized Hornet fighters—*holy shit!*—getting very big very quickly.

Shrike was closing fast. Too damn fast. She had seventy knots too much closure speed. Suddenly she realized she was about to over-run the lead section.

She extended her speedbrakes and yanked the jet hard to the right.

Which was where her wingman, Dash Four, happened to be.

"Yeeeoowww, watch it!" she heard on the radio, and she got a glimpse of her terrified wingman yanking his own jet up and over her to keep from being rammed. She kept her eyes on him, trying not to lose sight of the maneuvering jet, which was wobbling its wings like a confused gooney bird. He was above her now, his belly down so that she was no longer visible to him.

She swung her eyes back to the lead section, on whom she had been joining. They were gone.

Oh, shit! Where were they? High, low, where? In the space of two seconds, while she was observing the oscillations of her escaping wingman, she had lost sight of the other section.

Now things *really* were going to hell. There she was, overrunning a join-up, with her wingman flopping around just above her canopy, and her lead section somewhere in the same airspace, *no longer in sight.* It was a scenario for disaster. Four Hornet fighters were about to become one with each other. It would be spectacular.

Cool, laconic fighter pilot talk gave way to radio bedlam:

"Dash Three, where are you?"

"Four, is that you? Where are you, Four?"

"Hey, who just flew across my nose?"

"Look out! Look out! Dash Three, Dash Four, whoever the hell you are, look out, you're descending through the TARCAP [Target Combat Air Patrol] altitude!"

Then an instructor's voice cut through the bedlam: "Shrike, listen up. Level your wings and maintain thirty-one-five." He was telling Shrike to level off at 31,500 feet, between the layers of other fighters.

They missed each other. Somehow none of the sightless fighters collided. They had scattered like a flock of shotgunned crows, and it took ten minutes for the mission commander to get them back together and resume the exercise.

Meanwhile, the adversary pilots, hearing the melee on the radio, were cracking up. They *loved* it! Waiting out there in their red-starred pseudo-MiGs, listening to this gaggle of amateurs trying to get their shit together, they could already taste the free rounds of beer they were going to collect that night. It was easy to sort out the individual pilots' voices in the radio babble, and it wasn't hard to tell *who* among them had made such an ungodly mess out of what should have been a simple rendezvous.

After all, it was a voice that by now they all *knew*. It was female.

CHAPTER TWENTY-ONE

FNAEB

That was it. Shrike had used up all her slack.

There was no arguing with the "Unsatisfactory" that she was assigned for the class strike mission. It *was* unsatisfactory, and it had nothing to do with esoteric skills like radar intercepts or weapon employment or sorting out who you were going to shoot with your missile. She had demonstrated an unsafe tendency in basic formation flying—the essence of all fighter tactics.

Shrike's problems came down to the old catchall: *situational awareness*. If you couldn't effect a simple join-up with the other fighters in your flight, you were considered to be short in the SA department.

Back at Cecil Field, the commanding officer ordered a FNAEB to be convened for Lieutenant Sally Hopkins.

★

They called it the Room of Pain. It was a conference room on the second deck of the VFA-106 hangar. In it was a long table. On one side sat the four members of the board, and on the other, the aviator whose career was now on the line.

FNAEBs were yet another layer of the eternal Fine Mesh, the weeding out of naval aviators on their way up the ziggurat. A

FNAEB was a ritual, everyone figured, that had its origins in the Spanish Inquisition. Or possibly the Salem witch trials. It had all the merry frivolity of third-degree interrogation, flogging, walking the plank, and tar-and-feathering.

FNAEBs were conducted with dismal regularity at RAGs like VFA-106, where untested young naval aviators often stumbled on the way to becoming fleet-qualified strike fighter pilots. In more than half such evaluation boards, the student would be found worthy of retention and returned to the training pipeline. The student would receive a few extra periods of training and in most cases would graduate and leave the whole nasty experience behind.

But not always. In certain instances, when a nugget had shown himself to be an airborne hazard to most forms of human life including his own, the board would recommend that his training be terminated.

The board would choose one of several dispositions: The aviator might be transferred to another "community" of naval aviation, say transports, or patrol planes, or helicopters. Or he might be grounded altogether, removed from flying duty. The gold wings on the breast would become purely honorific, like a medal from a forgotten war. In the most unredeemable of cases, the aviator would not only be removed from flying status, he would be "undesignated"—stripped of the precious wings of gold.

Dewinged. For an aviator, it amounted to the ultimate emasculation.

Because Shrike Hopkins was a senior lieutenant, two lieutenant commanders were assigned as members of her FNAEB. A third, the head of the board, was a Navy commander from the staff of the Atlantic Fleet Strike Fighter Wing. The fourth member was the Air Wing flight surgeon.

From the beginning everyone knew this was not going to be an ordinary, open-and-shut evaluation board. Shrike let it be known she was going to play the gender card. But she had also been keeping a secret: She was having pains—*real* pains—in her abdomen. And lately they had been getting worse.

★

One by one, the instructor pilots were called before the board and asked to make written statements. They were supposed to recount incidents they remembered about Shrike's training flights. And they were asked for opinions about her aptitude for duty as a strike fighter pilot.

It was an outpouring of anger. Shrike's troubled relations with the instructor pilots came tumbling down like a spring avalanche. Most of the opinions were derogatory:

"I would not want to serve with her in my command because . . ."

"She is putting excessive pressure on herself because she is a female aviator in a male community . . ."

"She is too defensive and adversarial . . ."

"She is not humble enough."

"She takes the slightest criticism poorly and is very resentful . . ."

The commander with whom Shrike had gotten into the "verbal assault" scrap at Fallon was asked to make a statement. Would he want her in his squadron? "No," he answered. And why? "Because she's more trouble than she's worth."

Not all the statements were so damning. A few instructors *did* think Shrike had the potential to be a strike fighter pilot. One was Barney Barnes. Would Barney be willing to serve in a fleet squadron with her? "Yes," he answered without hesitation.

She also provided copies of fitness reports written by her previous commanding officers. Her performance, said one of the skippers, "was exemplary. She is an officer of the highest caliber, and will be a strong achiever in her future career."

Shrike had to laugh when she read that part. *Future career.* Some future career, she thought. Her future career was being decided by people who hated her guts. People who thought she was "more trouble than she was worth"!

★

The board deliberated for nearly two weeks. On a Monday morning in the spring of 1995, the senior officer of the FNAEB delivered the board's findings—one and one-half inches thick—to the commanding officer of the RAG. Shrike's recommended fate was contained in the last sentence of the cover letter:

"The board unanimously recommends that Lieutenant Hopkins's flight status be terminated."

It was the worst possible verdict. *Terminated. Dewinged.* It meant the end of a career. The end of a dream. It was the most devastating event of Shrike Hopkins's life.

★

The pains were getting worse. For several weeks now Shrike had been ignoring them, sure that they must be in her head. She had read all about such ailments. Psychosomatic disorders were a common affliction of people under severe stress.

Stress. That sure as hell described her situation just now. If having what seemed to be the entire male contingent of the U.S. Navy on your heels like a pack of jackals could be considered stressful, then, yes, she was learning more than she ever wanted to know about stress.

The pain was in her abdomen. She had been feeling it ever since the fighter weapons detachment in Key West. Although she knew she couldn't blame her erratic performance on the stomach pains, she knew it was going to look that way. She could already hear them talking about it in the ready room: Shrike was inventing some physical ailment to negate the report of the FNAEB. Just like a woman: She had an excuse for everything.

Then it got worse. The pain came in waves, seeming to swell and intensify each day as the FNAEB lurched toward its dismal and damning conclusion.

Now this. Now her stomach felt like a vat of molten lava. She didn't care anymore whether the pain was psychosomatic or a voodoo curse, and she most certainly didn't give a flying flatus *what* they were saying about her in the ready room. It hurt like hell, and she couldn't ignore it any longer. She turned herself in to the naval hospital for tests.

It wasn't in her head at all. The pain she had been feeling was in her abdomen—and it was real. In a two-hour surgery, a grapefruit sized tumor was removed from her right ovary.

★

The board's report worked its way up the chain of command. A FNAEB's decision was a recommendation, not a final disposition. It would be reviewed by the commanding officer of the RAG, then the commodore of the strike fighter wing, going all the way up to CNAL—commander, naval air forces, Atlantic—who was a three-star admiral.

Endorsing the FNAEB's report on Shrike Hopkins would be one of Captain Matt Moffit's last tasks as commanding officer of the RAG. Moffit was on his way to a grander assignment—command of a Carrier Air Wing, the ultimate flying job in naval aviation. It was the last rung before promotion to the rank of admiral. The last thing Matt Moffit needed was the Gender Thing running amok in his command.

He disagreed with the FNAEB's recommendation—but only a little. He thought that "undesignating" her—removing her wings of gold—was unwarranted. Moffit recommended that Shrike change communities, meaning that she go fly something else—transports, antisubmarine airplanes, helicopters. Anything but strike fighters.

And so it went, up the chain of command. The commodore of the strike fighter wing, Captain Fleming, dittoed Captain Moffit's recommendation: Let her keep her wings, but send her somewhere else. Anywhere but strike fighters.

From there the report landed on the desk of Admiral "Sweepea" Allen, who commanded all the naval air forces in the Atlantic fleet. Allen had the final say. With a thumbs up or down, he could decide the fate of officers like Lieutenant Hopkins. And before he decided, he wanted to have a talk with her.

★

Shrike had never felt so alone in her life. Even before the acrimony of the board hearings, she had sensed a chasm widening between her and the other nuggets. Each time she clashed with the instructors in the RAG, her fellow students scuttled for cover. Shrike was a lightning rod, and anyone who knew what was good for him was staying out of range.

Not everyone stayed away. A handful of instructors, notably

Barney Barnes, came by the hospital to see how she was doing. Barney told her he hoped she would be back in the cockpit soon. He said he looked forward to seeing her someday in the fleet.

Her classmates in 2-95 had all checked in by telephone. Each made the same polite inquiries: *How're ya doing.... What's the prognosis. ... Keep your chin up. ... Hope you get back on your feet soon. ... See you around. ... Well, gotta run now.*

And that was it.

So much for class camaraderie and the brotherhood of pilots. So much, for that matter, for the *sisterhood* of pilots. She sure wasn't hearing much in the way of support from the other women aviators out there. It was as though they were relieved that Shrike Hopkins wouldn't be attracting any more unfavorable attention to women in naval aviation. Even Angie Morales, the only other woman in strike fighter training, was keeping a safe distance from the Shrike Hopkins battle zone.

Shrike felt like a lost child. But she could understand their attitude. From her time in the Naval Academy and then in flight training, she knew about casualties. She knew that once you've stumbled and fallen behind the pack, your colleagues didn't come running Samaritan-like to your aid. Whatever it was you had, they didn't want to catch it. It was nothing personal, just a matter of winners and losers. That was the way it worked in the Fine Mesh.

★

Shrike Hopkins was continuing her string of bad luck. She had been home from the hospital for a week. She was still weak and unsteady on her feet. One night she was on her way to the kitchen for a glass of milk and something happened—she didn't remember what. She lost her equilibrium and fell, knocking herself senseless and opening a large gash in her head. Her neighbor found her on the floor, dazed and bleeding. Back to the hospital Shrike went for more stitching and more tests.

Two days later, her surgical incision split open. She was back on the table, undergoing yet another medical procedure.

Shrike was beginning to feel like a one-woman medical experiment. She was spending more time in the hospital these days than anywhere else. The medical technicians had even presented her with a new name tag. Instead of Shrike, they had a more appropriate call sign: *Lab Rat*.

★

Shrike had changed. She had lost weight, probably due as much to the stress of the FNAEB as to her medical condition. She looked not only slimmer but, to everyone's surprise, softer, as though the medical ordeal had excised some of her legendary contentiousness. To whomever she met when she visited the squadron, even the instructors, she managed a cheerful smile.

Still recovering from the latest round of stitching and restitching, Shrike packed her bag and journeyed northward to the naval base in Norfolk, Virginia, to make her pitch to the admiral. It would be her last chance to save her sinking career as a fighter pilot.

Admiral Richard Allen was a bespectacled naval flight officer who had survived each of the Navy's upheavals—the Cold War, Vietnam, Tailhook—since beginning his career in 1959 as a naval aviation cadet. He seemed sympathetic. Allen listened to Shrike's version of the events that led to the FNAEB. He asked questions about her relations with the instructors in the RAG. He seemed particularly interested in the problem of integrating women into the Atlantic Fleet combat squadrons.

This was Allen's last tour of duty before he retired. The Navy had already taken flak from the media in recent months over the Gender Thing. They'd had the Hultgreen crash, the post-Tailhook witch-hunts, a spate of sexual harassment charges. Allen wanted to head off another firefight over the Gender Thing here on his doorstep.

When he finished with his questions, Admiral Allen reached a decision: Lieutenant Hopkins could keep her wings. She could keep *everything*. He was throwing out the FNAEB recommendation. In the admiral's opinion, her case involved too many extenuating circumstances, and the board had overstepped its purview. It had gotten personalities mixed up with performance.

Shrike would be reinstated in the FA-18 strike fighter training pipeline and resume training.

★

The admiral's decision hit Cecil Field and the RAG like an incoming Scud. The instructors who had clashed with Shrike during her training were outraged.

Whaaaaat? Why the hell do they bother to appoint evaluation boards if they're gonna throw out any decision they don't like? It means you can't fail—if you're a female!

It was impossible for anyone to be neutral about the matter. To the outraged instructors, it was a clear signal that political correctness had become the order of the day. Excellence, integrity, quality of product—all had been thrown to the hogs. The Fine Mesh had been replaced with a gender-based quota system.

To women like Shrike it meant something else. It was a signal, at least for the moment, that justice would be served. A woman pilot had finally received fair treatment. It wasn't a *man's* Navy any longer; there really was a place for women like Shrike Hopkins.

Shrike had won a victory—against her male opponents. But before she could ever fly Hornets again, she had to win yet another battle: She had to regain her physical qualification to fly. And that was beginning to look like an even tougher fight than the Gender Thing.

She had a growing list of maladies—the aftereffects of the tumor, the blow to her head, a pituitary gland problem—that threatened to keep her off flight status indefinitely. She felt like she was earning the new call sign: *Lab Rat.*

The flight surgeon gave her the bad news: She might be grounded for a year. Maybe longer. Maybe forever.

PART THREE
DAS BOAT

★ ★ ★

Why is America lucky enough to have such men?
They leave this tiny ship and fly against the
enemy. Then they must seek the ship, lost
somewhere on the sea. And when they find it,
they have to land upon its pitching deck. Where
did we get such men?

—JAMES A. MICHENER
THE BRIDGES AT TOKO-RI

CHAPTER TWENTY-TWO

WHITEHOUSE

It was an old air strip, one of those military auxiliary fields that you found scattered all over Florida. Most had been constructed back in the war years when the Navy was taking advantage of the superb Florida flying weather to train thousands of aviators. These days almost all the old fields were abandoned, reverting back to pine thickets, or they had been turned over to nearby towns to serve as municipal airports.

This one was still active. They called the place Whitehouse Outlying Field. It was stuck up in the piney woods five miles north of Cecil. For nearly half a century now, Navy fighter pilots had been going up to Whitehouse for FCLPs—field carrier landing practices.

There wasn't much there—a single eight-thousand-foot strip of concrete, a ramshackle control tower that was only manned when they were conducting FCLPs, and a crash and rescue shack that housed a couple of fire trucks and crews. The crash and rescue crews, like most such units, didn't have much to do out there at Whitehouse. Only about once a year.

Whitehouse was a spooky place. Some would even tell you it was haunted. Over the years, going all the way back to before the Korean War, naval aviators had come out to Whitehouse to learn the craft of

*landing on an aircraft carrier. Almost all had lived through the
experience. But a few had not.*

*They all came here to practice: the A-4 Skyhawks, the F-4
Phantoms, the F-8 Crusaders (a particularly dangerous carrier
jet)—every fighter in the Navy's inventory had been represented
out there at Whitehouse. And at least one example of each had
crashed here.*

*The north Florida landscape is a wonderfully resilient ecostruc-
ture. It repaired itself like a quick-healing wound. In only a matter
of weeks you no longer saw the blackened cavity in the earth, the
unnaturally cleared spot out there in the trees that looked like a
meteor had struck. Or the long trench gouged through the runway
approach path, like an archaeological dig.*

*That's the way it was in Florida: The rains came and washed
away the soot and detritus. Vines and weeds and wildflowers covered
up the scarred earth. The grass grew back almost before your eyes.
Pine trees took root and filled in the clearings.*

*And soon there would be no trace of what happened out there. It
was only when you stood alone, just before dark, listening to the
wind sifting through the pines. Then you could hear them: the ghosts
out there at Whitehouse.*

★

Lieutenant Chris "Pearly" Gates walked back out of the LSO shack
and stood in the weeds gazing up at the empty Florida sky. Pearly
was alone out there, except for his writer, a new kid named Nelson
who was a stash waiting for a slot in a new Hornet class. Nelson was
fiddling around inside the shack, getting the radio set up for the
field carrier landing practice period.

Pearly glanced again at his watch. Four-twenty. Where the hell
were they? His nuggets were due overhead five minutes ago. "The
ship doesn't wait for you," Pearly always told his students in carrier
qualification. "You wait for the ship." Now everyone was waiting for
them, the pissants. He scribbled a note to himself to rip a strip off
their collective asses at the debriefing.

Pearly busied himself adjusting the Fresnel lens, making sure the glide path angle was exactly three degrees, not a smidgen more or less. He checked that the lights were the right intensity. He test-flashed the red wave-off lights to make sure they worked.

He tried his radio: "Whitehouse tower, this is Paddles. Radio check."

"You're loud and clear, Paddles. How me?"

"Loud and clear also. Thanks."

Everyone called the LSO "Paddles." That was an anachronism dating back to before the optical landing system came into use in the mid-fifties, back when the landing signal officer actually waved a pair of signaling devices that looked like huge Ping-Pong paddles. In those days he wore a set of coveralls with luminescent ribbons on the arms and legs. From the cockpit, the pilot would see this stick figure standing at the stern of the carrier, "mimicking" the airplane's attitude, flapping the paddles, and using a kind of body English to signal how he was doing. They called it "waving," and even though LSOs long ago stopped waving real paddles, being equipped instead with radio, telephone, and a trigger for the wave-off lights, the Navy still clung to its obsolete terminology. "Paddles" still "waved" pilots aboard the boat.

It was a hell of a job. Sometimes Pearly wondered why he did it. Why did *anyone* do it? Being an LSO was supposed to be a volunteer assignment. It was something you were selected for when you were a nugget new in a squadron, and it became your job for the next several years, until you were a lieutenant commander or commander. For a junior officer, it entailed enormous responsibility, more than any other squadron assignment, which was why it attracted people like Pearly Gates.

During difficult carrier flight operations, the LSO was the guy in the vortex of the action, standing out there with *everyone's* eyes on him, from the captain on the bridge to the poor sweating shit-scared pilot out there in his jet trying to land aboard the carrier.

At times like that, everything rode on the coolness and the judgment of the LSO. It was a heady moment for a young lieutenant. He could be the biggest hero on the ship. Or he could blow it big-time.

Which was precisely why Pearly Gates did it. He was an LSO because he *wanted* to be out there under the gun. Pearly was a young man who liked having the responsibility.

What he didn't like was this: standing out in the weeds at the end of some miserable, wind-scoured, sun-bleached runway, waiting for a gaggle of screeching jets to show up so they could come pounding down, one at a time, on the concrete thirty feet away from you, hammering your eardrums like pile drivers from hell. It was now nearly five o'clock, the hour at which most of his buds would be converging on the Rocket to tell stories and slam down a few beers. Everyone would be there. Everyone but the LSO.

It would get worse. Tomorrow night, when the rest of the world was knocking back their toddies, catching the news, sitting down to a proper dinner, Pearly would be just going to work. Tomorrow night his students started *night* FCLPs and Pearly Gates, LSO, would be standing in this same miserable weed patch, out here in the black-assed Florida night, hoping some cottonmouth or rattlesnake wasn't slithering his way, watching the eerie gray shapes of Hornet fighters materialize out of the black goo to come pounding down on this same slab of concrete. Pulverizing his eardrums.

That's the way it would be *every* night for the next two weeks, until his nuggets were ready for Das Boat. After that, of course, he wouldn't be standing in this forlorn, wind-scoured place. He'd be standing in *another* forlorn, wind-scoured place—out on the LSO platform of the U.S.S. *Nimitz*. The *real* Das Boat. Day and night. Getting his eardrums pulverized.

It was a bitch of a job. Pearly often thought of quitting, saying to hell with it, just being a normal, everyday fighter pilot.

And he *would* have quit too—except for one compelling reason: He couldn't. Pearly Gates loved this job.

★

Hook to steel. It was written up there on the wall board for them all to see.

"That's what separates us from the Air Force," LSO Chip "Plug" Neidhold told his class of nuggets. He said it again, liking the hard, mean-sounding ring to it: "Hook to steel. That's what it's all about.

That's what separates you from all the other fighter pilots in the world. You're gonna plant your tailhooks on the steel deck of an aircraft carrier at sea."

It was the first day of their last phase of strike fighter training: CQ (carrier qualification). It began, like every training activity began in the Navy, with a lecture. This one, according to the FA-18 Pilot Training Syllabus, was "ACQL 001: CQ (Carrier Qualification) Introduction."

Pearly Gates and Plug Neidhold were the LSOs who would be qualifying Class 2-95 aboard the carrier. They were a team. Pearly, who was senior and would be the "controlling" LSO, was a muscular young man, about five-ten and a trim hundred-sixty-five pounds. His brown hair was cropped in the ubiquitous crew cut that made him indistinguishable from the hundreds of young men in flight suits who populated naval air stations.

Of the two, Pearly was the more serious. Knowing the value of a little levity in the CQ briefing, Pearly usually let Plug get the students loosened up with a couple of jokes before he hit them with the life-and-death stuff.

Seeing Plug Neidhold the first time, you didn't need to be told where he got his call sign. He looked like a miniature sumo wrestler, standing about five-five, with a girth like a cement mixer. Plug had a round, cherubic face and an unquenchable passion for carrier aviation.

Plug was one of those kids who grew up never doubting what he would do with his life. He was going to be a fighter pilot. Period. He had been a Navy brat, his father retiring from a career as a naval aviator with the rank of commander. Plug migrated directly from high school to the Naval Academy to flight training, right into the cockpit of an F-14 Tomcat fighter. And after a three-year stint in the Tomcat squadron, based at Oceana and deploying on various carriers to the Mediterranean, he received orders to VFA-106, where he transitioned to the FA-18 Hornet. Along the way he earned his qualification as a landing signal officer. To Plug Neidhold's thinking, that was as good as it got in naval aviation.

The VFA-106 CQ briefing room was outfitted just like a squadron ready room aboard a carrier: rows of high-backed, airliner-type chairs, all facing a wall covered with the ubiquitous giant grease-board. Pictures of long-ago naval aircraft, carriers, and battles covered the walls. The nuggets sat in the high-backed chairs, doodling on their kneeboards while Pearly and Plug delivered their motivational briefings.

There were briefings every day on FCLP procedures, on the FA-18 specialized carrier landing equipment, on the shipboard equipment of an aircraft carrier, on night vision, on night flying procedures at the carrier, on divert procedures in the event they *couldn't* land aboard the ship, on instrument-flying techniques in the carrier landing pattern.

There was even a lecture about shipboard etiquette.

"Etiquette?" groaned a nugget.

"For the Marines, mainly," said Plug.

They sat through a two-hour lecture on seagoing protocol, both in the air and belowdecks—the niceties to be observed in the officers' wardroom, what to wear, whom to salute, how to find your way around the labyrinthine innards of a ninety-thousand-ton warship. Even what to call the parts of the ship. ("Don't call the floor a floor, stupid. Out there it's a deck.")

At the end of the lecture series came, of course, a two-hour exam. Everyone passed.

★

This was the Big One. The nuggets of 2-95 would meet their last—and biggest—challenge. The final test. They had learned to fly formation, make instrument approaches, fire guns, shoot rockets, launch missiles, drop bombs, refuel in flight, intercept bogeys—all the rudimentary chores performed by fighter pilots around the world.

These were all important skills to a fighter pilot, things you had to know. But if you were a Navy or Marine fighter pilot—one supreme skill outweighed them all. Nothing else counted if you didn't possess the single supreme qualification: landing aboard the boat.

Only naval aviators, of course, could get away with calling a ninety-thousand-ton ship-of-the-line belonging to the U.S. Navy a *boat*. But that was part of the game, speaking flippantly about that which scared the peewilly out of you. Somehow referring to that wallowing, griddle-topped death barge out there in the ocean as a *boat* made it seem less intimidating.

The idea was to maintain a lively sense of black humor about the whole thing. You joked about becoming a "ramp roast"—referring to the spectacle of a jet sinking below the approach path and fire-balling against the carrier's ramp—the aft end of the flight deck—during a landing attempt. You were supposed to hoo-haw about missing the wires with your jet's tailhook (what they called a "bolter") and hurtling off the far edge of the deck, back into the thin air over the ocean.

Sitting there in the ready room, you were even supposed to watch with fascination the video records of carrier landing accidents—jets pranging into the ramp, careening off the edge of the deck, splattering into the ocean after failed catapult shots—like they were replays from *Monday Night Football*.

It was a high-stakes form of whistling in the dark. If you stared the prospect of violent death in the face, swaggered up, and spat in its eye, then the whole terrifying specter seemed less terrifying.

For a naval aviator, landing aboard a carrier was the most essential skill in his repertoire, an ability as basic as breathing. Without it, nothing else mattered. You could be the best dogfighter in fighter-dom, the most uncannily accurate dive-bomber since Charlton Heston in *The Battle of Midway*, the best formation pilot outside the Blue Angels. None of it counted for zip if you couldn't catch a wire with your tailhook.

Long before it became the icon of the Navy's greatest public relations disaster, the tailhook was an indispensable item of hardware in naval aviation. Appended to the aft belly of Navy airplanes, the tailhook was the singular feature distinguishing Navy fighters from those of any other military force in the world. When the jet was configured for landing—gear and flaps down—the hook was extended, looking like the stinger on a hornet.

On most jets the shaft of the tailhook was about four feet long, round, and had a barbed flange—a "hook"—on the end. When the jet plunked down on the carrier deck, the tailhook scraped along the deck and snared one of the four arresting wires stretched like banjo strings across the flight deck. The fast-moving jet was yanked to a stop like a tethered dog hitting the end of its leash. The tail-hook was an immensely strong item of hardware, which it had to be to arrest the flight of a thirty-five-thousand-pound hunk of machinery traveling a hundred fifty miles per hour.

The idea was to fly an unwavering path, at a constant glide path angle, right down to the flight deck landing area, skimming low over the ramp of the deck. The ramp was the implacable, unyielding butt end of the boat, the edge of the flight deck that hung out over the ship's fantail. The ramp represented instant, violent death. Every pass you made at the deck was a flirtation with the ramp. Too high over the ramp and you "boltered"—missed the wires and went hurtling off the end of the ship, back into the sky. Too low—and you became one with the ramp. End of game.

It was the "ball"—that shimmering yellow blob down there on the Fresnel lens at the port edge of the flight deck—that kept you off the ramp. If you kept the ball exactly in the middle of the lens, between the datums, you sailed over the ramp with a clearance of about fifteen feet.

The ball was impersonal. The ball would settle off the bottom for anyone, nugget or Air Group commander, who screwed up and let his jet go low on the glide path. If the ball was low, *you* were low. If you were *real* low, you hit the ramp. If you hit the ramp, no matter *who* you were, you were dead.

★

Flying the ball could be maddeningly difficult. It was one of those elusive skills that seemed to reside at a subliminal level, beneath conscious thinking. Some days, the more you focused on it, the harder you tried to analyze your actions, the slipperier the damn ball became. *Why is the ball going up, off the scale?* You were just sitting there, working the throttles, keeping everything in the middle—and there it went. Or worse: *Oh, Christ, it's going low, turning red!* You cram on the power just as the LSO frantically hits the wave-off lights.

Some days were like that.

On other days, the ball seemed cemented in the middle. It never moved. Your left hand twiddled the throttles, making fine adjustments to the power setting, seemingly directed by some higher intelligence. You were focused, yes, but the conscious brain was letting some other facet of its cognitive machinery call the shots.

Days like that were magic. It was like finding the "sweet spot" in a golf shot or a tennis stroke. "An okay pass," the LSO would say in the debriefing. That was all. No other comment. "Okay" was the ultimate grade, with no niggling little qualifiers like "a little low start, a little high at the ramp."

Okay, with no comment. End of critique. That was as good as it got.

★

On a brisk spring afternoon, the seven remaining members of Class 2-95 took off, individually, headed for the traffic pattern at Whitehouse Field, five miles north of Cecil. Waiting at the edge of the runway in the dilapidated LSO shack were Plug and Pearly, radio-phone in hand.

The first one in the pattern was Burner.

"Three-oh-six, Hornet ball, seven-point-five, Bunsen," Burner said into his microphone.

That was the standard script. When the pilot rolled into the groove—turned his jet onto final approach—he was supposed to transmit a long string of information to the LSO: his aircraft number (three-oh-six), confirmation that he *saw* the glide slope "ball," his fuel remaining (seventy-five hundred pounds), and his name. The carrier landing pattern was an exception to the standard use of call signs. The ship's air bosses didn't care about cool call signs. They needed to match pilots up with their correct names.

"Roger ball," answered the LSO, Lieutenant Pearly Gates. With that acknowledgement—*Roger ball*—Pearly was sealing the "contract" between the LSO and the pilot in the groove. The pilot was flying the ball, while the LSO kept him under his very personal, positive control.

One by one, at sixty-second intervals, they made the same call:

"Three-twelve, Hornet ball, six-point-eight, Quinn."

"Roger ball."

"Three-oh-two, Hornet ball, eight-point-zero, Van Doren."

"Roger ball."

"Three-oh-niner, Hornet ball, seven-point-five, Morales."

"Roger ball."

All seven nuggets, one after the other. Down they came, flying the ball to a tooth-cracking arrival on the concrete "carrier" deck, then jamming the throttles up to take off again and repeat the whole process.

Their ball-flying passes were rough, which was standard for the first official FCLP session.

"A little power," Pearly transmitted to J. J. Quinn. "More power!" And then, not liking J.J.'s response to the call for power, "Wave off! Wave off!" A wave-off was an indisputable signal: Push up the throttles and get the hell out of there.

"Right for lineup," Pearly said to Angie Morales. She responded by dipping her right wing, changing the direction of the jet a couple of degrees to the right.

Pearly would issue "test" commands to everyone, checking their response time. Everyone got a lineup call to the left or right. Everyone got an unexpected wave-off command. It was part of the training, to execute the LSO's command—without question or hesitation—whether or not they agreed. Do it now, talk about it later.

"Three-oh-niner, after this pass, your signal is bingo," Pearly radioed.

"Three-oh-nine, roger," Angie Morales replied.

"Three-twelve, your signal is bingo."

"Three-twelve, roger," answered J. J. Quinn.

"Bingo" meant divert. Go home. When each pilot had completed his required number of passes and had reached the predetermined minimum fuel quantity, the LSO issued the bingo command. One by one, they "cleaned up"—retracted the landing gear and flaps— and pointed their jets southward to Cecil Field.

★

The best part was the debriefing. They usually did it *away* from the squadron, at the LSO's favorite pub. Pearly's favorite pub was Hop's, in Orange Park. Here he would hold court at a back table.

Like a priest at confession, Pearly would go over each pass made by every nugget that day at Whitehouse.

"A high start, Rick. A little low in the middle, slow at the ramp. Fair pass."

Rick McCormack nodded.

"Next pass, same thing. High start, then going low and slow in the middle. Get a better start, Rick, work it down sooner, and it's gonna be easier for us both. Y' got that?"

McCormack got it. "Yes, sir."

Pearly worked his way through all seven nuggets, debriefing each one individually. The barmaid came by with fresh pitchers of beer. To her, the bunch at the table looked just like anyone else. They were just another bunch of kids having a good time.

★

The second FCLP period was difficult. The sun had set two hours before, and the Florida landscape had turned as black as the inside of a manatee.

The biggest problem with flying at night at Whitehouse turned out to be *finding* Whitehouse. In the daytime, you could see runway 11/29, the nice eight-thousand-foot-long strip of concrete at Whitehouse, from miles away. All you had to do was fly right down the runway at six hundred feet, turn downwind, and enter the traffic pattern. A piece of cake.

But not at night. Out there on their very first night FCLP period, the nuggets discovered a discomforting truth: At night, you couldn't *see* the freaking runway! The reason you couldn't see the freaking runway was because someone had turned *off* the runway lights that ran down each side of the eight-thousand-foot runway. All you were allowed to see at Whitehouse was a little pattern of lights arranged just like the lights on a carrier deck, which, of course, was what they were supposed to be practicing for.

But, *holy shit*! That miserable little cluster of lights was indistinguishable from the trailer parks and fish camps and convenience stores and chicken farms that sprouted like swamp cabbage out there in the scruffy woods outside Jacksonville.

So here they came, groping through the dark, all of them peering inside their cockpits at the navigation displays on their instrument consoles, trying to aim their jets at the darkened little airfield out there in the piney woods.

They succeeded. Hornet jets arrived simultaneously, zipping across the field from all directions like incoming Scuds.

"Three-oh-eight, two-mile initial—hey, who's that on downwind?"

"No one's downwind!" called the LSO. "You're coming cross-field. Break it off and reenter on a one-one-zero bearing."

"Three-fourteen, downwind for, uh . . . oh, hell, sorry about that . . ."

"Three-oh-two, I'm in the break—I think . . ."

"Yeah, you're in the break. But you're never gonna see the runway from that angle, three-oh-two. Break right and exit the pattern."

It was chaos. For ten minutes the LSO played air-traffic controller, getting his charges aligned with the correct runway. Finally he had them all in the pattern, more or less sequenced in the right order.

Then the fun *really* began.

★

J. J. Quinn was seeing about what he had expected: the "carrier" deck lights, the shimmering little yellow ball out there at the left deck edge. In his HUD on the windscreen, he saw his angle of attack, which was optimum, and his airspeed, one thirty-four, and his altitude, five hundred fifty and decreasing. The little illuminated "velocity vector"—the computer-generated image on the HUD that showed where the airplane was actually aimed—was superimposed right over the landing area.

He had it wired.

Except for the ball, which was slipping to the low side. *A little power . . . oops, don't yank the nose up . . . fly the ball . . . fly the ball with the power . . . don't hike the nose up and down like that. It skews the angle of attack, destabilizes the approach. . . .*

J.J. was working hard. The ball was a damned slippery thing, sliding up and down like an eel in a jar. The LSO was not saying much, letting J.J. solve his little self-induced problems.

Closer, crossing the threshold of the darkened runway, J.J. forced himself to stay locked on to the ball . . . *Don't let it move, keep it in the middle . . .*

BaWhonk! The jet landed squarely in the middle of the tiny landing area. J.J. shoved the throttles up. He watched the lights flashing past.

And then . . . nothing. Darkness.

Instant darkness. Darkness so dark, J.J. blinked, thinking he must have gone blind.

One instant he had been looking outside, peering through his HUD, focused on the slippery yellow ball, watching in his peripheral vision the little pattern of lights that delineated the centerline and the edges of the landing area. In the next instant the lights had flashed by and were gone. There was nothing more to see.

Darkness. Black, impenetrable, evil darkness. But J.J. was still looking outside, trying to see *something*.

"Holy shit!" he exclaimed on the radio, involuntarily.

"Say again?" said the LSO.

J.J. didn't say it again. He was too busy trying to find something to look at.

It was a normal transition, of course, switching your eyes from a lighted deck to the blackness beyond the deck. A pilot *had* to force his eyes back inside the cockpit and fly his jet by instruments. Otherwise, he would be like J. J. Quinn, flying blind, gazing off into black, empty space, with no idea where his fighter was going. It was a potentially deadly scenario—one that had been killing aviators since the first wobbling night flights.

J.J. caught himself. He locked his gaze back on his instruments and reverted to basics: *Wings level, nose above the horizon, positive rate of climb, airspeed steady, altitude increasing.*

"You okay, Sniper?" Pearly called on the radio.

"I'm okay," J.J. said, his pulse whanging away at a hundred eighty beats a minute.

"You owe a round of beer for that 'Holy shit' on the radio. Pay up at the debriefing."

On the second night in the pattern at Whitehouse, J.J. got another wave-off—a *real* wave-off—with the LSO yelling on the radio and flashing the two vertical rows of red lights on either side of the Fresnel lens.

J.J. was rattled. Still thinking about the wave-off, he didn't notice that the LSO was not answering him on the next pass.

"Three-oh-nine, Hornet ball, seven-point-six, Quinn," he called on the radio.

No acknowledgment. The LSO was being *deliberately* silent. It was part of training. The LSO had to make sure his student was paying attention. One unwavering rule in carrier aviation was that when you called the ball, you *must* get an acknowledgment—a "Roger ball"—from the LSO. Without the acknowledgment, it meant you were *not* under an LSO's control. The "contract" was not sealed. You could *not* continue the approach to a landing.

J. J. Quinn, in his frustrated, hypertensed state, forgot all that. He continued the approach. He flew it right down to landing— *KaWhonk!*—and took off again.

All without clearance.

"Three-oh-nine, did you get a 'Roger ball' from Paddles?"

J.J. was surprised by the question. *Aw shit!* Did he? Hell, he didn't know. What kind of question was that?

Now he was *thoroughly* out of touch. On the next pass he did it again. J.J. called the ball and received no acknowledgement. And he landed anyway.

★

It was an expensive mistake. For the night's mistakes, as well as the generally unsteady ball flying, J.J. received a grade of "Unsatisfactory," which translated to yet another SOD.

It was his third. J. J. Quinn was nudging frighteningly close to FNAEB territory. Like his classmate, Shrike, had already done, he would stand before a panel of unsmiling senior officers who would question his fitness to be a strike fighter pilot.

In fact, J.J was already questioning his own fitness. One of J.J.'s assets, one that his instructors had always noted, was that he was receptive to criticism. Which was a good thing, because he was getting a hell of a lot of criticism lately. Much of it was from himself.

A thought was taking root in J.J.'s mind: Maybe, just maybe, he really *wasn't* cut out to be a fighter pilot. Maybe this whole idea was a colossal mistake. Maybe his wife was right. Maybe his pals back in the Marine helicopter community were right. Maybe he *was* too damned old, too fixed in his slow-moving, whop-whopping, rotor-headed helicopter mind-set. Maybe he should just say to hell with it.

CHAPTER TWENTY-THREE

DELIVERANCE

Burner Bunsen, who was turning out to be the best ball flyer in Class 2-95, was a Marine. And J. J. Quinn, the student having the *most* difficulty, was also a Marine.

That's the way it often happened in strike fighter training. Marines were the wild cards. A Marine would be the outstanding student of a class, while another entire contingent of Marines would fill the bottom tier of a class, causing the instructors fits. Proportionally, more SODs and evaluation boards were handed out to Marine students than to the Navy nuggets.

The reason for this oddity was hazy—and controversial. Navy pilots tended to make it into strike fighter training purely on their flight training grades. The top of a graduating class traditionally got fighters. The next, in descending order, were assigned to attack, antisubmarine, and lastly to shore-based patrol planes and helicopters. Sometimes, of course, a top student *wanted* something besides fighters, but that was the exception.

The Marine Corps was less elitist in the way they distributed talent. Top students *did* frequently receive assignments to jets, either AV-8 Harrier vertical-takeoff aircraft or FA-18 Hornets. But not always. The Marines practiced what they called "quality spread," meaning certain top students also were assigned, like it or not, to helicopters or transports. And lower-graded students were assigned, like it or not, to jets. It was not uncommon in the Marine Corps for a senior aviator to have experience in two or three communities—helicopters, fighters, even transports. The Marines believed in well-rounded backgrounds.

The Navy operated in a more specialized way. If you started out in fighters, you probably stayed there. If you were a helo pilot, that's where you remained. If you spent your career snagging wires on a carrier with a tailhook, you snagged a *lot* of wires.

In years past, it would have been unlikely that Burner or Sniper or Road, being Marines, would see carrier duty after finishing initial training. But times had changed. Now the strike fighter community—Navy and Marine—was becoming increasingly integrated. They flew the same airplanes; had the same procedures, manuals, checklists; and underwent the same training. And it was a normal situation now for seagoing Carrier Air Wings to have at least one Marine squadron onboard.

Burner Bunsen was one of those gifted aviators for whom such things came easy. Just as he had led the class in the strike and fighter phases, he was now the top dog in the ball-flying department.

J. J. Quinn, for whom things had never come easy, was having his usual slow start. His passes continued to be erratic. The harder he concentrated, it seemed, the more elusive the ball became for him.

It was maddening. J. J. Quinn *wanted* to be the best in the class. He was the senior pilot of the bunch, about to become a major, and by far the oldest. Hell, he was *supposed* to do better than these kids. Instead, J.J. was plodding along, trying to keep up.

In every new phase of the FA-18 program, J.J. had gotten off to a slow start. It seemed to take him longer than most students to get the hang of new techniques—dive-bombing, strafing, air-to-air. But he *did* always catch on, and once he'd gotten the picture, J.J. had shown that he could do as well as any of them.

Until now. J.J. wasn't getting the picture. Flying the ball out there in the pattern at Whitehouse was becoming an exercise made in hell. Now J.J. was furious with himself for having gone out there, two periods in a row, making the same damn clumsy mistakes. The more furious with himself he became, the worse it got. Worst of all, it was doing a number on J.J.'s self-confidence.

★

The nuggets ran into their old classmate, Shrike Hopkins, from time to time. She sometimes showed up at the officers' club bar for the Thursday afternoon beer sessions. She asked how everyone was doing. How was FCLP going? She updated them on her medical condition. She was still grounded, she told them. How much longer? She didn't know. No one knew. What was she doing? Administrative jobs. Bullshit work. But no, she hadn't given up. She was still hoping to get back in the cockpit.

Shrike looked good. Even though she was wearing Navy khakis, they could see that she had slimmed down. Her blue eyes sparkled, and she seemed to be paying more attention to mundane items like makeup and hairstyling.

At such beer sessions there was, of course, a glacial coolness between Shrike and some of the instructors. She didn't seem intimidated. Shrike smiled at them like a cat teasing terriers. Which, everyone figured, was the *real* reason Shrike came to the club: to maintain a presence among the old adversaries who had wanted to take her wings and ground her forever. It was her way of letting them know that she was very much alive and ready to come back. They hadn't seen the last of Shrike Hopkins.

★

With a load of self-doubt riding on his shoulders like a sixty-pound field pack, J. J. Quinn returned to Whitehouse to do battle with the slippery ball.

It was a night just like the previous night. J.J. watched the yellow ball slide up and down on the lens. He struggled to fly his jet down an exact glide path, feeling his confidence wane a little more with each pass.

And then on one pass, while he was still a hundred feet over the blackened scrub brush approaching the runway, he let the ball go *very* low. So low, it turned red, dropping off the bottom of the lens.

"Wave off! Wave off!" yelled the LSO, flashing the red lights. "Burner! Burner!"

A wave-off for being low in the groove was bad enough, but when the LSO called "Burner," which meant he wanted you to light the two afterburners on the jet engines—an effect like igniting two rockets behind you—you were *really* in trouble. J.J.'s Hornet roared back into the night sky, trailing two twenty-foot columns of blue flame behind the afterburners.

Twice this happened, J.J. making burner wave-offs for settling dangerously low in the groove.

And then, thoroughly demoralized, J.J. delivered the coup de grace to himself: He repeated the same unpardonable sin of the night before. On his last pass he called the ball and, missing the fact that he had received no acknowledgment from the LSO, landed anyway.

That did it. SOD number four. J. J. Quinn had used up all his slack.

★

The debriefing was in Bennigan's, a popular watering hole in Orange Park. J.J. looked like a man on his way to a firing squad. His morale had hit rock bottom. He sat there at the table, his face drained and expressionless, listening to the recapitulation of his night at Whitehouse.

When the LSO finished with his critique, J.J. just shook his head and said, "I should have known better."

"You should have known better than what?" said Pearly.

"I should have known better than to try this. I'll never be a fighter pilot. I don't have what it takes. I shouldn't have tried."

"Don't be so hard on yourself," the LSO said. "Try to lighten up a little."

"I can't. I'm just getting worse instead of better. I should just quit."

No one knew what to say. It was a painful thing, seeing a pilot lose it. J.J. had crawled into a black hole, and no one could coax him out of it. All the worry and uncertainty and residual fear of his decision to be a fighter pilot had come sliding down on him like snow from a roof.

Now J.J. was talking about quitting. And no one was talking him out of it.

★

It was J.J.'s turn in the Room of Pain, the same chamber where his classmate, Shrike Hopkins, had gone through her trial. And the board's recommendation in Shrike's case—*dewinging*—was now very much on J.J.'s mind.

Because J.J. was a senior captain, each of the three officers on the board were senior officers: a senior Marine captain, a Navy lieutenant commander, and the senior board member, a Marine lieutenant colonel. The fourth member, as usual, was the Navy doctor who served as Air Wing flight surgeon.

The board members already knew about J.J.'s problems. They had also heard all about his self-flagellating. The word was going around that J.J. would probably spare them all the trouble of deciding his fate. Everyone figured that the poor demoralized bugger would probably just quit.

They figured wrong.

★

People had been figuring wrong about J. J. Quinn all his life. J.J. always surprised them. He wasn't a superstar, one of those guys who began a race like a sprinter off the starting blocks. J.J. was a plodder, at least in the first stages of every new endeavor. He had a learning curve like a gooney bird. He floundered, stumbled, tripped over himself before he finally took off. But then, to everyone's astonishment, he always *did* take off.

J.J. spent that weekend in May holed up at home. He talked the matter over with Dorothy, but he didn't consult any of his classmates or peers in the Marine Corps. After much soul-searching he reached some hard conclusions. He was playing several roles—career Marine officer, family man, naval aviator, potential fighter pilot—but there was one role he would *not* play: quitter.

J.J. became a man with a purpose. And a goal. He climbed out of his black hole. He *charged* out, teeth bared, guns firing. Gone was the melancholy, down-on-himself hangdog student of three nights ago.

On a Monday morning, he showed up in the Room of Pain wearing his dress green Marine Corps uniform. His shoes were spit-shined. The creases in his trousers and tunic looked sharp enough to slice apples. The burnished naval aviator's wings glinted like Spanish gold above his left breast pocket. J.J. looked like a man on a mission.

"Captain Quinn, I understand you have a statement you would like to submit to the board?"

"Yes, sir, I do."

J.J. gave them the sales pitch of his life. He wanted the board to understand that he was motivated, in the most urgent way, to complete FA-18 strike fighter training. Further, he respectfully requested that the board review his entire naval aviation record, which would show that he had succeeded in *every* phase of training he had ever undertaken. Just as he knew he could succeed with this one.

J.J. told them that he realized he was having difficulty at this moment. Yes, he knew he was proceeding at a slower pace than expected. But the situation, he felt certain, was transient. He had already proved that even when he got off to a slow start, he always rose to a level of excellence.

In other words, he had the ability to succeed as a strike fighter pilot. He would accomplish the objective—*if* this board saw fit to give him an additional shot at it.

The four board members looked at each other. This was a surprise. They had heard that this guy Quinn was probably going to make it easy for them, that he would come in here and drop his wings on the table. Now they had to do some serious considering.

They listened to the flight surgeon's report. Based on his interviews with J.J., the flight surgeon thought that the Marine was simply being too hard on himself. Because he was older and more senior than the hotshot young nuggets in his class, J.J. felt that he should be leading the pack. *He* ought to be turning in the best performance. And since it wasn't working out that way, it was causing

J.J. a case of the fits. He felt like he was letting everyone down—classmates, himself, the Marine Corps.

The board also noted something else about J. J. Quinn: He was candid. Unlike many aviators with problems, J.J. wasn't making any excuses. Yes, he had screwed up. Yes, he knew he was performing below the acceptable standard. And yes, he could do a hell of a lot better.

To an evaluation board, candidness counted for a lot. It was an accepted fact that the most dangerous aviators were those who refused to acknowledge their shortcomings. To make mistakes was natural. To deny them was an express ticket to a casketless funeral.

★

Some FNAEBs were open-and-shut proceedings. An easy call. By an aviator's woeful training record, the board members could see exactly what lay ahead in his fighter-flying career: a classic, debris-filled, smoking hole in the earth, probably greased with the aviator's own fricasseed carcass.

In such cases, the board's duty was clear. They saved the maladroit aviator from his own grisly fate. They yanked his gold wings and ordered a transfer to another duty assignment, usually several light-years removed from the strike fighter community. All for his own good, of course.

But most FNAEBs were not so clear-cut. Just the fact that the subject aviator had gotten that far in naval aviation—all the way through flight training to the cockpit of an FA-18 Hornet fighter—was strong evidence that he wasn't a total klutz. So the board would scratch its collective head and wonder: Why was this guy having difficulty *now*?

They would sort through the aviator's past record, looking for those overlooked but repetitive little clues in his flying history that this guy just might *always* have been headed for the bottom of the great smoking hole.

Or maybe not. Maybe he was just going through a rough patch, like a ball player having a bad season. Was he having family troubles? A discontented spouse? Was he going through a confidence crisis, shaken by some aerial occurrence?

Like bullfighters and race-car drivers, fighter pilots lived on self-confidence. It was an elixir, the substance that made them invincible. With it, they were kings of the earth and the sky. When it slipped away, they became fragile, fearful, hollow-eyed mortals, haunted by the specter of the smoking hole.

The trick was to get the aviator to face up to it. There was a huge amount of pride involved. Rare was the fighter pilot who would say, "You know, flying these things just scares the living shit out of me. I think I'll quit before I get killed."

Instead the troubled pilot wrestled with his demons in private, praying that he might somehow live through the whole experience, stay out of the smoking black hole, survive until his time was up and he could get on with a sensible earthbound life. For such an airman, a FNAEB was a merciful exit. It spared him the gut-wrenching—and humiliating—exercise of clipping his own wings. The board did it for him, usually over his own manly protests.

And then everyone was happy. The Navy was finished with its problem aviator. And the aviator was finished with his problem, which was the morbid certainty of his own imminent demise. The aviator would be reassigned either to another community, like transports or patrol planes, or quit flying altogether and perform a ground-based job.

It was hard, of course, for the board not to remember other FNAEBs. The Ricochet affair was still on everyone's mind. In retrospect, everyone wished Ricochet's *first* FNAEB, the one he received while still in the RAG, had yanked his wings. Ricochet was one of those guys who never got better, just more dangerous.

And then there had been Shrike Hopkins. The Hopkins FNAEB had turned into a political melee. Every subsequent board now had to deal with the fact that even if they *did* decide to remove an aviator from training, the decision was likely to fly back at them like a boomerang. The Shrike Hopkins reversed FNAEB was a still-simmering issue in the strike fighter wing.

★

The board sifted through four and a half pounds of J. J. Quinn's military records. There were no surprises. J.J. had been an average student during his initial flight training thirteen years before, a credential that had helped get him assigned to helicopters. He had gone on to distinguish himself both as a pilot and an officer in the helicopter community. For two years he served as a flight instructor in fixed-wing T-34 trainers. When he made the fateful choice to transfer to fighters, he went through the Navy's advanced training unit out in Kingsville, Texas. He qualified in the T-2C basic jet trainer, then advanced to the TA-4J. J.J. completed the course with a ranking of third out of twenty-two students in his class.

Nothing jumped out at them. J. J. Quinn was not a ticking bomb.

Even his family life was prosaic. For eleven years he had been happily married. He had three kids, stair-stepped in ages two through six. J.J. had no stressors from home.

Each of J.J.'s instructors in VFA-106 made a written statement about his prospects. The statements all finished with a similar thought:

"Captain Quinn has given 100% effort through his training and definitely has the capability to complete the syllabus."

"Although slightly slower than average, Capt. Quinn honestly assesses his shortcomings and expends the extra effort to become proficient in all phases of flight."

"His integrity as a Marine officer is unquestionable. This quality will make him an asset to any fleet FA-18 squadron."

"He has heart. He can complete the syllabus and graduate to the fleet."

"A hard worker who may not catch on quite as fast as others, but once he learns, he doesn't forget."

The evaluation board didn't deliberate for long. In the time it took each of the four members to sign their findings, J.J.'s case was decided.

★

The nuggets of Class 2-95 got the word in the ready room as they were briefing for an FCLP period. *Sniper's back!*

And he was. His heels clicked on the hard deck as he strode down the passageway. A grin as broad as Pennsylvania covered his face. To everyone he saw, he flashed the same succinct message: Thumbs up.

CHAPTER TWENTY-FOUR

A MINOR GLITCH

One morning a notice appeared on the ready room bulletin board:

> Memorial Service: for Lt. Glen Kersgeiter. 1300 hours, Base chapel, Lemoore Naval Air Station.

"Did you know him?"

"No. Some of the instructors did."

"What happened?"

"Nobody knows for sure. It happened during a catapult shot off the *Lincoln.* He went into a roll to the right, ejected too late, nearly inverted. Some kind of a control problem."

The discussion was followed by a brooding silence. *Some kind of a control problem. . . .*

It was not the kind of thing fighter pilots liked to hear. When a jet crashed they wanted to know: *Who* screwed up? What egregious blunder did the guy commit that caused him to make a smoking hole in the earth? It was one thing when a fighter pilot made the ultimate mistake and bought the farm. At least that was understandable. You could learn from it and tell yourself that *you*, in the same situation, would do something different. But a *control problem* . . .

that was a different matter. Now you were talking about the *airplane* doing something malevolent. This was getting close to the thing with Hal, the smartass rogue computer in the movie *2001*, who acquired sentience and then took it in his cyber-brain to kill the spaceship's crew.

The FA-18 was one very smart jet, with its inertial guidance navigation and mission control computer and fly-by-wire flight control system. In all previous generations of flying machinery, the *pilot* had direct control over the aircraft's control surfaces. You moved the stick, and an aileron or elevator responded in exact proportion to your input. The surfaces were mechanically linked to the pilot's controls by cables or pushrods or hydraulic actuators.

No more. The FA-18 Hornet had fly-by-wire controls, wherein the direct mechanical connection was replaced by electric circuitry. Computers interpreted the pilot's inputs and decided *for him* how much control deflection the airplane really ought to have. Never mind that the pilot wanted *this* much elevator or *that* much aileron deflection; the smartass computer knew better. *Okay, pal, I know you feel like whonking this jet into a gut-busting nine-G turn, but that's too much. I'm only gonna let you have, oh . . . about seven Gs.* So the pilot got a seven-G turn, no more, regardless of how hard he hauled back on the stick.

The computer, of course, was right. It was programmed to keep the pilot's control inputs within the jet's allowable parameters. By monitoring and limiting control deflections, it prevented the pilot from overstressing the airplane.

It did more than that. Watching an FA-18 on takeoff or in landing configuration, you could see the tail surfaces—the horizontal stabilators and the V-shaped vertical stabilizers—moving left, right, up, down, in myriad combinations, flapping like the wings of a headless chicken. It was doing all this control-flapping *independent* of the pilot's actual stick movements. The flight control computer was interpreting the pilot's stick inputs and issuing its own digital signals to the jet's control surfaces. *Okay, pal, I know what you really want . . .*

During a catapult launch in the Hornet, the pilot wasn't even supposed to *touch* the control stick. He sat there with his right hand up on the canopy bow, removed from the controls. The idea was that during the acceleration of the catapult launch the pilot's hand would only get in the way. The flight control computer was already programmed to impart the exact amount of elevator deflection when the jet roared off the end of the flight deck. Any input from the pilot would only confuse the computer and disrupt the jet's smooth transition to a flying attitude.

Such a surrender of authority amounted to a huge leap of faith. Letting yourself be hooked up to a merciless, steam-driven catapult, being flung off the front end of a carrier like a stone in a slingshot—*with your hands off the controls*—would at one time have been unthinkable. In the older jets, the pilot's hand would be fastened on the control stick like a vise. Now they were supposed to do it *hands off*! Fighter pilots were betting their lives on a computer program written, most of them figured, by some ponytailed geek in Silicon Valley.

It was enough to make them wonder: Weren't computer programs, like any other item of technology, subject to flaws? The Hornet's flight control software, just like applications for desktop computers, received frequent revisions, which were supposedly enhancements and improvements. Pilots couldn't help thinking: Did my flight control software have a "bug"? Were flight control computers, just like home PCs, subject to fatal viruses?

★

The crash of the Hornet off the *Lincoln*'s catapult was not the first such accident. Exactly a year earlier, a Cecil-based pilot from VFA-83 was lost in nearly identical circumstances: a catapult launch, an uncontrollable roll, a too-late ejection.

Why?

It was spooky. What made it spookier was the explanation: "A flight control anomaly." That was aeronautical techno-speak, which meant that . . . nobody really knew. It was just something that happened.

The nuggets of 2-95, still learning to fly the Hornet, couldn't help wondering: If the accidents were unexplained, and if there really was a flaw in the flight control system, then wasn't such an accident likely to happen again?

Yes, they concluded. It was.

★

Peggy McCormack, Rick's wife, kept having this dreadful vision. She could see these three grim-looking Navy officers in starched whites coming up the sidewalk, marching right up to the front door at their little house in Jacksonville. Rick would be away somewhere.

Oh, Christ, it's them! The three starched-white bearers of grimness. That was the way they delivered the news, if you were a fighter pilot's wife and your husband had just made a smoking hole in the earth somewhere. The doorbell would ring. One of the three, usually the senior officer, would clear his throat and utter the bad tidings: "Ummm, good afternoon, ma'am, aaahhh . . . we're awfully sorry to have to tell you that . . ."

It was all imaginary, of course. A nervous wife's daydream. But she wasn't alone. Most of the young wives had the same dreadful vision from time to time. For some, it was a recurring nightmare. They dreaded seeing *anyone*, particularly anyone in uniform, looking grim-faced and walking up their sidewalk.

The best way to handle the awful visions and dreams, they learned, was to talk about it. So that's what they did: They would get together for lunch or drinks or tennis and laugh about the whole thing, make light of their fears, giggle about the silliness of their runaway imaginations. Being with the other young wives with the same anxieties and dreadful visions made it all seem somehow less frightening.

It was not a subject the nuggets liked to chat about with their spouses. *Death? The casketless funeral . . . the missing man formation flyby . . . the folded flag?* The subject was too grim. Such discussions always danced around the same old throat-catching question: *What if . . . ?*

For Fine Meshers still in their twenties, newly married, in the rude bloom of perfect health and with a universe of unlimited opportunities waiting out there for them, the whole dismal topic just seemed far-fetched. *Who, me? No way.*

Sure, you signed up for life insurance, and you filled out all the emergency notification forms the military gave you, and, of course, you made a will. But hell, man, a sudden smoking-hole-in-the-dirt finale was not a possibility you let yourself dwell on, or you'd be thinking about it every time you went out there and strapped into a jet. You'd turn into some kind of quavering, psyched-out mushwit. Every flight would be an exercise in terror. You'd eventually turn in your wings and become a ground-pounder.

They all knew aviators who had done that. Some did it because they couldn't push out of their minds the specter of the smoking hole. Others did it for family reasons. The stress at home just became too much. Too many casketless funerals, too many bad dreams and visions of widowhood, and a young wife would freak out. The next thing that would happen would be the *clunk* of a set of gold wings dropping on the commanding officer's desk. The aviator would be quietly reassigned to a ground job, usually to another station where he wouldn't have to confront the quizzical stares of his former squadron mates.

Early in his career, Road Ammons received a piece of advice from his astronaut mentor, Colonel Bolden. Bolden was a Marine Corps aviator who had been around long enough to know something about the "What if" subject. "Whatever you do," Bolden told Road, "be honest. Tell your wife *everything* about your job, the good and the bad. Tell her what the risks are. Don't skate around the hard truth. In the long run, that will make it easier for you both."

So that's what Road did: He told Lowanda everything. He kept her informed even when he was away. Wherever he was, at the squadron, away on a training detachment, he checked in by phone at least once a day.

It seemed to be working. Lowanda knew what Road was doing, why they were there, where he was going. It was fine with her.

Dorothy Quinn was another wife who had no illusions about her husband's job. During their thirteen years in the Marine Corps she and J.J. had attended their share of funerals and missing-man formations. And though she hadn't become so hard-shelled that the prospect of death and widowhood slipped her mind, she refused to dwell on the subject. For the Quinns, the Marine Corps was like a marriage. They were in it for the long haul. For better or worse.

Russ and Tracy McCormack had their own way of dealing with the "What if." In the first weeks of their marriage, they had made a pact: If they had a spat, they would patch it up before Russ went on his next flight. They would *never* separate while they were angry over something. Just in case.

★

Deedle deedle deedle. It sounded like one of those electronic alarm clocks.

Burner Bunsen glanced down inside his cockpit. What he heard was a warning to the FA-18 pilot that *something* wasn't right. It was a general alert, not necessarily a life-threatening emergency, but some sort of problem that the pilot ought to take care of before things went to hell.

Burner was on takeoff roll on Cecil's runway nine-left, already accelerating through a hundred knots. In a couple more seconds, he'd be lifting the Hornet's nose and barreling into the sky.

Deedle deedle deedle. There it was again, like the sound effect in a computer game.

What the hell? Burner tore his eyes from the HUD in the windscreen and glanced inside the cockpit. On the left DDI—digital display indicator—was a message: CHECK TRIM FUNCTION.

And then Burner felt it—a distinct yawing of the jet's nose to the left. He jammed in the right rudder pedal to counteract the yaw. He was already at takeoff speed. It was decision time: Either go flying, or snatch the throttles back and try to stop the thing on the runway before he ran off the end. High-speed aborted takeoffs were a dangerous proposition. They usually ended up in a fireball off the end of a runway.

Burner decided to go flying. He eased the nose of the Hornet upward.

Which only aggravated the yaw problem. Now the jet *really* wanted to slew off to the left side.

Whoa! What was going on here? Another glance inside. He saw the problem.

The Hornet had two rudders—the two big nearly vertical tail surfaces that provided the jet's directional guidance. For takeoff, both on a runway and from an aircraft carrier catapult, the rudders were computer-programmed to "toe in"—to deflect inward by thirty degrees to provide additional downward push on the jet's tail, which helped rotate the nose upward to a flying attitude. After the Hornet was airborne and accelerating, the rudders were programmed to "fair"—return to their normal streamlined, undeflected position.

On his display indicator, Burner saw the positions of his two rudders. The left rudder was deflected thirty degrees inward, like it was supposed to be. The right rudder showed *zero* degrees. No deflection.

The rudders were asymmetrical. Only one, the left rudder, was working, which had the effect of slewing the fighter's nose around to the left.

Burner had his right rudder pedal jammed nearly all the way in. The Hornet was responding. The nose slewed back to the center, to the straight-ahead direction.

The jet was airborne, accelerating like a drag racer. With his left hand Burner reached for the gear handle and snatched it up. He could feel the jet *trying* to pull off to the left, like a dog yanking against its leash. Burner had the rudder pedal shoved nearly to its limit. The Hornet was responding; the nose was pointed straight ahead.

Speed was solving the problem. As the Hornet accelerated—a hundred eighty knots, two hundred, two-twenty—the left rudder returned to the faired position. Just like it was supposed to. Burner glanced again at the display indicator. Now both rudders were streamlined. Zero degrees deflection.

Back to normal.

For the next hour and a half Burner concentrated on the mission—a BFM (basic fighter maneuvering) exercise. All the flight control systems on his jet performed perfectly. No problems.

By the time he landed back at Cecil, Burner had almost forgotten the problem on takeoff. Standing there at the maintenance desk, trying to describe the circumstances on the maintenance write-up page, Burner wasn't even sure it had been a problem. He didn't want to sound like one of those alarmists who were always finding something wrong with their airplane. It was just one of those minor little flight control glitches that come and go. Hell, that's the way it was with computerized, fly-by-wire airplanes like the Hornet. No big deal.

CHAPTER TWENTY-FIVE

HIS OWN MAN

The nuggets of 2-95 were nearly ready for the ship. Three more FCLP periods and they would be finished with Whitehouse.

J.J. was back, and he was feeling good about it. During a four-day holiday weekend and a couple of bad weather days, J.J. received some pump-up training in the OFT (operational flight trainer, or simulator) practicing carrier passes. Then he went out to Whitehouse with an instructor in the "trunk" (the rear seat of a tandem-seat FA-18D model), where he practiced the real thing while an instructor coached him.

It was working. J.J.'s confidence returned. He was flying acceptable passes on the ball and, even more amazingly, he was enjoying it. Gone, at least for the moment, was the habit of sinking below the glide slope while on final approach, scaring hell out of himself and the LSO. Gone was the necessity for the flashing red lights and screams of "Wave off! Wave off!" from the hyperventilating LSO and the inevitable afterburner wave-off to keep J.J. out of the weeds.

The seven nuggets were not alone in the pattern. Now they were joined by other students from another class. These were experienced fighter pilots who had been away from the business and were there to requalify in carrier landings.

One was Commander Jim "Harpo" Hillan, a former Tomcat pilot and a test pilot who had been detached from carrier duty for the past three years serving as an exchange pilot with the U.S. Air Force. As soon as he had requalified, Hillan would take command of his own FA-18 squadron. Another old hand was Lieutenant Commander Dave "Smoke" Morgan, a former FA-18 pilot who had been off in Washington for the past three years at a desk job.

★

With only a few more periods out there at Whitehouse before going to the ship, it was time for an old ritual.

They called it "U.S.S. *Whitehouse*." It was one of the rare occasions when the pilots could invite their loved ones—wives, girlfriends, kids, relatives of every stripe—out to see what they *really* did there.

It was a gorgeous spring Sunday afternoon. They all trooped out to the piney woods at Whitehouse Field, to stand there in the weeds by the LSO shack at the end of runway 11. They came to watch their sons, husbands, boyfriends, and, in the case of Roger Yeates, his *wife*, Angie Morales, show them what they had been practicing these past three weeks.

Pearly Gates and Plug Neidhold, the LSOs in charge of Class 2-95, were like tour guides at the Smithsonian. Plug loved dispensing arcane facts about carrier flying. "Did you know," he was saying to a couple of wives, "that your husbands belong to a group of only about two thousand aviators *in the whole world*?"

"Really? What group is that?"

"Those who are qualified to land aboard aircraft carriers."

They didn't know that.

"Did you know that in the French Navy, there are only six pilots—*total*—who are qualified to land aboard a carrier at night?"

They didn't know that either.

Plug and Pearly were wearing their own gray-green flight suits. They showed the visitors the equipment: the LSO shack with the big glass windows from which they would control the landing jets; the Fresnel lens, the big optical ball mounted at the edge of the runway behind the LSO shack. They flashed the wave-off lights for them. They explained how the jets would come roaring overhead, just as they would next week when they went out to the real carrier, and break to the left, one by one, to join the traffic pattern.

Both the McCormacks' wives were there. Peggy McCormack, who was dark-haired and petite, was the senior of the two McCormack wives, having been married to Rick for nearly three years. The newest Mrs. McCormack, bride of Russ, had been a family member only four months now. Tracy McCormack was a pretty girl, youngish-looking in her short skirt and auburn hair. In keeping with the spirit of the Heckle-Jeckle duality, she, too, had a three-year-old son from another marriage.

J. J. Quinn's wife, Dorothy, was there. She had already endured plenty of these Navy and Marine Corps class performances. Dorothy looked like she would be happy when this whole show—not just today's performance but the whole strike fighter training program—was finished. Then she could settle down again to being a Marine Corps wife in a more or less permanent house up in Beaufort, South Carolina, where J.J. would be assigned when he finished.

Pearly Gates's new girlfriend came out for the show. She was a leggy blonde in tight jeans. Her name was Ivy, and Pearly was taking the greatest pleasure in showing her off.

The best-looking of them all, though, was Greta, the girlfriend of Burner Bunsen, to whom she had now been engaged for one week. Greta had long blond hair and a happy smile. She listened carefully, seeming to be genuinely interested in what the LSOs were telling them.

Also there to watch the action was a trim, gray-haired man in designer jeans and polo shirt. Pearly and Plug had seen many such fathers out there at Whitehouse. Every class, it seemed, had one. This one was the father of Burner Bunsen.

There was a certain smugness to him. He had that master-of-the-universe countenance that let everyone know he was being a hell of a good sport by taking time out of his busy career to come out here for this little show. He was wearing all the distinguishing insignia of a successful career: Gucci loafers on sockless feet, tortoiseshell sunglasses, sixty-dollar Manhattan haircut. Accompanying him was the current wife, a tall, attractive woman twenty years younger than he.

You could tell by the expression, by the questions he asked, that Burner's father wasn't thrilled about his kid's choice of professions. It was easy to imagine the shock when he heard that his son wanted to be, of all things, a goddamned fighter pilot! *Now, look, son, I know it probably seems glamorous and cool and all that, but damn! Think about your future. Why do you want to waste all the expensive education. . . . I mean, hell, you ought to be in business school this very minute. I can get you into the firm at . . .*

No, Burner's father definitely wasn't happy about all this. It was hard for him to contain his disappointment. Why, for Christ's sake, the *military*? Wearing that bristle-headed haircut, tearing around in those jet-propelled scooters like some kind of speed freak.

But here he was, doing his fatherly duty, standing out there with the wives and kids and girlfriends in the weed patch at Whitehouse Field, waiting and watching the afternoon sky where it touched the Florida pine trees.

Then the jets came. From over the pine trees appeared the first flight of three Hornet fighters, in echelon formation, stacked to the right. They made a circling pass around the field, then came boring straight down the runway at six hundred feet. They looked like killer angels swooping down on the spectators.

A fan of wrinkles appeared at each of the father's eyes as he squinted into the sun. He was staring intently at the jets swooping down the runway. One of them was Burner, his kid. Burner? That was the call sign he'd acquired. Where the hell did they get these names, anyway? Why couldn't they use real names?

Abruptly the lead jet banked hard to the left and pulled away from the formation, entering the carrier traffic pattern. Three seconds later, the number two jet broke to the left, then number three. From the weed patch the relatives could see them flying downwind now, opposite the landing direction, extending their landing gear and wing flaps.

"Burner's in the lead jet," called out Plug.

The father nodded. His son would be the first to land. He

watched the first jet bank toward the runway, skimming the pine trees. Two plumes of gray trailed from the Hornet's engines.

The noise of the engines swelled as the jet approached. It came closer, growing in size until it was *big* . . . a hell of a lot bigger than when they first saw it whistling through the distant sky at six hundred feet. Now he could see the long pointed snout of the fighter, the sleek wings and strakes, the sinister missile racks at each wingtip. And the noise! Jesus, the engine noise was swelling, rising in pitch and volume, approaching the threshold of pain, even with the foam earplugs they had been given. The spectators, all in unison, covered their ears with their hands.

The father's mouth was open. The master-of-the-universe expression was fading . . . replaced by a perplexed expression . . . something he was trying to figure out.

The jet crossed the threshold. It swept down on the landing zone marked on the concrete, thirty yards away from the weed patch where the spectators stood holding their hands over their ears. *Kaaplooooom!* The fighter's tires screeched onto the concrete. In the next instant the pilot shoved both throttles to the stops, and the jet's afterburners kicked in.

Baaaroooom! Flame belched from each engine's tailpipe. The fighter leaped back into the air, trailing a twenty-foot inferno behind the engine tailpipes. Dirt and grass and concrete dust and rubber and jet exhaust revolved in a whirlwind behind the fighter.

The thunder rattled the windows of the LSO shack. The earth beneath the spectators' feet shook. Heat waves shimmered through the dirt and debris on the runway. Back into the sky the jet roared, thrusting upward like a hurled spear.

And out there in the weed patch the spectators stared. They had expected to see some action, hear some jet noise, be a little impressed, but this . . . Christ! This was *awesome*.

Something had happened to the father in the designer clothes and expensive haircut. He was standing transfixed. His jaw hung open. He looked like he had been walloped with a mallet.

From his lips came a single utterance: *"Ho-leeee shit!"*

You could tell that he was struggling to understand what the fuck was going on here. Here was his kid, his bright and good and some-times misdirected kid, who had *always* needed his help with tough tasks. Here was the kid whom he had raised and whom he thought—until this very moment—he was *still* raising. Here was *his* kid commanding that goddamned earthshaking fire-breathing behe-moth, doing a job that *he,* with his money and success and experi-ence, would never—*could* never—dream of doing.

It was beyond his comprehension.

Something peculiar had happened. Gone was the smugness. Gone was the father's disappointment, at least for the moment. When the Hornet fighter slammed down out there at Whitehouse Field, then roared like a rocket back into the Florida sky—the father's relationship with his son had changed forever. His kid was no longer a kid. He was his own man.

CHAPTER TWENTY-SIX

RUNWAY ONE-ONE

One more FCLP period and the nuggets would be ready for the ship. It was a Friday afternoon, and they were in the pattern again at Whitehouse.

Deedle deedle deedle.

Burner looked inside his cockpit. The aural warning again.

Terrific, thought Burner. *Now what?*

Deedle deedle deedle. And then the "deedle" was followed by another warning, this one a woman's recorded voice. "Flight Control," said the synthesized voice. She repeated the message: "Flight control."

Burner was in the daytime FCLP pattern at Whitehouse. He was on the downwind leg for runaway one-one, flying at the carrier landing pattern altitude of six hundred feet over the ground.

He checked all his systems displays. In the lower left corner of the left DDI was the yellow-lettered, illuminated message: FCS. And on the line beneath: RUD OFF.

FCS was a general warning that meant "flight control system." Since all the Hornet's flight controls were "fly-by-wire," it meant that one of the computer-directed control surfaces on the fighter was not getting the correct input. RUD OFF was a more specific warning identifying the affected surface: A rudder was "off." One of the Hornet's two rudders was not working.

Sure enough. On the flight control display, Burner saw that the right rudder presentation, a pair of boxes, showed X's in each box instead of the normal blank spaces.

"Roman three-twelve has an FCS caution. I'm gonna go up and do a reset."

"Roger, three-twelve. Take the delta pattern overhead," replied the Whitehouse tower controller.

The "delta pattern" was a holding pattern at two thousand feet over the airport, above the normal FCLP traffic.

Burner eased the throttles forward, selected the landing gear handle to the up position, and then raised the landing flaps. At two thousand feet, he leveled the fighter off and started a shallow left-hand orbit over Whitehouse.

A "reset" was a simple procedure. Like all the nuggets, Burner had memorized the steps:

1. MENU FCS—IDENTIFY FAILURE
2. FCS—RESET

If no reset and second failure exists, land as soon as possible.

No problem, thought Burner. *Let's get this thing reset and get on with the period.*

This afternoon's session was the last FCLP period for Class 2-95 before going out to the carrier. Any makeup periods would have to be done over the weekend in order to complete the FCLP syllabus. And that was something Burner definitely *did not* want to happen. He had some serious plans this weekend.

In fact, Burner had some serious plans for the rest of his life. He had now been engaged for exactly ten and one-half days. Until he met Greta, he had expected that he would be a carefree bachelor fighter pilot for years to come, probably until he was *really* old. Maybe even beyond age thirty.

All that had changed. Burner was in love, and it was tough

enough just to keep from thinking about her *all* the time, let alone while he was out here in the FCLP pattern.

But he had to. At the moment he had to deal with this damned FCS nuisance, so he could get back in the FCLP pattern and finish up this period so he could get home and spend the weekend with his girl.

The reset switch was on the lower left cockpit quadrant, just behind the throttles. Burner found the switch and—voilà!—just as advertised: the X's went out in the little squares on the rudder display. Both the FCS and the RUD OFF messages extinguished on the flight controls display screen.

Back in business. Things were looking good for the weekend.

"Whitehouse tower, Roman three-twelve has a reset and I'm on a three-mile initial to rejoin the pattern."

"Roger, Roman three-twelve. Your interval in the pattern is just lifting off. You'll be number six."

★

Lieutenant Roger "Fudd" Elmore, flying the number five Hornet in the pattern at Whitehouse, was going through a domestic crisis. His wife, a cute brunette to whom he had been married since his last year at Colgate, had been having these horrible visions. The realization had struck her like a thunderclap that what her husband did for a living just happened to be very, *very* dangerous. So dangerous, in fact, that she was having these anxiety attacks. She had seen enough news reports about Navy fighter pilots getting killed. And the prospect that it might happen to her husband—leaving her and their young daughter alone—was making her crazy with fear.

When her husband had gone into naval aviation straight out of college, she hadn't thought much about it. She didn't even know what naval aviation meant.

And then she found out. It was something that got people killed. By now several classmates of Roger's had already been killed in accidents. Now she *hated* the whole grisly business.

It was becoming a serious problem for Fudd Elmore, trying to keep his wife from flipping out. Every time she heard about a Navy jet going down somewhere, she would go into a neurotic fit, becoming convinced that if it wasn't *her* husband who had made that particular smoking hole in the ground, then he would surely be smack in the middle of the next one. Morale at the Elmore household had dropped off the scale.

Not all of her pessimism was unfounded. Fudd Elmore *was* having problems. Only a month before, he had completed RAG training in the FA-18 and reported to his fleet squadron, which was about to deploy aboard the U.S.S. *George Washington*. But during the squadron's predeployment workup training—the carrier landing exercise every squadron goes through—Elmore had scared the hell out of his new squadron commanding officer and the squadron LSO by flying several *very* ugly passes out there on the *Washington*, getting waved off and finally being sent back to the beach.

So the commanding officer sent Fudd Elmore back whence he came: the FA-18 RAG, to repeat the carrier qualification phase. "I'm running a strike fighter squadron, not a training unit," said the commanding office. "Either get this guy qualified—or he's yours to keep."

So here was Fudd Elmore, going through the whole drill again, droning around the pattern at Whitehouse, qualifying all over again with the nuggets of Class 2-95.

And this time around, he was doing okay. Elmore was making acceptable passes on the ball. Things were looking good. It was even beginning to look as though his commanding officer might be pleased to have him back.

And then Elmore had an idea: His wife thought this business was dangerous, right? But that was because she'd never seen it close up. She'd never actually seen what he did.

He had a word with the LSO, and permission was obtained for Debbie to drive out to Whitehouse that afternoon and watch the FCLP period from the LSO shack. Just like they did on family day with all the new classes. The closeness to the jets out there on the runway would make it all seem less scary to her. She would see that it was actually quite routine. Not at all dangerous like she'd been imagining. She'd see that it was all in her head.

★

"Roman three-twelve, Hornet ball, two-point-four, Bunsen."

"Roger ball," acknowledged Pearly Gates, the LSO.

Burner nudged the throttles back, squeezing off a tiny bit of power, as he started down the glide slope. He could see the yellowish blob of the ball centered between the two rows of green datum lights. Exactly where it was supposed to be.

It was a bright spring afternoon. The wildflowers were in bloom in the meadow around the approach path to the runway. A gentle westerly breeze was stirring the tops of the piney woods along the north edge of the field. High overhead, the Florida sky was dotted with puffs of cumulus.

Burner had a good pass going. "The easiest way to fly a good pass is to fly a good start," Pearly Gates always said. If you started down the glide slope with the ball already locked in the center, with your jet on the correct speed and attitude, lined up with the centerline of the deck, the rest was easy.

And Burner had gotten a good start. Everything locked in place. Ball in the center. On the runway centerline. He hoped that he could do as well out there on the ship next week . . .

Deedle deedle deedle.

There it was again. Damn! An FCS caution.

What the hell was it? The rudder again? Maybe he could get a quick reset, fix the problem and . . .

"Flight controls," said the electronic woman's voice. "Flight controls."

Yeah, yeah, I know, thought Burner. *Go away. I know what to do.*

Then he felt it. The jet was decelerating.

And yawing to the right.

He pushed the throttles up.

"Power," called the LSO, who could see the jet settling.

Burner pushed the throttles up some more.

The jet was yawing more. And rolling to the right.

"Wave off! Wave off!" the LSO called. The red lights on the lens were flashing.

Burner obeyed. He shoved the throttles to full power and nudged the nose upward. He felt the power come up on the jet.

But something wasn't right . . . the jet wasn't responding like it should . . . and now it was *really* yawing to the right . . .

And rolling. Rolling right.

Nothing was working. Burner fought the airplane. He had the stick all the way to the left, against the stop.

And it was still rolling.

★

They looked so graceful.

Debbie Elmore stood there by her minivan in the little parking lot at Whitehouse Field and watched the jets in the traffic pattern. Her two-and-a-half-year-old, Stacey, clutched her hand.

Seen from this perspective, she thought, the FA-18 fighters didn't look menacing at all. They looked like great, gray swans out there, flying along one behind the other, taking turns alighting on the field and then lifting off again.

They weren't even flying very fast.

Already she was feeling better about the whole thing. Probably, she thought, she *had* been exaggerating the hazards of her husband's job. This was obviously a very ordered, structured, disciplined business. And it certainly *looked* safe enough.

This was going to be fun, she decided. She was glad she had agreed to come out here to Whitehouse and watch them practice. And to think that Roger, her husband, was out there this very minute, flying one of those jets.

She and her daughter started across the parking lot, holding hands, toward the van where the driver waited to take them out to the LSO shack by the runway.

And then something caught her attention. The jet that was on final approach to the runway wasn't behaving like the others. . . .

Its wings were wobbling. Like it was having some kind of problem.

Debbie Elmore stood transfixed. Her gaze was locked on to the jet out there on final approach. *No*, she thought. *This isn't happening. This can't be real. . . .*

★

Every experienced LSO had seen it. It went with the job. If you stood there on the platform on a carrier long enough, or out at the end of lonely runways like Whitehouse, you eventually saw it all: ramp strikes, loss-of-control accidents, successful ejections, unsuccessful ejections. Crashes of every variety.

Pearly Gates had seen most of it. But it never got easier. And nothing in his experience made moments like this one any more believable.

"*Wave off! Wave off!*" he was screaming in the microphone.

The Hornet in the groove was *trying* to wave off. But it wasn't working. Pearly could see that something had very badly gone to hell with the jet. One minute he was coming right down the rails, everything locked in place, then suddenly . . . the goddamned jet went out of control!

Burner, thought Pearly. Of all the nuggets now in CQ phase, Burner had been doing the best. Pearly wished that all his students were as trouble-free as this guy, the Marine who, in all likelihood, would never have to fly off a ship after he completed RAG training. He'd be going to a Marine squadron up in Beaufort, South Carolina, where he'd probably spend his entire career based on land.

Though Pearly refrained from expressing such sentiments around the squadron, he thought such assignments were a waste. Sharp guys like Burner ought to be in seagoing squadrons. On the boat.

Now this.

Pearly had never felt so helpless. He stood there with his thumb mashed on the wave-off button. The red lights on the Fresnel lens behind him were flashing like a Las Vegas casino front.

It no longer mattered. The Hornet in the groove was a wallowing, out-of-control mass of hardware. It was hurtling toward the earth like a runaway freight train.

Pearly watched, his stomach tightening. He *knew* now what was going to happen. The jet was skidding and rolling to the right. It was angling toward the open meadow a hundred yards short of the runway.

"Eject! Eject! Eject!" Pearly yelled into the microphone.

The jet went into the meadow inverted. A geyser of dirt and weeds and airplane parts filled the air like a volcanic eruption.

KaaaWhoooooom!

The orange fireball rolled across the meadow. The impact made the earth shake—the result of a sixteen-and-a-half-ton object striking the earth at a hundred sixty miles per hour.

They felt it in the LSO shack. Pearly Gates and Nelson the writer stared in horror out the window.

They felt it in the parking lot, where Debbie Elmore and her daughter stood screaming.

They felt it in the Whitehouse control tower, where the startled controllers were already screaming on their line down to the fire and rescue shack: "Roll the trucks! Approach end of runway one-one. Roll the trucks!"

★

Every phone in the Strike Fighter Wing was ringing.

"Who was it?"

"Bunsen. First lieutenant. Class 2-95."

"What's his condition?"

"They don't know for sure."

"Whaddya mean, they don't know? Did he eject or not?"

"They don't know. They haven't found him yet."

★

This went on for several hours. In the meantime no one was willing to say. The crash and rescue team combed the woods around the approach end of runway 11, poking through the thornbushes and vine tangles. They walked over every square inch of the weeded approach area, sifting through the still-smoldering airplane parts, hoping to find some sign that the pilot of the crashed jet had ejected.

Not until just before dark, when the cherry picker—an eighteen-wheeler with a winch and hoist—arrived from Cecil could they determine what happened to the pilot. The cherry picker managed to lift the upside-down hulk of the fuselage.

Then they knew where the pilot had gone.

Nowhere. He was still in the cockpit. Burner had stayed with his jet.

CHAPTER TWENTY-SEVEN

REFLECTION

So they weren't immortal after all.

Of course, no one had ever actually *told* them that they were immortal. But it didn't matter. That's just the way you thought if you were twenty-six years old, in possession of perfect reflexes, good looks, superb education, rocket-scientist brains, and the best job description in the world: *fighter pilot.*

With all that going for you, you just *knew*—hell, yes, man—I'm immortal! And more than that. Invincible! Indestructible! Maybe even bulletproof. A nugget fighter pilot was all those things—until something happened to alter his perception of immortality.

For the nuggets of Class of 2-95, it had happened. The best and the brightest among them, the one with the most indisputable claim to immortality, turned out to be mortal.

The effect was devastating.

★

The ultimate bummer. The nuggets were wandering through the passageways at the squadron looking like they'd been poleaxed. For most, it was the first time they'd lost a friend in a flying accident. Now they didn't know what they were supposed to feel. Grief? Sure, they were having plenty of that. But there was more.

Shock. Disillusionment. Disbelief. Fear. Their emotions were running wild.

For the nuggets, now in the fifth month of their strike fighter training, it was a critical moment. Some were reevaluating their choice of professions. Some were even questioning whether they wanted to continue with strike fighter training. Some had young families at home. The prospect of leaving them fatherless and widowed was too much to cope with.

Only a few weeks ago, Commander George "Rico" Mayer had taken command of VFA-106 from Matt Moffit, who had gone to Oceana, Virginia, to take charge of a Carrier Air Wing. Mayer realized that he had to do something to preserve the morale of his young nugget fighter pilots.

What he did was order a two-day stand-down of all flying in the RAG. The detachment in Key West—another class just finishing air-to-air phase—was ordered to knock it off and come on home. Every jet sat parked and quiet on the sprawling ramp at the RAG. The idea was that everybody should take a breather and get their emotions under control.

Mayer called an AOM—all-officers meeting. Every student and instructor assigned to the RAG crammed into the big briefing room on the second deck.

"These things happen," Mayer told his people. "This is an inherently dangerous business. But it's not nearly as dangerous as it used to be."

Which was true. The fighter community lost approximately a dozen FA-18 Hornets and F-14 Tomcats each year in operational accidents. At least half the crews survived.

Twelve jets from a fleet of hundreds was a minuscule loss rate, really. It was a quantum improvement over the previous generation. Only a few years ago, a single aircraft carrier's Air Group might account for that many losses.

One of the old hands in the RAG, Commander Moe Vazquez, told them how it was when he was a nugget. He and his newly winged colleagues were put in a room. A captain came in and said, "Take a look at the man on each side of you." So they did, swiveling to either side to look at each other. "Take a good look," said the captain, "because one of the three of you isn't going to make it."

One out of three. It was a terrible ratio. But that's the way it worked out, at least in the bad old days, which included not only heavy training casualties but horrendous losses in Vietnam.

Times had certainly gotten better. Until Burner's accident, the FA-18 RAG had not lost a jet for more than a year, when a Marine nugget had catapulted off the ship after carrier qualification and then inexplicably flown into the water.

Now the nuggets of Class 2-95 were trying to cope with their loss.

Angie Morales and Burner Bunsen had been classmates since they were students together back in Meridian, Mississippi. They had been through it all together—basic, advanced flight training, selection for Hornets. They were fellow Fine Meshers. Burner Bunsen was the first friend Angie Morales had lost.

Now her face was a mask. The diminutive pilot had never been given to outbursts of emotion. Looking at her pretty, oval-shaped face, you couldn't read anything about what she was thinking.

Of them all, Chip Van Doren was taking it the hardest. Chip was walking around the base, ashen-faced and morose, looking like he had lost his best friend—which, in fact, he had.

Chip and Burner were the only two bachelors in the class, so they had become natural allies. While the other students were home with their young families, Chip and Burner were out there laying siege to the watering holes of Orange Park, learning the first names of all the cute barmaids at places like Hop's and Bennigan's, cutting a swath through the contingent of groupie girls who flocked there to meet some *real* fighter pilots.

The Chip-and-Burner hunting team disbanded after Burner met Greta. Burner, the hunter-killer scourge of the Orange Park hard-body bars, had been disarmed.

But the friendship endured. Burner and Chip still managed to get together a couple of times a week, usually rendezvousing at the officers' club, to put away a few beers and talk about the usual subjects: Women. Airplanes. Neat cars. The essential fighter pilot subjects.

They were numbers one and two in the class ranking, Burner managing to stay ahead of Chip Van Doren by just a few hundredths of a grade point. But his lead was never secure.

The two were as different as goats and geese. According to the Navy's aviation aptitude criteria, Burner, the liberal arts, philosophizing, belly-crawling Marine, shouldn't even have been there. He wasn't a techno-geek, lacking as he did a background and a passion for things mechanical and electronic. Burner was an abstract thinker. Burner didn't fit the rocket-scientist profile of the modern naval aviator.

But Burner, of course, surprised the hell out of everyone. Burner was one of those rare aviators, like a musician with perfect pitch. Flying was just something that came to him naturally.

Van Doren, the techno-geek, had never been struck by an abstract thought in his life. People accused him of liking computers so much he was even *thinking* like a damned computer. Chip Van Doren addressed every problem, airborne or earthbound, in binary terms. One or zero. Yes or no. Go or no go. Win or lose. Kill or be killed.

Chip and Burner were opposites, both in temperament and background. They should have been repelled by each other like opposing ends of a magnet. Instead, they were the closest of all the 2-95 nuggets except, of course, for Heckle and Jeckle.

★

The McCormack twins had already lost a classmate. They had a buddy, Steve Begeher, with whom they had pinned on their naval aviator's wings after flight training. Begeher was a Marine. Instead of FA-18 Hornets, like the twins, he had been assigned to AV-8 Harrier training at the Marine Corps air station at Cherry Point, North Carolina.

The Harrier was the "jump jet," the Marines' vertical-takeoff-and-landing attack jet. The Harrier was a hybrid animal, performing both like a jet fighter and a helicopter. The problem with the Harrier was that sometimes it confused its role, behaving like *neither*. It was considered a tricky beast, subject to fits of misbehavior and bizarre crashes. It was *not* usually the first choice of nugget aviators. Since its introduction to naval aviation, the Harrier had killed more than a score of Marine pilots.

Steve Begeher was one of them. Only two weeks ago, the McCormacks had gotten the news: Begeher crashed at Cherry Point. The details were skimpy: a landing accident, a problem with the jet's vertically deflected thrusters, a loss of control.

Now Burner. Two friends in less than a month. The McCormacks weren't doing much of their Heckle and Jeckle routine these days. In the old days, back when they were sailors, and then midshipmen at the academy, the twins had always been able to count on each other, with their data-linked brains, for morale reinforcement.

Times had changed. They still had each other. But they had families. Now it was *their* morale they had to worry about.

★

The least affected by the accident was J. J. Quinn. One of the few advantages to being senior and experienced was that he had been through all this. You didn't spend thirteen years in Marine Corps aviation, even in helos, without seeing a fair amount of violent death. And losing a few buddies.

Sure, you mourned the loss of a friend. And sure, you shared the grief of his family. And for sure, you tried to learn something from it. But then you put it away. You went back to business.

J.J. was also lucky: He had backing at home. For all Dorothy Quinn's skepticism about his choice to be a fighter pilot, she happened to be an experienced Marine wife. She knew that now was definitely *not* the time to get hysterical about the hazards of the fighter business. Even if every fiber in her body was screaming at her to do just exactly *that*.

So she didn't. Dorothy was too good a team player. Instead, she did the most difficult thing a Marine Corps wife could do: She bit her lip and shut up.

★

Shrike Hopkins, released from the hospital and still recovering from her surgery, was stunned by the news about Burner. Like J.J., she had been around naval aviation long enough to have lost friends. When she was still in flight training, two of her classmates perished in a midair collision. Another friend ejected from a T-2 and was gored when he came down in a tree. "He lived, but he was a mess," she remembered. And then during carrier qualification in the T-2, another friend had crashed and died on the deck of the *Lexington*. And then, last November, she had lost Kara Hultgreen.

Shrike was still on a medical grounding. These days, especially after the rancor of her FNAEB, she didn't hang out with the squadron pilots. And anyway, it was painful for her to see her former classmates now in the last phase of training. After carrier qualification they would be going to their fleet squadrons.

But still, she felt badly for all of them now. It was tough, real tough, coping with the loss of a classmate. But Shrike was a fatalist: "If you're gonna go," she liked to say, "it might as well be in an airplane."

★

It was hard to tell how the crash was affecting Road Ammons. He showed up at the bar to down a few beers with his classmates, but good ol' Road wasn't saying much. The grin was gone from his round face, and in its place he wore a stoic, impassive expression.

Of all the nuggets, Road had been the most focused. He always seemed to be on a programmed track, guided by his invisible mentors. Now his friends wondered: Had he been coached about how to handle trauma and the loss of a buddy? Had Road somehow steeled himself against letting such an event affect his own performance? Or was he reverting to football training, treating the crash like the loss of a player on his football team? A tough break, you know, but the game had to go on.

Or did Road still think *he* was immortal?

★

Lieutenant Commander "Zoomie" Baker looked at the long faces gathered around him at the table in the officers' club. The faces all belonged to nuggets, most of them students from Class 2-95. Zoomie couldn't remember seeing so much grimness in a Navy officers' club since the time Congresswoman Pat Schroeder came to visit.

Zoomie filled every glass at the table from his pitcher of beer.

"Look," he said, "for most of you, this is the first friend you've lost in naval aviation. It won't be the last. I know, because I've lost several. I'm sorry, and I'll miss him too.

"But let's do what Burner would expect us to do if he were here: *drink*." Zoomie raised his glass. "Here's to Burner. And here's to blue skies."

Solemnly, one by one, the nuggets around the table raised their glasses. "To Burner," each mumbled. "Here's to Burner."

They downed the pitcher of beer. Then they ordered several more and downed them all. Someone proposed another toast to Burner. Then they ordered more pitchers of beer and made some more toasts. They toasted good ol' Burner again, and blue skies again. They toasted each other. Then they ordered more beer.

This went on for several hours. During the course of the evening they toasted the Navy, the Marine Corps, the Air Force, Pat Schroeder, Saddam Hussein, and Fidel Castro. The toasts continued until closing time. Before they left, someone even had the presence of mind to toast good ol' Zoomie for getting them so royally shitfaced.

★

Most accidents involved more than one factor. It was a sequence of events, some of them seemingly innocuous. But the combination, like a mix of chemicals, became lethal.

So it was with Burner's accident. There was no doubt that he *did* experience a flight control malfunction. One of the rudders on his jet clearly did fail and freeze in the streamlined position.

But therein was the mystery. Why did he crash? It just didn't make sense that a rudder failure, all by itself, would make the jet uncontrollable. After all, Burner himself had experienced a similar failure—a RUD OFF problem—only a couple of weeks before the accident. And the jet *had* been controllable. In repeated tests, both in the simulator and in a real Hornet, the jet was manageable with a single rudder failure.

Something else must have failed.

Gradually, as the investigators sifted through the wreckage of Burner's Hornet, the missing parts of the mystery began to fall in place, like pieces of an intricate jigsaw puzzle.

Something else *did* fail.

The right engine of Burner's jet had lost power. And it had lost power in the most insidious way: *without warning*. It had "spun down" slowly, giving no audible alert, while Burner was preoccupied flying the ball *and* coping with the flight control failure. When he "waved off"—applying full throttle to the jet—only *one* engine, the left one, kicked in with full power. The asymmetric thrust caused by one good engine versus one bad one caused the jet to yaw and roll toward the side of the failed engine.

It was a critical moment. At that point, only one control input would have saved Burner's jet: both rudders, fully applied. And one had already failed.

From that moment on, Burner Bunsen's Hornet was doomed.

★

To the nuggets, there was only one logical explanation: *Shit happens*.

It was chaos theory capsulized in two words. After all the facts were heard and conclusions reached, that's what it came down to: the existentialist manifesto of the nineties. It explained everything—and nothing. For the nuggets learning to fly the FA-18 Hornet, it was a simplistic philosophy—and the only explanation for an unthinkable event.

Nothing else made sense to them because in the modern world shit really *did* happen. It happened in business, in government, in computers, in relationships.

And in jet fighters.

But why did he stay with it?

That was the most troublesome question. Now that they knew why the jet crashed, they wanted to know the rest: Why didn't Burner just grab the ejection handle and punch out?

Every ready room had in its collection of videos a compilation of horrendous carrier accidents taken from shipboard cameras—everything from cold catapult shots to ramp strikes to stall-spin accidents. In many of the scenarios you could see the airmen eject, usually with microseconds separating them from survival and extinction. Some made it. Some didn't.

Some didn't eject at all.

Back in the ready rooms the pilots would stare morbidly at the video of a doomed jet and wonder: *Why didn't he punch out? He had the chance . . . maybe a two- or three-second window . . . and he didn't do it!*

Why?

Did he think he could save the jet? What was he waiting for? Was he paralyzed with indecision, fear, false hope?

Every pilot who saw such a scene locked it up inside his head and took it home with him. Later, in his most secret thoughts, the fighter pilot would replay the scene. He would place himself in the cockpit of the doomed jet and he would ask secret questions:

When *his* turn came, how would he handle it? Would he decide to eject while he still had time? Would he wait? Would he make the fatal choice to stay with it, thinking that he could save the jet?

The decision to eject was a highly personal thing. You had a second, maybe two, to make the most critical decision of your life: *Grab the handle and eject. Or stay there and fly the beast.*

Eject, and you might be abandoning a salvageable airplane. You looked like a schmuck. And you stood a good chance of getting killed anyway, because ejections were, by definition, a violent and risky way to exit an airplane. But if the jet was doomed—and you *didn't* eject—you were toast. If you waited, trying to figure the thing out, then ejected too late—you were toast anyway.

When your turn came, nothing else in life mattered. You no longer had a past or a future. Nothing that had ever happened to you—or would ever happen again—had any significance. There was only *now*—an entire lifetime condensed into one tiny flashpoint in time.

Make the right choice, and the show went on. Extension of engagement.

Make the wrong choice, and the curtain dropped. End of run.

Most fighter pilots liked to think that when their time came they would make the right decision. But still, in their secret thoughts, they kept replaying the old videos. And they kept asking themselves the same old questions:

What was that guy thinking about? Why didn't he eject?

Would I?

CHAPTER TWENTY-EIGHT

REQUIEM

It was one of those Florida postcard days: high scattered cumulus clouds, temperature in the low seventies, light east wind, morning sun sparkling through the pines like a jeweler's lamp.

A crowd of a hundred fifty showed up to say good-bye to Burner. They came from all ranks and strata, wearing everything from jeans to starched whites. There were civilians, mostly family of the deceased. The Marine pilots from the RAG came in their "Charlies"—short-sleeved khaki shirts and the ceremonial blue, red-striped trousers, topped with the white-covered uniform cap. Navy officers wore their summer whites, though a few were in khakis. Half a dozen pilots came over from the squadron, still wearing sweat-stained flight suits. Thirty or forty enlisted men and women from the Air Wing, sailors and Marines, came to pay their own respects.

Entering the chapel, they passed a linen-covered table on which someone had arranged a collage of objects, like icons in a museum: a pilot's flight helmet, a pair of leather flying gloves; a Marine officer's polished, ceremonial sword; a set of gold naval aviator's wings.

And a framed eight-by-ten photograph of Burner, wearing his Marine Corps uniform and gold wings, grinning his standard lop-sided Burner grin.

The young pilots' wives all wore the same stunned expression, like they'd just been walloped with a croquet mallet. Each was staring at the front of the chapel, at the front pew where the family was sitting. On a little dais lay the triangularly folded American flag, waiting to be handed over to a family member.

On each of the young faces you could read the thought that was branded into their consciousness: *That could be me sitting there in the first pew . . . listening to the eulogies of my husband . . . waiting for someone to hand me that god-awful folded flag.*

It had been a tough weekend. Some of the wives were having trouble accepting this new aspect of their husbands' jobs. Sure, they had already been told, at least in an abstract way, that this was a dangerous profession. They understood that flying jet fighters entailed a certain amount of risk.

Until now it had all seemed so unreal. *Okay, maybe bad things did happen. But not here, for Christ's sake! Not to people we actually know! This is supposed to happen other places, to other families, in other lives. . . .*

Burner's classmates were there, sitting behind the family in the first pew. Sitting with the family in the first pew was Slab Bacon, who had been designated the official "CACO," a Navy acronym meaning "casualty assistance contact officer." In every incident involving injury or loss of life, the Navy appointed a CACO to help the bereaved family cope with the labyrinthine maze of the military bureaucracy.

Chaplain James Wetzel, who had already officiated at many such events, delivered his standard invocation. "God gives, and God takes away," intoned the chaplain. He told the assemblage that they "could draw comfort from the knowledge that Lieutenant Bunsen was a man who believed in God and in his country. Now he's gone to a better place."

The chaplain's invocation was followed by a short soliloquy from Captain Fleming, commodore of the Strike Fighter Wing, who talked about the "sacrifices that were made in the defense of our country." And then came eulogies from two officers of the Marine Aviation Training Group, who talked about how Burner had "kept faith with the Corps." He had loved his country, done his duty to the end.

And so on.

During it all you could hear scattered snuffling, a few stifled sobs. But no one seemed in danger of losing it. Most of the heavy weeping had taken place over the weekend. Now the community of naval aviators was doing its damnedest to stay dry-eyed.

Trying the hardest were the wives. Some of the instructors' wives, of course, had been around awhile and had seen enough memorial services. Now they boycotted them altogether. Others were sitting there with their husbands, looking stone-faced.

To everyone's amazement, one wife who was *not* flipping out was Debbie Elmore. Of all the nuggets' spouses there at Cecil, Elmore's wife was the one they thought for sure they'd have to haul away in the looney wagon. After all, the poor woman had *been* there, standing in the parking lot at Whitehouse . . . *watching* the crash . . . absorbing one of the rarest and most in-your-face exposures to a flying calamity anyone could have without actually sitting in the cockpit. She hadn't even known whether it was her husband or not! Debbie Elmore, everyone figured, should be a certifiable nutcase.

Just the opposite. The experience seemed to have transformed her. When the accident investigating team asked her, in their most delicate manner, for a statement about what had happened out there, she gave it to them. In a dispassionate, matter-of-fact voice, she described what she had seen during those critical five seconds prior to the crash. She did it with a dry eye and a clear memory. And then she even put it in writing for them.

It was most remarkable. Debbie Elmore was not only *not* traumatized by the accident, she seemed to have gained a grip on reality. Gone was her anxiety and hysteria about unthinkable disasters. It was as though she didn't need to imagine the worst anymore. She had already seen it.

It was time to recite the most-recited lyrics in aviation. A young Marine captain took the podium and read "High Flight," the classic poem by John Gillespie Magee, Jr.

> *Oh, I have slipped the surly bonds of earth,*
> *And danced the skies on laughter-silvered*
> *wings;*

Sunward I've climbed, and joined the tumbling
   mirth
Of sunspit clouds—and done a hundred
   things . . .

Tears were now flowing in abundance. Even some of the older, battle-hardened wives were cracking.

The poem concluded:

And while with silent, lifting mind I've trod
The high untrespassed sanctity of space,
   Put out my hand, and touched the face of
      God.

That did it. You could hear sobs, snuffles. Out came the handkerchiefs, dabbing at the rivers of salt water.

But the *real* gut-wrencher, the guaranteed wringer of tear ducts, was the finale—the ritual that ended every military memorial service. The audience of mourners was asked to rise. From a wing of the chapel, somewhere out of view, a bugler played.

The melancholy sound of taps filled the chapel. Each long note swelled, reverberating like syllables from the grave.

The effect was stupefying. No one could move. No one could speak.

The bugle was finally silent. So was the chapel.

But that wasn't the end of it. The ushers nudged the assemblage toward the door of the chapel, out into the bright sunshine on the front steps.

Someone pointed to the south and said, "I see them. Here they come."

Four specks, swelling in size, approached from over the trees, beyond the runways at the south of the field. The Hornets were in a tight diamond formation, aimed right at the chapel and the hundred fifty people outside.

They were coming in low, going like hell, something well over four hundred knots. As they crossed the perimeter of the field, the thunder of the jet engines swelled in a crescendo.

And then, directly over the assembled crowd, the right wingman pulled up from the formation—*barrooom!*—lighting the afterburners of the Hornet's engines. Trailing plumes of flame, the fighter pointed its nose up . . . up . . . up toward a great puffy cumulus cloud that had *somehow* appeared at precisely the right place over the field. . . .

The jet vanished in the cloud.

The three remaining Hornets streaked on to the north, the right wingman's position now empty.

It was a perfect performance—the missing-man formation. The classic farewell to a fighter pilot.

★

For a while the nuggets hung around. Each paid his condolences to the parents. Burner's father, who had been so opposed to his son's becoming a fighter pilot, no longer wore the prideful look of the successful executive. Even in his impeccably tailored dark blue suit, he looked subdued and old. He nodded grimly, shaking the hand of each young aviator.

And each nugget tried to pay his respects to Greta, the pretty blond-haired girl from Gainesville to whom Burner had been engaged for not quite two weeks. Greta had held up well—until the missing-man formation. That was when she lost it. Now she was sobbing uncontrollably. No one knew what to say or how to console her. The young woman was crying, mopping at her eyes, trying to acknowledge the well-wishers. Under her arm was the folded American flag that the squadron had presented to her. She was clutching it under her arm like a security blanket.

By now everyone was drained. The nuggets wanted to get the hell away from the chapel. Chip Van Doren caught the McCormacks and Road Ammons on their way to the parking lot. "What do you think Burner would expect us to do now?"

"I dunno. What?"

"What do you think? Get your drinking clothes on. I'll meet you at the club."

CHAPTER TWENTY-NINE

NIMITZ

Pearly Gates sucked in a lungful of the clean-smelling ocean air and gazed at the white wake of the ship. For half a mile behind the carrier, the wake gurgled like a white highway in the brilliant sunshine. In the distance, Pearly could still make out Point Loma and the skyline of San Diego.

The *Nimitz* was making, he figured, nearly thirty knots. They were steaming in a straight line for the operating area between San Clemente and Santa Catalina Island. In half an hour's time, when they had reached the area, the carrier would reverse course and turn into the wind. Then the action would begin.

His nuggets would show up, roaring over the ship in what he hoped would be a spiffy-looking echelon formation, ready to land aboard.

Sometimes Pearly had to marvel at the way the Navy made everything so complicated. California, for instance. Why the hell did they have to come all the way to the Pacific freaking Ocean for this?

It wasn't as though they were lacking a perfectly good ocean right there at home, a mere twenty or so miles east of Cecil Field. Off the shoreline of Florida they had plenty of open sea in which to perform the carrier qualification ritual.

But that wasn't the way the Navy worked. Each of the half dozen or so carriers assigned to the Atlantic fleet was busy with missions deemed more urgent than playing nursemaid to a gaggle of shave-tailed nugget fighter pilots. Three carriers were already committed to the Mediterranean, where, should the order be given, they would commence the pulverization of the Bosnian Serb army. The other three were variously preoccupied with fleet chores, either standing down or working up from some other readiness exercise.

So California it was. The U.S.S. *Nimitz* was operating in the friendly waters off southern California—and had an open deck.

The logistics of such an operation looked like the supply route for the D-Day invasion. Six FA-18s had to be ferried to Miramar Naval Air Station in San Diego, which would be the staging base for the fly-out to the ship. A thirty-person maintenance crew had to be hauled by a C-9 military airlifter to North Island Naval Air Station, also in San Diego, three days in advance so they could walk aboard the *Nimitz* with all their tools, spare parts, and support equipment. Another contingent—LSOs, administrative personnel, and several squadron officers—would be flown out to the ship aboard a twin-engined C-2 COD (carrier on-board delivery) aircraft.

All of this so a handful of kids with expensive educations could land their airplanes on a ship.

It was chilly out there, standing in the wind that swept over the flight deck. Pearly was wearing his LSO costume, the same old outfit he always dug out of his locker when he went out to sea for carrier qualification periods. The costume was his talisman. So far, it had brought him—and his students—good luck.

Not that Navy LSOs were superstitious. But they *were* steeped in ritual and tradition, and one time-honored tradition was that LSOs, alone among the starched and pressed seagoing Navy, were expected to affect bizarre costumes.

So Pearly was wearing his special old turtleneck jersey, the same one he had worn for two cruises on the *Saratoga* and for a dozen or more CQ detachments with the RAG. Over the jersey he wore the survival vest that everyone who worked on a carrier deck was required to put on when they went topside. The vest contained a flare pencil and had inflatable bladders that were supposed to keep you afloat in case you were swept off the deck into the ocean below.

Every deckhand's vest had a label, identifying the wearer. Pearly's vest had stenciled on the back: VFA-106 LSO. On the front he wore the special LSO embroidered patch—a view of the back of a carrier with the pseudo-Latin motto: RECTUM NON BUSTUS.

Pearly looked like a panhandler, walking around the ship in his fatigue pants, jersey, and vest, his old black wool watch cap pulled down to his ears. Some LSOs took the weirdness license to extremes. They showed up on the platform with ski masks, babushkas, red fezzes, Russian fur hats, capes, gorilla face masks, and in one instance on the carrier *Lincoln*, a stuffed Seeing Eye dog.

Pearly busied himself setting up shop on the platform. The LSO platform was an eight-by-eight-foot wooden grid jutting out the port side of the flight deck, hanging out eighty feet over the water. The platform was just aft of the first of the four arresting wires stretched across the flight deck. Beneath the platform, hanging out over the water, was the safety net. The net was there to catch anyone who fell off the platform and to provide an escape for the LSOs if a jet in the groove veered toward them.

The LSO platform faced aft, toward the aircraft approach path to the flight deck. Directly behind it was stretched a piece of canvas that served as a windbreak and a deflector from the jet blast up on the forward flight deck. At the forward edge of the platform was a console containing the communication equipment, a television monitor showing the image shot from a deck-mounted video camera, and displays indicating the approaching aircraft's type, speed, and distance from the ship. Also displayed were readouts of the ship's speed, the wind direction and velocity, and the magnitude of the deck's pitching.

On the platform with Pearly was a petty officer wearing a sound-powered headset. His job was to stay in constant communication with Pri-Fly, the glass-enclosed nerve center up on the sixth level of the ship's superstructure, and with Air Ops, the carrier's air-traffic control center down in the bowels of the carrier. The petty officer would relay to the LSO any urgent information about the deck or the airplanes in the traffic pattern.

Pearly checked his equipment. He tried out his radio handset. He checked the "pickle"—the black handle at the end of a long cable with two switches: one for the red wave-off lights on the sides of the ball, and one for the "cut" light. He flashed the wave-off lights and then triggered the cut light by which, in an emergency landing, he would signal the pilot to "cut"—chop the throttle on his jet—as he crossed the ramp. Pearly then adjusted the intensity of the ball, the yellow blob of light on the Fresnel lens that delivered glide slope information to the pilots.

The Fresnel lens was an offshoot of the British-invented mirror landing system. Originally, a mirror was mounted at the port edge of the deck. A high-intensity light was shone against the mirror and reflected upward at the precise angle of the glide slope. A set of green reference lights was rigged midway up the mirror, serving as a datum—an "on glide-slope" reference. A pilot making his approach would see the reflected light on the mirror as a "ball," and its position above or below the datum lights would tell him he was high or low on the glide slope.

The Fresnel lens, developed in the 1960s, took the mirror idea a step further. It still looked like a ball on a mirror, but instead of a real mirror, the lens was actually a vertical row of five glass boxes. The green datum lights were extended outward from the middle, or third, box. Each box projected a beam of light at a different angle, so that the pilot, seeing the light—the "ball"—from one of the boxes could know his relative position, high or low, on the glide slope.

The beam of light narrowed as the aircraft flew closer to the ship. As the jet passed over the fantail of the carrier, the beam from the middle lens—the "centered ball"—was only two feet high.

That was the target: a window *two feet high*. The pilot landing his jet aboard the carrier had to fly through that tiny aperture in order to clear the ramp and catch a wire with his tailhook. He had to fly through it in all conditions—day, night, and when the deck was heaving up and down like a rowboat in a rapids.

It was the most demanding feat in aviation. And it was a feat that *every* carrier-based naval aviator had to perform again and again. Without fail.

★

The nuggets wore the standard gray-green flight suits, wandering the passageways of the great ship, knocking heads on the low overheads, banging shins on the step-over "kneeknockers" that you passed at every bulkhead along a passageway. Everyone got lost.

There was a *smell* to an aircraft carrier. It was a redolence you only noticed when you first walked down from the sprawling, open-aired flight deck to the labyrinthine interior of the great ship. It was not unpleasant—an olfactory blend of machine oil, paint, jet fuel, sweat. Every aircraft carrier was different. Each had its unique belowdeck atmosphere.

The *Nimitz* was enormous. Ninety-five thousand tons—a statistic that exceeded the average aviator's computational power. It was like a floating city. How could anything that heavy float? How could it *move*, for that matter?

But move it did, at something in excess of thirty-five miles per hour, faster than most frigates and destroyers. The *Nimitz* knifed through the oceans of the world on the energy of two Westinghouse nuclear reactors, powering her four steam turbines and propellers.

The *Nimitz* was a supercarrier, first of the Navy's fastest and most powerful group of carriers called the *Nimitz* class. Her normal seagoing complement included a crew of 5,550 men and women. When the *Nimitz* went on overseas deployment, she took on board a nine-squadron Air Wing, numbering from eighty to ninety aircraft. The Air Wing had two F-14 Tomcat squadrons, shore-based at Miramar, California, and two FA-18 Hornet squadrons from Naval Air Station Lemoore, California. Included in the Air Wing was a squadron of A-6 Intruder attack jets; a unit of four EA-6B Prowlers, which were tactical electronic warfare versions of the A-6; a squadron of S-3B Viking antisubmarine warfare jets; a detachment of at least two E-2C turboprop Hawkeyes, which were early warning and strike control aircraft; and a detachment of SH-60F Seahawk antisubmarine helicopters.

With her nuclear power plant, the *Nimitz* possessed nearly

unlimited mobility. Already she had gone more than eighteen years without refueling. Consumables, like food and jet fuel, could be replenished under way by supply ships and seagoing tankers.

Being aboard a mighty warship like the *Nimitz*, marveling at the modern American technology, it was hard to believe that the most critical technology on the aircraft carrier was not American. Modern aircraft carriers would not be possible except for two major developments since World War II: the angled landing deck that made safe arrestment of jet airplanes possible, and the steam catapult that permitted the *launching* of high-performance jets from flight decks.

Neither was invented in America.

That these developments came from Britain, of course, always caused glee among visiting Royal Navy pilots. When a Brit deigned to come aboard an American carrier, it was always with just the slightest trace of superiority. He would glance at the modern equipment and smile. "Hmm, it looks like you Yanks may be finally getting the hang of it."

It was the steam catapult that made ships like the *Nimitz* possible. Without the catapult, supersonic fighters like the Hornet and the Tomcat could not fly from the tiny parcel of real estate available on a carrier's flight deck. Thin, swept wings, heavy weapons and fuel loads—such aeronautical luxuries required a vast amount of energy to reach flying speed.

Nor could the jets return to the flight deck without another British invention—the angled deck. In the old days, before supersonic jets and steam catapults, all aircraft carriers had a single fore-to-aft flight deck. Airplanes landed on the aft portion—and stopped. There were no "bolters"—touch-and-go landings—because other airplanes and equipment were parked on the forward half of the deck. The straight-deck ships had as many as thirteen arresting wires and a huge nylon barricade to prevent airplanes from hurtling onto the forward deck.

But then the British designed a carrier deck with the landing runway aligned about eleven degrees to the left of the ship's centerline, thus permitting airplanes to touch down and then take off again from the *side* of the deck. The new V-shaped carrier deck had, in effect, *two* runways: the aft, off-center (angled) deck for touch-and-go landings, and the forward, straight deck used exclusively for launching.

The four "wires" stretched across the *Nimitz*'s landing deck were actually 1.375-inch-thick steel cables, suspended five and a half inches above the deck. Each of the cables ran belowdeck to its respective "engine"—a giant hydraulic cylinder that worked like a shock absorber. When a jet's tailhook snagged one of the cables, the cable pulled a piston in its hydraulic cylinder, absorbing the energy of the arriving jet and braking the jet to a metered stop up on the flight deck.

For each aircraft that approached the carrier, a signal was sent down to all four arresting engine rooms to adjust the pressure for the weight of that particular aircraft. A heavy Tomcat fighter would require a different setting than a much smaller, lightly loaded Hornet. Each arresting cable was able to bring a fifty-four-thousand-pound jet, moving at a hundred forty miles per hour, to a stop on the flight deck in two seconds, within three hundred forty feet.

After a jet rolled to a stop and pulled the power back on its engines, the cable slackened and dropped from the hook, back onto the deck. The hydraulic engine belowdeck then retracted the wire back to its taut position across the deck, ready to trap the next jet.

It was not a foolproof system. Accidents happened. Death sometimes struck with numbing suddenness on a carrier deck. Everyone who had gone to sea for extended cruises aboard aircraft carriers had seen it happen: A cable would be snagged by the tailhook of a landing jet. The cable would pay out just like it was supposed to, while the hydraulic arresting engine down below absorbed the kinetic energy of the landing airplane. The cable would strain against the pull of the twenty-ton jet . . .

And then it would break.

It didn't happen often. The cables were regularly checked for fraying, and the total number of "hits"—arrestments—on each cable was carefully logged. After a hundred hits, a cable was retired and replaced with a fresh one.

But still, it happened. One night on the *Saratoga*, an A-3 caught the number three wire. As the wire paid out, slowing the big jet, the cable snapped. With its engines already at full power, the A-3 floundered off the end of the deck and managed to fly again. The crewmen in the jet escaped.

The crewmen on the deck did not. The separated number three arresting cable lashed across the surface of the flight deck like a scythe. It mowed down everything in a seventy-foot arc—maintenance equipment, antennas, tugs . . . and half a dozen deck crewmen, severing their legs like a laser gun.

★

There was no such luxury in naval aviation as idle time. You were supposed to be either flying or doing your collateral ground job. If you were doing neither, then they scheduled you for a briefing.

And so it was aboard the U.S.S. *Nimitz* for the nuggets of Class 2-95. This one was the pre–night qualifications briefing. It was Pearly Gates's chance to play Vince Lombardi.

It was already well known in the squadron that Pearly took his briefings *very* seriously. And he expected everyone else to take them just as seriously. Any poor fool who ignored the red BRIEFING IN PROGRESS light over the ready room door and blundered into one of Pearly's briefings would get his head snapped off at the shoulders.

This was the occasion for a Pearly Gates bravura performance. For six weeks now he had been working with his young charges, coaching, critiquing, praising, encouraging. He had nursed them through the first awkward FCLP periods, through the inky-black night sessions at Whitehouse, through the trauma of losing a class-mate, through the adrenaline-surging, catapult-firing, first-trap exposure to the *Nimitz* at sea.

Now it had come down to this: the final test. This was the last— and most difficult—test the nuggets would face in their path to becoming fighter pilots. Pearly knew that his kids were ready. They had all the tools.

All they needed was confidence. And that was the reason for his Vince Lombardi briefing. A pilot's confidence was the most fragile and irreplaceable substance in aviation. Without it, all the skill, training, and experience of a lifetime counted for nothing. The specter of fear could slither into a cockpit like a serpent. It crippled a pilot, poisoned his mind, stole his skill. Fear killed more aviators than all the mechanical malfunctions that ever afflicted flying machines.

On the wall-sized greaseboard, he had written "Pearly's Pearls." They were more like commandments:

1. Dominate the Ball!
2. BE the Ball!
3. You Are Not Alone!
4. Trust the LSOs!
5. There Is No Life Below the Datums!

Pearl number five referred to the bottom half part of the Fresnel lens. The datums were the horizontal row of green datum lights, protruding at midpoint from both sides of the lens, that served as the on-glidepath marker for the pilot. If the pilot landed with the ball high, he would either catch the last—number four—wire or miss the wires altogether and get a "bolter," taking off again from the angled deck. If he let the ball go low, beneath the row of datums, it meant that he would get an early wire—a one or two instead of the ideal number three wire.

It also meant that he came perilously close to the blunt, unforgiving killer ramp. He had come close to being a ramp roast.

★

The movies on the *Nimitz* were endless. Day and night, twenty-four hours straight, they flickered up there on one of the three ready room television monitors. The only time the movies stopped was when an LSO briefing was taking place.

The *Nimitz* had a supply of movies that exceeded the gross inventory of Blockbuster and Turner Broadcasting combined. You could check out everything from newly released Stallone groaners to Bogey classics from the thirties.

That's what they did, the off-duty sailors, pilots, and maintenance personnel of the CQ detachment. The big, cavernous ready room with its upholstered airliner seats became the between-shifts hangout. It didn't matter what the movie was. They plopped down in one of the deep chairs, relieved to be away from the nerve-numbing havoc of the flight deck—and stared glassy-eyed at a flick.

The other two monitors were for ship's business. One was used for routine messages, like a community television channel announcing the times of church services, opening and closing of the ship's store, birthday greetings. It could even relay cable stations like CNN.

Another monitor was the PLAT (pilot landing aid television)—the deck-mounted video camera that recorded every approach and landing to the ship. You could sit there and observe each jet roll into the groove and swoop down toward the camera. If the jet landed precisely on target, it looked like it had plopped down right on the camera. Then another camera, mounted up on the island super-structure, would follow the jet as it rolled out on the deck, caught by the arresting wire.

The PLAT tapes could be replayed for LSO debriefings, just in case someone wanted to argue about his grade from the LSO.

The PLAT had another purpose. On those rare occasions when someone *really* botched a pass to the ship—when he and his jet became one with the killer ramp—the investigators could retrieve the tapes and see just why things had so badly gone to hell: "Ah-ha! See that? Sucking power at the ramp, getting slow . . ."

Kabloom. There it was, recorded for posterity on videotape.

CHAPTER THIRTY

THE TREBUCHET

Rick McCormack was the first onto the catapult.

He could see the director down there on the flight deck, just under the nose of the Hornet, moving his arms in the come-forward motion, urging McCormack to move his jet onto the number one catapult shuttle.

This was it. McCormack felt his pulse rate shift into high gear. Ahead he could see the three hundred feet of catapult track—the distance in which he and his Hornet fighter would accelerate to flying speed. At the end of the catapult track was the squared-off, precipitous forward edge of the flight deck. Beyond, thin air. And the heaving blue Pacific ocean.

It was the most vulnerable—and unnatural—moment of a pilot's life. Once he was in the mechanical grip of the great, merciless steam catapult, the aviator relinquished all control of his destiny. His life—or death—was at the whim of a detached, mindless power beneath the surface of the flight deck.

That was the part that took getting used to: the powerlessness. A fighter pilot, by chemistry and divine right, was supposed to be *in control.* But here he was, for three interminable seconds, caught like a cat in the jaws of a pit bull. The pilot sat there while the catapult propelled him from zero to one hundred sixty miles per hour. Nothing he could do during that infinitesimal flea-speck in time— snatch back his throttles, stomp on the jet's brakes, scream epithets in his radio—nothing would halt the forward rush of that behemoth steam catapult.

For Rick McCormack, taxiing onto the *Nimitz*'s number one cata-pult, this was the first time, at least in the Hornet. His previous two dozen catapult shots and arrested landings in training jets while he was still a flight student now seemed like ancient history. That was in another, safer life. This was the real thing, in a real fighter, on a real carrier. With real danger.

All the things that could go wrong on a catapult shot ran through McCormack's brain. The most awful thing, of course, and the one that haunted the worst dreams of carrier aviators, was a cold cata-pult shot. "Cold" meant that the catapult, for whatever reason, failed to accelerate the jet to flying speed. On a normal cat shot, the jet went off the bow of the carrier at about fifteen knots above stall speed. As the jet soared off the front of the ship, the pilot took over control of his jet and flew away.

At less than sufficient speed, something closer to stalling speed, the pilot would have his hands full. He would wrestle with the slug-gish controls, wondering what the hell was going on. If he was smooth on the controls, quick enough to jettison the external stores hanging beneath the airplane, like an auxiliary fuel tank or a load of weapons, he might be able to fly away.

At anything below stall speed, the jet was doomed. The pilot had only one option: eject immediately. The problem was time. The malfunction would have to be recognized, analyzed, and acted upon in the space of about three seconds.

Cold catapult shots were rare these days. A more likely failure was with the jet itself. Firing a fifty-thousand-pound package of whirling turbines, computers, gyros, pumps, valves, and switches like a stone from a siege gun *did* sometimes cause things to break. Engines failed. Instruments quit. Sometimes entire displays came out of the instrument panel, hitting the pilot in the chest or, worse, jamming the control stick. Wheels broke from landing gear struts. Controls froze. Computers crashed.

Three seconds. All his life's experiences, training, instincts—it all came down to that: three critical seconds. *What the hell was happening? Will this sucker fly or not? Should I punch out now, or stay with it?*

The force of the catapult shot affected the pilot too. His body was crushed back against the seat as the jet hurtled down the catapult track, his internal organs wrapped around his spine. His eyeballs flattened in their sockets, distorting his view out the windscreen. His left hand maintained a death grip on the throttles to keep from involuntarily snatching them back to idle thrust.

And his right hand, in the most unnatural act of all, was up on the "towel rack," the catapult grip on the canopy rail. The idea was to keep the pilot's hand out of the way of the control stick during the catapult shot, because the force of the acceleration would cause him to yank the stick too far back, to the nose-up position. In the Hornet, the jet's flight control computer did it for him, "flying" the jet off the catapult, commanding the correct amount of nose-up deflection from the fighter's tail surfaces.

Even after a successful catapult shot, jets sometimes flew into the water. The next-to-last flying accident in the RAG, the one before Burner's crash, had been out here on the carrier. A Marine captain, finishing his carrier qualifications, had been sent from the carrier traffic pattern back to an airfield ashore at night. Everything seemed normal about his departure from the ship. The jet was performing perfectly. The landing gear and flaps were retracted on schedule, and the fighter was accelerating. The pilot checked in on the control frequency.

Then he flew into the ocean.

That was all. No one saw it happen. Lacking hard evidence, it was impossible to say with certainty what caused the crash, but the circumstantial evidence was abundant. Because the jet struck the water at the time after takeoff when the pilot was preoccupied with inside-the-cockpit duties—retracting the gear and flaps, changing frequencies on the radio, selecting a navigational function on the horizontal display indicator—he probably was not devoting full attention to the most important of duties: staying out of the water. With his head down, performing cockpit cleanup chores, still adrenalized from the rush of the night carrier operations, he failed to notice on his instruments that the nose of the Hornet had tilted downward. And because it was a night over the Atlantic, with no perceptible horizon and the surface of the ocean only a dimensionless black void, the young Marine didn't realize that his jet was losing altitude, that it was slipping ever closer to the ultimate danger.

The FA-18 Hornet and its pilot sank to the floor of the ocean, leaving not a trace.

★

Rick McCormack shoved all this from his mind as he jockeyed the Hornet up over the catapult shuttle. Deck crewmen were swarming beneath the nose, attaching the nose gear of the jet to the shuttle, which was the only part of the catapult that could be seen abovedeck.

The shuttle was the jet's only connection to the mighty steam catapult. When the catapult fired, the shuttle traveled down a narrow slot in the deck the entire length of the catapult, pulling the jet with it.

Beneath the slot in the deck lay the catapult's two steam cylinders, each eighteen inches in diameter, mounted together like a double-barreled shotgun. Each cylinder contained a piston. The two pistons, through slots in the top of the cylinders, were mated to each other and to the shuttle. When the two pistons shot down the length of their cylinders, the shuttle—and the attached jet—went along for the ride.

A device called a "holdback" was attached to the back of the nose gear to hold the jet in place while the catapult applied tension. On a signal from the catapult officer, the catapult was fired by opening valves, letting steam surge into the cylinders. A tension spring in the holdback fitting released when the catapult fired, and the jet was propelled down the 309-foot length of the slotted deck.

In two and a half seconds the catapult could accelerate a sixty-thousand-pound jet from zero to one hundred fifty miles per hour.

At the end of the catapult were two water brake cylinders, which were tubes mounted at the end of the steam cylinders. The shuttle came to a halt when a tapered spear on each piston rammed into its respective water cylinder, squeezing water out the narrow escape orifices. From its terminal velocity of well over a hundred miles per hour, the shuttle mechanism crunched to a halt in only nine feet of travel when the spears hit the water brakes, rattling every compartment in the forward half of the ship. The shuttle was then hauled by a cable and pulley assembly back to its starting position for the next launch. The *Nimitz*'s four catapults could launch a jet every thirty seconds.

The awesome power of the catapults never failed to astonish young aviators. When given his first orientation tour of the aircraft carrier's internal machinery, standing there at the end of the catapult cylinders when the spears slammed into the water brakes—*whaaabooom!*—rattling every rivet on the giant ship, a nugget fighter pilot's eyes would expand to the size of Frisbees. The standard utterance was always something like, *"Ho-lee shit!"*

★

The catapult officer was in view out the right side of McCormack's windshield. He wore the green jersey and helmet signifying that he was a member of the ship's division responsible for the catapults and arresting mechanisms. Across the back of the jersey was stenciled his title: SHOOTER.

McCormack had met him in the ship's officers' wardroom: a lieutenant commander named Dave Weed. Weed was a pilot who had already spent a tour in an A-6 squadron, and then an assignment as an instructor back in the training command. Now Weed was a shooter. It was his job to ensure that the catapult was set not only for the type of jet being launched, but for its exact weight. A runner with the "weight board" had already come around to each jet, holding up the board for the pilot to approve. On the board was written the jet's weight—36.5 for McCormack's Hornet. McCormack acknowledged the number with a thumbs-up. The catapult was then set to propel the 36,500-pound jet to its exact flying speed off the end of the deck.

At the port deck edge was an enlisted man, also in green jersey and helmet, hunched down and talking into a sound-powered telephone. He was monitoring the gauges and settings for the catapult and communicating with the crew down in the catapult machinery spaces. He waited for the visual signal from the catapult officer telling him to initiate the firing of the catapult.

Taxiing forward, McCormack felt the nose of the jet lurch as the nose-tow bar dropped into the shuttle slot. On the signal from the yellow-shirt standing by the jet's nose, he eased off the brakes. The catapult officer was whirling his right hand over his head, signaling the pilot to power up.

McCormack pushed the two throttles forward to full power.

Rick McCormack's heart accelerated another twenty bangs a minute. The Hornet was sitting there, both engines roaring, crackling, vibrating the entire airframe, held back only by the spring-tensioned holdback fitting down there on the nose gear.

The shooter was going through the time-honored ritual dance of the catapult officer: body arched into the wind, upraised right arm whirling over his head, waiting for the ready signal from the pilot in the cockpit.

McCormack "wiped" the cockpit one last time with the stick—rotating the stick through its full range of motion to ensure that all the jet's control surfaces were free—and scanned his instruments. All okay. He shoved his head back hard against the headrest. He wrapped his left hand tighter around the throttle grip. He brought his right hand up in a salute to the catapult officer—the signal that he was ready.

His life was now out of his hands.

The shooter cocked his head to each side, checking for last-second signals from the island (the carrier's six-story "control tower"), looking for unwanted obstructions in the path of the catapult. All clear. He lunged forward in a fencer's thrust and touched his right hand to the deck—the traditional signal to the crewman at the deck edge to initiate the firing.

McCormack waited for the catapult to fire. Nothing was happening. *Why isn't it firing?* It seemed like minutes, hours, were going by. *What's wrong?*

One and one half seconds, in fact, had elapsed. *Why isn't . . .*

The catapult fired.

Whoooom! Down the catapult track he went. The acceleration rammed him back into the seat. Rick McCormack felt as if he were in the grip of a giant hand. In his peripheral vision he saw the flight deck of the U.S.S. *Nimitz* sweeping behind him. Ahead was the sheer, precipitous end of the deck.

And then nothing. He was hurtling off the edge of a sixty-foot cliff. Beyond he saw only blue—water, sky, thin air.

The hard thrust of the catapult shot abruptly ended and—*hallelujah!*—he was flying. McCormack snatched the control stick with his right hand. *He* was in control again. *Okay, God, I've got it. Thank you. Thank you.*

★

Better than sex!

Well, almost. That was the consensus back in the ready room after the nuggets had completed their first day period on the carrier.

"What a rush!" said Rick McCormack.

"The first cat shot—wow!" said his brother.

"Holy shit! You talk about awesome . . ."

It was true. There *was* something sensual about it. It was an analogy dating back to the first Navy catapults, when scout planes were launched off battleships with explosive charges. It was the ultimate rush—something akin to a roller coaster, a sky dive, a rocket launch, all rolled into one two-and-a-half-second experience.

Carrier pilots always came back to the ship saying the same thing about that first catapult shot: It came *very* close to being . . . orgasmic.

CHAPTER THIRTY-ONE

SUGAR TALK

Road Ammons's pulse rate was hitting about a hundred sixty. Which was normal, at least for this little window in time. The window would last another thirty seconds. That was all. Half a minute from this point in his approach to the U.S.S. *Nimitz* until the last tingling millisecond when his tailhook skimmed over the blunt back end of the flight deck and—*whump!*—he slammed down on that postage-stamp-sized hunk of steel at one hundred thirty-seven knots.

"Roman three-one-nine, Hornet ball, eight-point-one, Ammons."

"Roger ball," came the comforting voice of Pearly Gates. "You're a liiii-tttle low."

Yes, he was. He could see the ball dwelling there on the lens just below the green datum lights. It should be right in the middle.

Road squeezed the throttles up just a bit, to bring the jet up on the correct glide path.

Thirty seconds. Thirty pulse-racing, adrenaline-pumping, shit-scared seconds. Would it be like this *every* time? Road wondered. Did landing jets on aircraft carriers ever become routine, ho-hum exercises, like parking your car in the driveway?

Road hoped he would never find out. He was a Marine, and one of the things Road *loved* about the Marine Corps was that they had enough sense to stay ashore, at least more often than their Navy counterparts. Most Marine fighter squadrons were land-based, and that suited Road Ammons just fine. Aircraft carriers were something he would be willing to turn over in perpetuity to the Navy swabbos.

But still, he had to *qualify* on the damn things, didn't he? The Marine Corps took this attitude that, hey, you guys are naval aviators just like the Navy jocks, and anything they do, you had better do just as well.

So here they were—he and J. J. Quinn, who despised and dreaded seagoing airfields even more than Road Ammons— qualifying on that great, gray, heaving death slab out there. There was no way around it. It was a credential they *had* to collect in order to graduate. It was Road's fervent wish that when it was over he could put it away in a drawer somewhere, like a medal from a war he wanted to forget.

"Pow-*werrrrrr*!" came Pearly's voice from the platform. Road recognized the tone. It was the LSO's sugar talk, a lilting, encouraging tone—but increasing in urgency. Pearly was telling Road to add power—nudge the throttles up, but just *some*. Not a lot. Correct the situation—but don't *over*correct.

Road overcorrected. He shoved the throttles up. The Hornet started to climb, to go high on the glide path. Road yanked the throttles back.

The Hornet settled.

"Eeeee—zzzeee," intoned Pearly. More sugar talk. He wanted Road to settle down. Make *little* corrections.

Five seconds to the deck. The blunt end of the carrier swelled in Road's windscreen.

The yellowish blob of the ball was hovering near the middle now, only a hair to the low side. Road knew from the constant lecturing by Pearly and Plug that now—*especially* now—it was critical that he stay with the ball.

That was the hard part. Stay focused on that yellow blob. Don't stare at the deck. Don't take your eyes off the ball. . . .

Road took his eyes off the ball. He had to! Shit, man . . . there was the deck . . . the whole freaking ship . . . coming at him like a goddamned steel mountain.

"Pow-WERRRR!"

KeerrWhump!

Road's Hornet fighter plunked down on the deck. In the next instant, as the tailhook snagged the number one wire, Road felt himself thrust hard against his shoulder straps. His left hand jammed the throttles full forward, to full power.

The jet had stopped.

For several seconds Road sat there stiff-arming the throttles, his engines bellowing at full power. The Hornet was pulling against the unyielding tug of the arresting cable stretched across the deck.

"All right, son, we've got you," came the voice of the air boss, sitting up in his windowed "office" high above the flight deck. "You can pull the throttles back now."

Road looked around. *Oh, yeah,* he thought. *Sure enough. I'm here. I'm alive.*

He pulled the throttles back. He had just made his first carrier landing in the FA-18.

★

"Don't spot the deck," said Pearly, down in the ready room. He said it again, glowering at Road Ammons. "Do—not—spot—the—frigging—DECK! Do you understand that?"

"Yes, sir," said Road.

"Spotting the deck" meant taking your eyes off the ball as you approached the ramp—which was what Road had done on each of his four arrested landings that day. It meant you zeroed in on the landing area of the deck, which almost always caused the pilot to drop the nose of his jet and land short of the target area.

Landing short was the worst thing you could do on an aircraft carrier. It meant that you came within a few feet, perhaps inches, of a spectacular, fiery union with the ramp. It was almost always terminal.

The idea was to stay focused on the ball all the way to touchdown. That was the only way to ensure landing exactly on target, which was the space between the number two and number three wires. The four cables on the carrier deck were spaced thirty feet apart. On a perfectly flown pass—ball in the center all the way to touchdown—the jet caught the number three wire. Your jet cleared the ramp by exactly *fourteen feet*.

If your hook caught a number two wire, or worse, a number one wire, it meant that you had cleared the ramp by something *less* than the optimum fourteen feet. You had come within ten or eight or perhaps only *three or four feet* of becoming immolated in a glorious orange fireball.

Number three wire was good.

Numbers two and four were all right.

A number one wire was, by definition, an "arrival." You had cheated death, but not by a comfortable margin. Enough number one wires, and the LSOs started looking at you like you carried the Ebola virus.

Which was the way Pearly Gates was looking at Road Ammons.

"No more deck spotting, Road," he said. "No more one wires. Got it?"

"Okay, Pearly. I've got it."

★

Everyone did it once in a while. Occasionally you missed the target wire and caught a number one or a number four. That little two-foot window was an elusive target, particularly when the deck was lurching up and down in a heavy sea, or the wind was buffeting your jet like a leaf in a storm. The tolerance was tiny. Too low, and the LSO would wave you off. Too high, and you missed the last wire, the number four, and boltered.

And *that*, of course, was the reason pilots were supposed to jam their throttles to full power on every touchdown, regardless of whether they thought they were going to catch a wire. If they *did* snag an arresting wire, so much the better. The jet would stop on the deck regardless of the power on the engines. If they missed, the engines were already spun up and delivering maximum thrust. Off they would go again, just like a normal touch-and-go practice landing out at Whitehouse.

Everyone in the detachment got four landings on their first day at sea. And *every* nugget—Road, Rambo, the twins, Sniper, Chip—snagged at least one number one wire. But none was doing it with the same deck-spotting consistency as Road Ammons.

The three senior pilots—Hillan, Morgan, Earl—all did well, as expected. Most notable was Commander Jim Hillan, whose passes at the ship looked like they were on autopilot. Hillan had a hot streak going: four "okays" for four passes, each one to the number three wire.

★

The conditions out there in the strait between Catalina and San Clemente were as close to ideal as the nuggets would ever see. The visibility was unlimited. The southern California sun beamed down from a cloudless sky, sparkling off the Pacific like a field of jewels.

It didn't take long for the sheer terror to wear off. After the pulse-pounding surge of the first catapult shot, and then the same thing in reverse with the first "trap," the nuggets were beginning to feel the glimmerings of something like cockiness. *That wasn't so tough! Hell, I even remembered to pull the power back after that last trap.*

By late afternoon, the golden California sun was becoming something of a problem. It was shining *too* brightly. The *Nimitz* was steaming westward, which meant that the pilots squinted directly into the low-hanging spring sun as they tried to pick up the ball on final approach.

"Clara," called Chip Van Doren on short final.

"Roger," acknowledged Pearly. "You're a little high. Keep it coming."

"Clara" meant that the pilot had lost the ball—his primary source of information during the last few seconds of a carrier landing. He was coming down the glide slope without any visual guidance.

Seconds passed. Pearly kept his thumb poised on the wave-off button while he watched the oncoming jet. If the pilot didn't pick up the ball in the next couple of seconds . . .

"Ball," Van Doren called out, four seconds from the ramp, as the shimmering yellow blob came back into sight.

"Roger, ball."

Kerrr-ploppp.

Van Doren caught a three wire. While he was taxiing clear of the landing area, the next jet, J. J. Quinn's, called out "Clara."

Pearly rogered. "Keep it coming."

And again, four seconds out, J.J. picked up his visual cue. "Ball."

"Roger, ball. You're a little low. Right for lineup."

J.J. corrected, dipping his right wing to align the jet with the centerline, then plunking down on the deck to snag a number two wire.

When the third jet in a row called Clara, Pearly made a decision. He picked up the handset that connected the LSO platform to the Air Operations office, up in the island. "It's no good, boss. The sun's in their eyes now. We gotta change course."

He already knew the answer. In the narrow channel between the islands, the giant ship had little room to change course. The *Nimitz*'s captain came on the phone: "No way, Paddles. If you can't work 'em this way, we'll knock it off until night ops."

It was as Pearly expected. This was a training exercise, qualifying new pilots, not an operational mission. Safety had to come first. "Yes, sir, we concur with that," said Pearly.

No more day ops. They would wait for nightfall.

★

Pearly Gates came down to the ready room, still wearing the wool cap and the vest with the RECTUM NON BUSTUS patch. Plug Neidhold was tagging along behind him, carrying the LSO book with the grades for every pass the nuggets made at the ship today.

Pearly knew the standard LSO debriefing techniques. You were supposed to hold the grade book so the pilot can't see it. You made eye contact with the guy you were debriefing. You gave compliments first, criticisms last. You didn't waffle or appear ambiguous in your critique. You didn't invite argument about a grade and you never, never, no matter how much a guy argued, changed the grade.

Every pass made to the carrier received a grade from an LSO. Back in the early paddle-waving days of carrier aviation, some hard-nose apparently decided that too much praise was bad for pilots. So the best grade a pilot could receive was "okay." On rare occasions, when a pilot distinguished himself by flying a perfect pass under adverse conditions, an LSO might assign an okay under-lined, which amounted to an oak leaf cluster on his grade. An okay in parentheses was a "fair." An ugly pass at the ship received a "no grade," a dash through the grade box meaning a below-average pass. The worst grade an LSO could hand out was a "cut," the equivalent to an "F" in grammar school. A "cut" grade was, by defi-nition, reserved for "gross deviations inside the wave-off window." It meant the pilot had scared hell out of himself—and the LSO.

But with RAG students, especially nuggets, the LSO was more than just a debriefer or a grader. In the RAG environment, he was also a teacher. The nuggets were expected to make mistakes as they learned. It was the LSO's job to coach them, nudge them along in the process of becoming competent carrier aviators.

Pearly debriefed each pilot. He had few comments for the three senior aviators, Jim "Harpo" Hillan, Dave "Smoke" Morgan, and Robert "Flounder" Earl. For two days' work on the ship, Hillan received seven okays for eight passes—a nearly perfect grade-point average.

Chip Van Doren too received compliments. "Nice work, Chip. Good tight ball flying." His first pass was a "fair," number two wire, with a "little low at the ramp" comment. His next two were "okay," three wire. Three more fairs, ending with two straight okays. It was a strong showing for a nugget.

Angie Morales started off erratically, then found the target wire. "Your first trap, you spotted the deck on me, Rambo."

"Yeah, sorry."

"But then you picked it up. No more one wires, but you're over-controlling some." Angie received two no-grades and two fairs—an average performance.

And then the twins. Sitting together in the second row, wearing identical flight suits, Heckle and Jeckle were once again indistin-guishable, even to Pearly, who had been seeing them now for four months. "All right, which one is Russ?"

"That's me," said one of the grinning redheads.

"High start, overcorrect, low in the middle, a little settle at the ramp, number two—fair pass. Second pass, high start, high all the way, settle at the ramp, number one wire—no grade. Third pass . . ."

And so on. Russ McCormack received two no-grades and three fairs. "Not bad, for your first day," said Pearly. "Start working it down sooner, try to avoid the high starts. Carry a little more power close in."

Then Pearly debriefed the second twin. It was a carbon copy of his brother's passes. "This is weird," said Pearly. "Can't you guys do anything different? If one of you gets a no-grade, does it mean the other has to do the same thing?"

"I promised our mother I wouldn't make him look bad," said Rick.

"The hell you did," said Russ. "You promised her you would try to be just like your smart brother."

Both the Marines, J. J. Quinn and Road Ammons, had flown sporadic passes—some good, several bad, a few ugly. J.J.'s first two passes were no-grades to a one wire. Then a bolter. Bolters were usually the result of overconservatism—flying too high over the ramp, carrying too much power, or "flinching" from the upcoming steel deck. Bolters weren't usually unsafe, just inconvenient. And unnerving. "I'll buy that bolter," said Pearly. "I called you for power close in, and you gave it to me. Too much, unfortunately, and it made you bolter. It won't count in your grade average."

Road was even more sporadic. After his deck-spotting passes of the previous day, Road overcorrected and got two bolters. Then he settled down for a couple passes—one okay to the three wire, one fair to the two wire. And then a cut—the worst grade you can get.

"You spotted the deck again," Pearly said. "Road, I want you to keep your eyes on the ball. All the way to touchdown. All the way, you understand?"

Road nodded. "Sorry, I just lost my concentration. I'll fly the ball."

It didn't sound like good old Road Ammons talking. He wasn't his usual animated self, flashing the Yamaha grin, doing the aw-shucks-I'm-just-another-Marine routine.

Good old Road seemed subdued. And worried.

★

Whaaaaboooom! Sssssssssssss. Whaaaaboooom! Sssssssssss.

J. J. Quinn lay in his bunk. The *whaaaaboooms* were coming every three minutes or so, each followed by the sound of steam hissing from the catapult cylinders. Every time the catapult fired, J.J.'s bunk reverberated like a tuning fork.

Above the junior officers' stateroom area, up there on the forward flight deck, jets were taxiing up, one after the other, onto the catapults—and were being blasted off the bow of the ship like shells from a cannon.

Fire, retract, retension, fire again. Like a steady artillery barrage. It went on incessantly, the nonstop *whaaaaboooom* and *sssssssss* of the two forward catapults.

It had been J.J.'s plan to get a nap before he went back to the ready room. Tonight would be his first night landing qualification. But he hadn't figured on those freaking catapults! The number one catapult was directly over his stateroom. It was like living inside a boiler factory. He wondered how the hell anyone got any rest on a carrier.

He gave up trying for a nap. J.J. decided to write a letter to Dorothy. He knew that in all likelihood he would arrive home before the letter, but it was something he always did. Writing to his wife was J.J.'s form of journal-keeping.

There was another reason why J.J. wrote to his wife. It was the same reason pilots had been writing letters home since the first aircraft carrier put to sea: *Just in case.* Of course, neither J.J. nor Dorothy believed that anything was likely to happen. But thirteen years in the Marine Corps had made them both realists. Things *did* sometimes happen. If anything—the worst of scenarios—actually did occur, at least this last letter would still be on its way to Dorothy. So J.J. wrote his letters. Just in case.

★

Listening to the steady *whaabooms* of the catapults, Chip Van Doren was struck by a thought. He was trying to remember . . .

something that had fascinated him in a history class back at the academy.

Then it hit him. "A trebuchet!" he said.

"A what?" said Road. They were sitting in the officers' ward-room, on the O-2 level. They were having dinner before the night launch.

"French word. Tray-boo-shay," said Chip. "A trebuchet was a medieval catapult—a long pole mounted on a fulcrum with a sling at the end. They'd lay this thing out on the ground, tilted over its fulcrum, then add weights to the short end of the pole. When they let go, the long end would flip through the air and fling whatever was in the sling way to hell in the air, maybe a quarter of a mile or so over the ground. When they were laying siege to a castle, they'd use this thing to sling boulders, or vats of burning oil, or dead horses or whatever. When they were really feeling nasty, they'd stick one of their prisoners in the trebuchet and catapult *him* up over the wall into the castle."

It was easy to visualize. Particularly now. They sat there in their flight suits, silently chewing on the solid Navy meatloaf, thinking about catapults. Sailing through the air, over castle walls.

"Is that what we are?" asked Road Ammons. "Prisoners being flung over a wall?"

"Yeah," said Chip, grinning. "Comforting, isn't it?"

★

Carrier landings demanded the utmost concentration from the pilot. But most Navy pilots, after they'd gotten over their initial anxiety coming aboard ship, would tell you they *loved* making carrier land-ings—in the daytime. Give the average Navy pilot enough fuel, and he would stay out there all day long, bagging one trap after another.

Until nighttime. Nighttime was a bitch. Darkness over the ocean was as bleak and void as the bottom of a mine shaft. Even the most crinkly-eyed, battle-toughened, steel-nerved Navy fighter pilot would, in a private moment, confess a lonely secret: *Night carrier landings scare the shit out of me.*

Nonetheless, they did it. They did it in all conditions—good weather or bad, smooth seas or pitching, roiling, heaving oceanscapes. Daylight or darkness. If they wanted to stay alive, they became very proficient at it.

★

Pearly was wearing his trademark wool jersey and fatigue pants. He stood in front of the greaseboard, hands on his hips, looking at his nuggets like a coach at a pep rally. It was time again for the Vince Lombardi act.

"Let me tell you something," he started out in his coach's voice. "You people are among the most elite pilots in the world. You know why? Because you are qualified to do something that only a handful of aviators on the entire planet can do: land on an aircraft carrier.

"You have had the best training that any aviator has ever received. Since your first day in the Navy, you've passed every test they could throw at you. You are the best of the best, and let me say, ladies and gentlemen, I am proud to have been able to work with you."

All this was ingratiating balderdash, of course, but it had a purpose. It was part of Pearly's Lombardi pump-up technique.

The nuggets weren't just hyped for the coming event. They were *wired*—more so than for any other phase of the Hornet training program. They fidgeted in their lounge seats. Rambo Morales had passed around a bag of chewing gum, and now each was gnawing a wad of gum the size of a softball.

The nervousness crackled through the ready room like a brooding storm. Everyone was talking too loud, cackling like hyenas over some nonsensical joke, fidgeting with their flight gear.

Each had his own nervous fetish. Road Ammons emptied out his entire survival vest and then restowed each item, one by one. Just to make sure. Sure of what, he didn't know, but it didn't matter. It kept him busy.

Angie Morales had the ability to drop into a Zen-like meditative state, closing her eyes while sitting upright and looking dead as a mummy. So that's what she did, slipping into her trance right there in her ready room chair.

Chip Van Doren had mapped out a jogging route around the perimeter of the hangar deck. While the others fidgeted in the ready room, he changed into sneakers and running shorts and did laps around the hangar deck, jumping over airplane tie-down chains and dodging tug tractors. About an hour later he came sweating back to the ready room. "Twenty laps," he said, poking at his calculator-wristwatch. "That makes, ah, let's see, six-point-eight-one-eight miles."

"You smell like a goat," said Angie Morales, emerging from her trance. "Are you gonna go flying like that?"

"Of course not. What do you think I am, an animal? I'm gonna change socks."

Meanwhile, Rick McCormack was running his mouth. His classmates had bestowed a call sign on him: "Yappy." Being half the Heckle-Jeckle duo, he was already the undisputed talkiest nugget of the class. Whenever Yappy McCormack was hyped about something, *anything*—an air-to-air adventure, a hairy low-altitude training flight over the high desert, or his first night qualifications on the carrier—his mouth ran like an endless tape. He was a one-man talk show.

Now no one could shut him up. Yappy was running his mouth about everything from the weather to the movie on the tube to the lousy cheeseburgers in the wardroom to how dark it was going to be outside. His mouth seemed to be wired to his adrenal gland. The closer it came to launch time, the more he yapped. His classmates, even his brother, were talking about sealing his mouth with duct tape.

★

The nuggets were becoming aware of another peculiarity: They had to pee a lot. Every ten minutes or so, it was the same thing—a gushing, urgent need to go dribble yet a few more drops. No one had ever explained it, but it was a historical fact: Before a night carrier launch the average naval aviator would need to void his bladder at least ten times. Maybe more.

★

Road Ammons poked his head out onto the catwalk adjoining the flight deck. It was like peering into an ink bottle. Beyond the rail of the catwalk, out there over the Pacific, he could see only blackness. A cloud layer obscured the stars. There were occasional pinpoints of light—ships, airplanes, but no horizon. No up, no down. Just the horizonless freaking ocean and the sky, all melded together in a bleak void.

Road stood there for a minute, letting his eyes adjust to the darkness. Up on the flight deck the yellow shirts were towing jets around, positioning them for the launch. Road switched on his goosenecked Boy Scout flashlight. Then he stepped up on the flight deck and headed for his jet.

306. That was the side number of Road's jet. The beam of his flashlight shone on the jet's number, painted on the long tapered nose of the Hornet. It was a "B" model, a two-seater Hornet, which meant he had to preflight the empty backseat also, ensuring that the straps and switches and ejection seat were all safetied.

Road finished his walk-around, poking his flashlight beam into the engine inlets, into every orifice and fixture of the jet's exterior. The plane captain, an enlisted kid named Miller, followed Road around the darkened jet like a watchdog, talking the whole time. He helped him into the cockpit, handing him the straps and radio cords.

"This your first night landing, Captain?"

"It's lieutenant, not captain."

"Yes, sir, Lieutenant. This your first time at night?"

"Yeah. My first on a carrier." *And it's gonna be my last, I hope.* Road wished the kid would shut up.

"Looks pretty dark out there to me, sir."

"Yeah, it's pretty dark out there." *Darker than a coal miner's bunghole. Where do they get these talky kids?*

"I mean it's, like, *really* dark. You wouldn't catch me out there in no—"

"Yeah, well, I guess I'm strapped in now. Thanks for the help. See ya later."

"Good luck, Captain. You sure wouldn't get me to go out there—"

Clunk. Road closed the canopy. It was quiet inside the closed cockpit. The silence was wonderful.

★

That was the hard part—the waiting. Road's jet was spotted in front of the island superstructure. He was number six in the sequence to be launched, so he had to sit there and wait his turn to start engines.

From his position in the cockpit, he had a view of the two bow catapults. A pair of F-14 Tomcats was going first, also doing night qualifications. The big fighters were taxiing forward into position on the catapults.

Road watched the fighter on the port catapult—the number one cat. The catapult officer was giving him the wind-up signal. The pilot responded by pushing his throttles to full power.

The roar of the Tomcat's engines flooded the deck.

"Suspend number one catpult!" said a voice on the radio. The pilot? The air boss? The catapult officer?

It didn't matter. Up in Pri-Fly, the air boss had a mushroom-shaped plunger he could push that suspended *all* four catapults at once. Nothing would fire if he punched the suspend button.

The suspend command was given whenever *anything*—an airplane problem, a traffic problem, a catapult problem—made it necessary to *not* fire the catapult.

The catapult was suspended—the equivalent of unloading a cannon. The Tomcat's engines were still roaring at full power. The cat officer waggled his lighted wand to the pilot in the cockpit, signaling him to pull the power back on the Tomcat fighter. It was okay to throttle down. The catapult was safe.

It was the pilot's first night catapult shot. Now he was confused. Something was wrong and he didn't know what. What the hell were they telling him? Here he was powered up . . . ready to be hurtled down the catapult track . . . and now they were giving him some kind of signal . . .

And then an awful thought struck the Tomcat pilot: *They're going to fire this fucking catapult!*

He did what came naturally: He jammed the throttles hard against the stops—*kaboom!*—lighting both afterburners. If he was going off the catapult, it would be with all the thrust his engines could deliver.

Two fifteen-foot torches of flame erupted from the tailpipes of the big fighter. The glow of the roaring afterburners illuminated the entire forward flight deck. The Tomcat was sitting there with its engines roaring at full power, belching flame like a space shuttle on the pad.

"Power back! Power back on cat one!" bellowed the air boss on the radio. "What the hell do you think you're doing down there?" He was yelling at the Tomcat pilot. "The catapult is suspended. Get the power off that jet before you hurt someone!"

Actually, he already *had* hurt someone. A deck crewman working by the jet blast deflector—the grated blast shield that raised up out of the deck behind the catapult to deflect the exhaust from the jets—had been caught out in the open by the sudden application of the Tomcat's afterburners. The heat and flame from the tailpipes flipped him end over end like a bowling pin.

The pilot finally got the message. He pulled the engines back to idle.

The medics were running across the deck toward the fallen crewman. Within seconds, they had him in a gurney and were hauling him toward the dispensary down on the second deck.

Up in the island, glowering down at the scene on the deck, the air boss was livid. How dare one of these peckerhead fighter pilots disobey a signal on *his* flight deck—and get one of *his* people toasted like a marshmallow! "Get the Tomcat off the catapult," he ordered on the bullhorn.

"He's supposed to launch for night quals, Boss," said the flight deck officer on his walk-around radio.

"Not tonight, he's not. Not on *this* ship. He's outa the game. You tell him to park that goddamn airplane and get his ass up here on the double."

"Yes, sir."

Thus began the night's flight operations on the U.S.S. *Nimitz*.

CHAPTER THIRTY-TWO

THE BLACK VOID

Road Ammons could see the shooter out there on the deck rotating his lighted wand. It was the power-up signal.

Road brought both throttles up to the full power detent. Sitting there on the catapult, engines rumbling away at full power, Road gave all his cockpit displays one more look-over. No warning or caution or advisory messages. No caution lights. No X's in the flight control display. Ejection seat armed. Radio altimeter set at forty feet.

All he had to do now was flip on the exterior lights switch with the little finger of his left hand. That was the nighttime signal—instead of the traditional daytime salute—to the shooter that the jet was okay for launch.

That was all: Flip the switch. Then his ass would belong to the shooter. And to God.

Road glanced one more time out the front windscreen—and wished he hadn't. It was *worse* than dark out there. The empty void out in front of the ship looked like one of those hypothetical black holes in space that could swallow you up and make you disappear.

He remembered asking a guy in the previous class what it had been like out there on the ship at night.

How dark was it out there?

Dark, man. Darker than a thousand assholes.

Road tore his eyes away from the black void. The shooter was still rotating his wand, urging Road to give the signal.

Road shoved his helmet back hard against the headrest. He put his right hand up on the catapult handle. He fixed his eyes on the HUD, which would tell him everything he needed to know when the catapult flung him off the bow—attitude, angle of attack, airspeed, rate of climb.

He flipped his light switch on. The navigation lights on the Hornet's wingtips and tail illuminated.

From the corner of his eye Road saw the shooter go through his little fencer's dance, lunging forward, touching his wand to the deck. The visual circuit was now complete, from pilot to shooter to the crewman who actually pushed the launch button.

Road waited for the shot.

And waited.

It was taking too long! Why the hell wasn't it—

Whaaarrrrrumph! There it was—jamming him back in the seat, flattening his eyeballs, squashing his guts . . .

Hurtling him down the catapult track. Toward the black void. At the end of the deck, the force of the catapult abruptly ceased.

He was flying. *Don't look out,* Road told himself. *Fly your instruments. Keep this sucker climbing. Don't look out there at the black freaking void.*

Road climbed straight ahead. With his left hand he slapped the gear handle up and brought up the flaps. Passing through three thousand feet, he called the ship's radar controller.

"Roger, Roman three-oh-six," said the controller. "You're cleared to marshal at angels two-one. Expected clearance time is two-zero-one-zero."

"Marshal" was a stack of holding patterns about thirty miles behind the ship, starting at twenty thousand feet. The jets were "stacked" in patterns a thousand feet apart. Road was cleared to enter the holding pattern at "angels two-one," which meant twenty-one-thousand feet. He could expect to be cleared for an approach to the *Nimitz* at twenty-ten (ten minutes past eight P.M.). He had fifteen minutes to wait.

Road heard his classmates, Chip Van Doren, Russ McCormack, then Harpo Hillan, checking in with the controller. The others— Yappy, J.J., and Angie Morales—would "hot seat," meaning that after the first pilots were finished and back on the deck of the *Nimitz*, they would climb out of their cockpits, with one engine still running, and the next group of pilots would strap in.

Up there in the marshal pattern, the night no longer seemed so black. The lights of San Diego were lighting up the eastern horizon. The coast of California stretched northward in a long ribbon of light. Down below, Road could see lights twinkling on the islands of San Clemente and Catalina.

"Roman three-oh-six, your signal is Charlie."

"Roman three-oh-six, roger."

"Charlie" was the signal to land. Road was cleared for his approach to the ship. Show time.

★

Pearly Gates was worried about the burble.

He walked out on the open flight deck, tilting his face to the wind like a hound sniffing the breeze. "The wind's right down the axial," he said. "The ship's making its own wind. There's gonna be a burble."

The ocean wind had died out after sunset. The carrier needed wind over the deck to reduce the closure speed of the landing jets from a hundred fifty miles an hour to an acceptable hundred twenty or so. Now it was calm, which meant that for landing airplanes the ship had to "make" its own wind. The *Nimitz* was driving through the water at thirty knots.

When the ship made its own wind, it caused two problems for the pilots. One was the crosswind, from right to left, complicating the problem of lining up the landing jet with the runway centerline. Instead of the wind coming down the angled aircraft landing deck, which was displaced eleven degrees from the ship's fore-and-aft axis, it was coming down the *straight* deck, from the bow to the stern.

The other problem, which was worse, was the "burble"—the eddying effect of the wind sweeping over the island, the carrier's superstructure. The wind spilled around the island like water over a rock formation, causing turbulence and a "sinkhole" behind the ship, where the jets flew their final approach. The landing jets had to fly through the eddy of turbulent air just before they crossed the ramp of the ship. It was like driving a sports car through the air wake of an eighteen-wheel truck. The burble was most pronounced when there was no wind over the ocean and the carrier had to make its own.

And so it would be tonight, Pearly knew. There was no damned wind. The giant ship was charging like a torpedo boat through the San Clemente channel in order to generate the wind they wanted over the deck.

★

"Roman three-oh-six, ball, seven-point-eight, Ammons."

"Roger, ball," answered Pearly Gates from the LSO platform.

Road's jet looked like a tiny firefly out there against the black backdrop. He was the second jet down the chute. Harpo Hillan had landed already and gotten his usual number three wire. Now Harpo was up on the forward deck, getting back on the catapult for another trip around the pattern. After the first arrested landing, the jets would stay in the traffic pattern at twelve hundred feet around the carrier instead of going back up to the marshal holding pattern.

Pearly didn't like the oncoming jet's position on the glide slope. "A liiii-ttle low," he said in his sugar voice.

Road's jet rose on the glide path. But only a little.

"You're still a little low."

A steady green light was showing on the Hornet's nose gear. A green light told the LSO that the jet's speed was too slow, too close to its stall speed. Red indicted that the jet was fast. An amber light told the LSO that the approaching jet was exactly on its optimum landing speed. Pearly wanted to see an amber.

The light flickered from green to amber. Then back to green. Slow again.

"Powww-werrr," said Pearly.

The light went to amber. Then to red. The jet started to climb. Road was overresponding to Pearly's call.

"Don't climb."

The jet steadied on the glide path. The Hornet was close now, only seconds from touchdown. He was on glide path, with an amber "on-speed" light.

Approaching the ramp, the Hornet began to settle. Its wings wobbled.

The burble.

"Power! Power!" called Pearly.

The jet settled as it crossed the ramp. *Kerrrplunk!* The hook snagged a one wire.

"Damn it," yelled Pearly, watching the jet roll past him on the deck. "He didn't give me power going through the burble. He spotted the deck."

★

Road wasn't the only one. They were all having trouble with the burble.

The problem was, the nuggets had been spoiled by the two sun-drenched California afternoons, making their daytime landings with a solid twenty-knot breeze coming right down the angled deck. It had even become fun—easy, almost—bagging daytime traps out there in the golden sunshine of the Pacific.

Now the golden sun was gone. So were the twenty knots of friendly wind down the angle. Now it was black as the inside of a heifer, and they had to fight the tendency of the jet, nudged by the crosswind, to keep sliding toward the left edge of the flight deck.

It was a different game. Even the old-timers, Hillan, Morgan, and Earl, were working harder than usual. Everyone was fighting the killer burble that grabbed them at the most critical moment in the approach.

★

"Who the hell is Roman three-oh-seven?" demanded the air boss. His exasperation level was peaking out. What he wanted to do now was wring some peckerhead fighter pilot's scrawny neck.

The air boss was trying to figure out what was going on with Roman 307. Some guy kept checking in on the radio, identifying himself as Roman 307. "Roman three-oh-seven airborne . . . Roman three-oh-seven leaving marshal ... Roman three-oh-seven commencing approach ..."

The only problem was, they didn't *have* any goddamn Roman 307, at least in the air. "Lemme get this straight, Roman three-oh-seven," said the air boss. "You say you're a Hornet and you're out there in the pattern tonight?"

"Yes, sir."

"Well, son, I'm looking down at the flight deck this very minute at a parked airplane with a pilot in the cockpit. Its number happens to be three-oh-seven. And my board says that pilot is someone named McCormack. Could you be that gentleman?"

A moment of radio silence. "No, sir. I mean, yes, I could be, but that's not me."

"Then just who might it be, pray tell?"

"Me, sir," said another voice. "I'm McCormack, the one on deck. That guy out there just thinks he's me."

"I see. He thinks he's you. Well, in that case, you out there, the one who *thinks* he's Roman three-oh-seven, would you kindly take a minute to look at your digital display and tell us what number your airplane thinks it is?"

"Yes, sir." After half a minute, "Ah, sir, it looks like I'm ... ah, not really Roman three-oh-seven. It looks more like ... ah, Roman three-ten. Sorry about the confusion, sir."

The air boss, of course, didn't know about the Heckle and Jeckle phenomenon—that the twins had been screwing up events all their lives with their proclivity for transposing identities. In this instance, Russ had mentally transported himself into Rick's jet, assuming his brother's call sign. It was a classic McCormack brothers mind-warp.

Up in his glass-paned aerie in Pri-Fly, the air boss was glowering at the blackened sky, out there where some peckerhead in Hornet number 310 was flying around. He lowered his microphone and tilted back in the high swivel chair. He rubbed his temples with his fingertips. "I've been doing this shit too long," he muttered. "I think it's making me crazy."

★

J.J. already knew about the burble. While he was descending from the marshal holding pattern, he could hear the radio transmissions from the pilots ahead of him as they took their turns approaching the carrier. He could hear Pearly sugar-talking everyone through the burble: "A liii-ttttle pow-*werrrr* . . ."

Now it was J.J.'s turn.

"Roman three-oh-two, Hornet ball, six-point-six, Quinn."

"Roger, ball."

J.J. could see the carrier out there, through the HUD in his windscreen. It looked like a faraway constellation—a cluster of little white lights—against the blackness of the sea and sky.

J.J. felt like he was flying jerkily. He was snatching and yanking at the controls like a spastic. He could feel his pulse pounding in his temples.

Settle down, he told himself. *Be smooth. Relax.*

Relax. That was a joke. He felt about as relaxed as a dog passing peach pits.

He was halfway down the slope now. From here the ball was just a yellowish little pinprick of light. Was it in the middle? Maybe. You couldn't tell from this far out.

But he was getting closer, descending toward the big iron slab that he knew was plowing through the ocean at thirty knots. The only thing was, it didn't *look* like a big iron slab. It looked like a little trapezoid of lights at the end of a dark tunnel. It was hard to believe that he was going to *land* on the damned thing—

"A liii-ttle power." Pearly's sugar voice.

J.J. shoved the throttles up an inch. It was too much.

"Don't climb."

He jerked some power off. Too much. He put some back on.

He knew he was being rough on the throttle. *Settle down,* he told himself. *Be smooth. Anticipate the burble.*

Approaching the ramp, J.J. anticipated the burble. He anticipated it too much. He crammed on some power—a *lot* of power. He saw the ball move up the lens, toward the top.

The dark mass of the ship came swelling out of the gloom. J.J.

was flying right into the trapezoid of lights. He saw the ball blurring off the top of the lens just as—*whump!*—he met the deck.

He waited for the hard, reassuring lurch of the hook snagging a wire.

No lurch. It didn't come. He'd missed the wires.

"Bolterrrrr!" called the LSO.

J.J. jammed the throttles full up, *past* the full throttle position, into the afterburner detent. Off the end of the angled deck he went, afterburners roaring and torching like Haley's comet, back into the black goo of the night. The mass of the ship disappeared in his peripheral vision.

There was *nothing* like a night bolter to get the juices pumping. J.J.'s system was now so adrenaline-saturated, he felt ready to fly *without* an airplane.

He leveled the jet at a thousand feet and entered the traffic pattern for another pass. "Three-oh-two, this is Paddles. You're overdoing the power. Settle down and fine-tune it a little for me, okay?"

"Roger, Paddles," said J.J. Settle down? *Sure thing*, he thought. *No problem.*

★

That's the way the night was going—bolters and one wires. Chip Van Doren got his first bolter of the carrier qualification session, and it so surprised him he almost forgot to shove the throttles up again.

The McCormacks, still carbon-copying, did one of each: a scared-myself-shitless settling pass to a one wire, and then an ain't-gonna-happen-to-me-again overcorrection to a bolter.

Not to be left out, Rambo Morales got *two* bolters, one after the other. Then a one wire, causing the LSO to growl at her on the radio. "Don't do that again!" Thereafter she found the groove. Angie settled down and finished with four straight passes to the target wire.

By the third or fourth pass, most of the nuggets were finding the groove. Van Doren finished up with three straight okay passes to a two or three wire. The McCormacks both settled down and found the middle wires.

That left the Marines. Road Ammons and J. J. Quinn were still out there, going around the pattern.

CHAPTER THIRTY-THREE

COOL HAND LUKE

Pearly Gates hated nights like this. It was smooth out there, with unlimited visibility. Black as sin, with no wind. He almost wished for a little more adversity—some wind, turbulence, a few handicaps. At least when the weather was bad, you usually had wind, which meant the ship wouldn't have to make its own. Then you wouldn't have this damned crosswind, and there probably wouldn't be a burble. And even if there was a burble, it wouldn't matter because there would be turbulence *everywhere*, not just behind the ship. His nuggets wouldn't get themselves all psyched up anticipating that little pocket of rough air each time they approached the ramp.

At least no one had badly scared him. Not yet. All he had to do was get his two Marines finished up.

Standing there on the platform, Pearly gazed off into the gloom behind the ship. He could see the faraway twinkling red beacon light of the next jet to come aboard.

★

"Roman three-oh-two, say your state."

J.J. glanced down at his lower left panel, at the engine/fuel indicator. "Roman three-oh-two has four-point-two." J.J.'s fuel supply was down to four thousand two hundred pounds.

Three thousand two hundred pounds was "bingo" fuel. That meant that when his fuel state reached three-point-two, the game was over. He would have to bingo, meaning he would discontinue trying to land on the ship and divert to an airfield ashore. Tonight's bingo field was Miramar Naval Air Station, on the outskirts of San Diego.

J.J. knew the numbers. And he knew at this very minute what they were talking about down there in Pri-Fly: *This guy has one more shot at the deck. Then he's outa there.*

Back to the beach. And the beach was where he would stay, because the CQ session would be concluded. The *Nimitz* was scheduled to return to North Island tomorrow.

The LSOs would grade J.J.'s CQ phase "Unsatisfactory"— another SOD—which, following his four previous SODs and the evaluation board, could have only one logical consequence: Captain J. J. Quinn, USMC, would be history. His career would be deader than yesterday's roadkill.

All this was going through J.J.'s mind. Twice he had boltered. Each time he had jammed the throttles past the full power notch into the afterburner detent. The extra power of the afterburners was nice, of course, when you were careening off the edge of the flight deck—but unnecessary. The Hornet's basic engines—even without afterburner selected—delivered enough thrust to stand the jet on its tail. Afterburners sucked up fuel at nearly twice the rate as the basic engines.

Now J.J. was running low on fuel. He *had* to get aboard. He had to log one more satisfactory arrested landing in order to finish his qualification. He didn't have the fuel for any more bolters.

He knew he was overcontrolling his jet—yanking and snatching instead of finessing his throttle and stick movements. J.J. knew he had to clamp down on his adrenaline-charged nerves. *Concentrate, man!*

He did. On the next pass, he started down the glide slope exactly on speed, with the ball holding in the middle. He had a good pass going. Pearly was keeping quiet, letting J.J. work the ball.

And then J.J. saw the red wave-off lights flashing. *What the hell . . .*

"Wave off! Wave off!" said Pearly. J.J. shoved up the throttles and pointed the Hornet's nose up, back to the traffic pattern. Now he was confused. And angry. *It was a damn good pass. Why did they wave me off?*

"Sorry about that, three-oh-two," said the air boss on the radio. "The deck went foul. Somebody decided to park an airplane with a piece sticking over the foul line."

"Roger."

"What's your state, three-oh-two?"

J.J. was almost afraid to look. If his fuel remaining wasn't as much as they thought he needed to make another pass, he was finished. And so, probably, was his career. "Three-point-six," J.J. said.

Silence on the radio. J.J. knew what was going on: The air boss was having a phone conversation with Paddles about whether this guy Quinn had a snowball's chance in hell of getting aboard before reaching bingo fuel.

"Three-oh-two," said the air boss on the radio, "here's the deal. We're gonna give you a tight pattern, bring you in for a short final. You won't have a lot of time to set up. Are you gonna be comfortable with that? If not, just say so, son, and we'll bingo you now."

Comfortable? Beneath his oxygen mask, a grin spread across Quinn's face. He keyed the microphone and said in his best matter-of-fact voice: "Three-oh-two, roger on the tight pattern."

★

It *was* tight. J.J. rolled out on final, with a centered ball, exactly on speed.

The ball stayed centered as J.J.'s jet came down the glide slope, descending toward the little trapezoid of lights.

And stayed there.

The gray mass of the ship materialized out of the darkness. He stayed focused on the ball, keeping it in the center. The trapezoid of lights was rising to meet him . . .

Kerrrplunk. A two wire.

Taxiing out of the wires, following the director's signals with the lighted wands, J.J. felt a wave of relief come over him. And satisfaction.

"Good job, three-oh-two," said a voice on the radio. It was the air boss.

"Three-oh-two, thanks, Boss."

★

That left Road Ammons. Road needed three more traps to qualify. He had gotten two successive one wires—settling at the ramp each time as he passed through the burble. And then he had boltered. Road wasn't having a great night.

Pearly watched Road coming down the slope. The jet's airspeed was too slow.

And then Road did what he had been doing all night. He saw the deck coming at him—and he went for it.

"Power!" called out Pearly.

Kerrrplunk. Pearly watched Road's jet roll past the LSO platform, snagging the first arresting wire.

"That's his third," said Plug. "What do you wanna do with him?"

Pearly stood there for a second. He watched Road's jet clearing the wires, taxiing to the forward deck.

Road had this trend going now—settling at the ramp and spotting the deck. It was a dangerous habit. It meant he wasn't flying the ball all the way to touchdown.

Pearly knew what he had to do. This was the part of the job that he hated. He shook his head. "Tell him to shut down. He's disqualified."

★

Disqualified. Road Ammons was crushed.

No one had ever seen him like this. They found him sitting in the back row of the ready room, staring at the PLAT video screen up there on the bulkhead like it contained some message of vast importance. There was nothing on it. Just a static view of the aft flight deck with parked airplanes. And the blackness out there behind the ship.

It was an awkward time. The other nuggets came yelling and laughing into the ready room, punching each other on the shoulder, swapping high fives. Hell, man, they'd done it! The final test! The Big One!

"Hey, did you hear the air boss chewing on Yappy when he thought he was Russ? . . ."

"Dark? You know how dark it was out there? . . ."

"So I hear Pearly giving that 'Pow-werrrr' call, and, man, I *know* I better put on some power . . ."

"The hardest part, I swear it, is just *sitting* on that freaking catapult, looking at all that blackness out there, waiting to get catapulted . . ."

"And I really thought I had a wire. But it didn't happen, and I was just, like, sitting there, waiting, you know, and—*shee-it!*—no more deck, nothing, flying off the end of the damn boat . . ."

"It wasn't as hard as I thought it would be. Easier, really. But ten times scarier! . . ."

Road was trying hard to smile, congratulating his classmates and being a good sport about the whole thing. He tried to explain what happened to him. "I clutched up," was all he could say. "I just clutched up. Like a kid in his first football game."

You could see the pain in his eyes. Road had failed his CQ period, and failing was something he had no experience with. He wasn't one of those kids he was talking about—the kind who clutched up in his first game. He was a Fine Mesher. Road Ammons had always been a winner.

★

Pearly and Plug came down to the ready room, still wearing their LSO vests and wool caps, carrying the grade book. Pearly motioned for Road to follow him into the little office behind the ready room.

"You're a good pilot, Road," Pearly said. "Hell, you're an *excellent* pilot. You've got all the skills. You just got myopic on me out there tonight, going for the deck. That happens sometimes, on a guy's first look at the ship. That's why I took you out. I want to get you back in the FCLP pattern and reinforce your basic ball-flying habits."

"When will I be coming back to the ship?"

"That's up to the skipper. There's another CQ det going out soon on the *Washington*, out of Norfolk. Maybe they'll send you out with that group."

While he was saying all this, Pearly was writing up Road's grade sheet, transferring his notes from the LSO book to the official squadron grade sheet. Road watched him scrawl an X in the "Unsatisfactory" column.

A SOD. A down. It was the first he had ever gotten.

★

The CQ detachment returned en masse to Cecil. Class 2-95, except for Road Ammons, was done. They had a few squares yet to fill—a couple of required instrument hops and an all-weather intercept problem. And then they would be, by official decree of the RAG and the U.S. Navy, *real* fighter pilots!

Each received a squadron assignment. J. J. Quinn was given orders to one of the strike fighter squadrons at the Marine Corps Air Station in Beaufort, South Carolina. Marine squadrons either stayed there in Beaufort or they deployed to the NATO base at Aviano, Italy, where they flew combat patrols over Bosnia. Occasionally a Marine squadron would be assigned to a Navy Air Wing, deploying aboard an aircraft carrier.

Chip Van Doren, Rambo Morales, and both the McCormacks all had assignments, just as they expected, to strike fighter squadrons based right there at Cecil Field. At regular intervals they deployed aboard carriers to the Mediterranean or the Middle East or the Indian Ocean.

They didn't see much of Road. The young Marine was keeping to himself. He showed up for FCLP briefings every evening. He joined the new class out at Whitehouse, going around and around the FCLP pattern just as he had with Class 2-95.

Pearly Gates wasn't the controlling LSO for the new CQ class. Pearly checked from time to time with the new class's LSO, Lieutenant Mark "Buddha" Young. How was Road Ammons doing?

Okay, he was told. Nothing to report. Ammons was doing okay.

Still, Pearly worried. He couldn't forget Road's face the night of the debriefing after he had disqualified on the *Nimitz*. Seldom had Pearly seen a student look so devastated. Road looked like he had received a death sentence.

It sometimes happened that way with the Fine Mesh generation. One of these bright young superstars would show up, having sailed through college, through flight training, to strike fighter training, all the way to the cockpit of an FA-18. The kid had the world by the tail. He was a winner.

Then he would fail. And it would blow him away.

It was more than he could handle because he had never failed at anything. He had thought of himself as one of the chosen—somehow exempted from the everyday calamities that afflicted normal humans. Failure was like death and acne—something that just didn't happen to hotshots like himself. *Fail? Me? No way, man. . . .*

When it happened, it changed his chemistry. He fell to earth like a disoriented duck. In some instances, the kid *never* regained his sharp edge—that grinning, *Top Gun* swagger of the cool-handed fighter pilot. There would always be that nagging seed of doubt . . . he had failed once . . . and he could not shake the feeling, the fear . . . the horrible expectation that it was bound to happen again.

Now everyone was wondering: Was that happening with Road Ammons?

You couldn't tell. Road wasn't a guy who poured his guts out to people. He showed up at the FCLP briefings and sat by himself, jotting notes on his kneeboard. He stayed out of the ready room talking-with-your-hands bull sessions.

One thing was for sure: It wasn't the old Road. Gone was the Yamaha keyboard grin, that aw-shucks-I'm-just-another-Marine shuffle. Gone was that understated self-assurance of the Mississippi black kid who had excelled in a white world. Now he looked like just another African-American G.I. with dog tags and a side-walled haircut.

Pearly and the other instructors were wondering: When Road got back to the boat, would he clutch again? If he did, he would disqualify again. And it would be the end of him.

★

Things started going to hell early. Road and his new class of CQ students were supposed to fly out to the U.S.S. *Washington*, cruising now off the Florida coast. The weather had turned lousy. A squall line was hovering a hundred miles offshore, with patches of rain and stiff winds and lightning. The carrier was reporting that the ceiling was down to seven hundred feet. It would be a hell of a challenge for a bunch of nuggets, everyone said, making their first landings in such conditions.

But from the *Washington* came the word: Crank up your engines and take off. This is as good as it's going to get, guys. You're going to give it a shot.

Off they went, the first flight of Hornets, out into the murk to land aboard the *Washington*. Road Ammons was in the first flight.

★

From the second deck window in the squadron hangar, they all watched. The Hornets were returning from the *Washington*. They'd been gone five days. When the jets had taxied through the fuel pits, they rolled up to the flight line and shut down the engines. One by one, the pilots climbed out of the cockpits and started across the ramp toward the squadron hangar.

The first guy in the ready room was Buddha, the LSO from the *Washington* carrier qualification detachment. While he was still pouring himself a coffee, he was hit with questions. They all wanted to know the same thing: What happened out there? How did it go? How did the nuggets do? Did anyone disqualify?

What about Ammons?

"Ammons? You mean Cool Hand Luke?" he laughed. "You wouldn't believe what happened. It was truly evil out there, that first night. Like something from hell—rain and lightning and low, black clouds. And here's your guy Road down in the ready room telling everyone it's gonna be 'no sweat.' 'A piece of cake,' he says. A *piece of cake*, for Christ's sake! Everybody shit-scared, which is normal for the conditions—and here's this *nugget* giving pep talks, like he's Cool Hand Luke."

"Well, what happened? Did he clutch?"

"Hell, he *was* cool. When it came his turn, he flew six straight *good* passes. No bolters. No wave-offs. The kid was a superstar."

It was amazing! Now they knew something about Road Ammons they hadn't known before. They knew he wasn't one of the prima donna Fine Meshers who let himself be blown away by his first setback. Cool Hand Luke! *No sweat. A piece of cake. . . .*

It made them wonder: Where had the coolness come from? Had he been pumped up by someone like his grandfather? His astronaut godfather? One of those salty old Tuskegee Airmen fighter pilots?

They would never find out, at least from Road. That wasn't his style, to talk about such things. It was personal. But one fact was apparent: Road Ammons had been forced to search somewhere deep inside himself. And he had come up with what he needed. He had found a source of inner steel.

You could see it now, watching him out there on the ramp. He was walking from his parked fighter toward the hangar. It was the old Road.

He saw all the faces peering at him from the second-deck window. He gave them a thumbs-up. He was flashing the Yamaha grin, giving them the aw-shucks routine, walking with just a hint of . . . a swagger.

EPILOGUE

On a wintry day in January 1996, the carrier *Washington* sailed into the Adriatic to relieve the U.S.S. *Roosevelt* on station off Bosnia. It was a time for reunion. On the flight deck of the *Roosevelt*, the McCormack twins hugged each other. They had been separated for six months—the only time in their lives.

Despite the twins' request to be assigned to the same unit, the Navy decided otherwise. Russ went to a Cecil-based squadron that was sailing for the Mediterranean. Rick's orders were to VFA-131, also based at Cecil, on an opposite deployment cycle. When Russ had finished his six-month cruise, it would be time for Rick to go.

Thus did Russ McCormack receive a distinction: He became the first of the Class 2-95 nuggets to fly combat missions. During four days in September 1995, McCormack's squadron carried out air strikes against Serb targets in Bosnia. For its performance, VFA-82 won the battle "E"—designating it the best strike fighter squadron in the Navy. Russ logged over a hundred day and night carrier landings, flew five combat sorties, and, during the height of the Bosnian crisis, spent sixty-one consecutive days at sea.

Meanwhile, Rick had received a separate distinction: He was selected for training as a landing signal officer. It meant that he, like his training LSO in the RAG, Pearly Gates, would spend count-less days and nights out on the lip of a runway or on the edge of the flight deck, willing his fellow airmen to a safe landing.

The reunion was brief. The twins practiced a little Heckling and Jeckling and exchanged brotherly counsel about everything—wives, kids, not busting your butt during night carrier landings, staying alive when the Serbs were shooting at you.

And they discovered something interesting. While they were apart, each had reached an independent conclusion: The Navy—and flying fighters—was dangerous work. It was demanding of their most precious time and energy, calamitous to family life, financially unrewarding.

They loved it. Heckle and Jeckle were both lifers.

★

Tom "Slab" Bacon, who *had* been a lifer, was jumping ship.

Slab's hoped-for assignment as an FA-18 instructor with the Swiss Air Force didn't come through. On the day he received the news that the coveted job had gone to someone else, Slab dropped his resignation letter on the skipper's desk.

Slab shook hands around the squadron, said his good-byes, turned in his ID card, and drove out the main gate. He was in a hurry because he already had a new job: He was beginning his new career as a junior airline pilot.

But Slab and the Navy weren't finished with each other. He kept his commission in the naval reserve. Because of a new policy in the Incredible Shrinking Navy that allowed reservists to be assigned to active duty units, Slab went right back to his old squadron, VFA-106. He could keep doing what he did best: instructing in the Hornet.

★

Though Shrike Hopkins prevailed in her battle to keep her wings, winning the right to reenter strike fighter training, she lost her medical qualification due to complications from her surgery. While in a nonflying status awaiting a final medical disposition, she requested that she be assigned to the Air Force's Space Command in Washington, D.C., where her unique qualification in astronautical engineering could be put to use. Instead, the Navy assigned her to administrative duty in the strike fighter training squadron where she had been a student. Shrike was a paper-shuffler.

From her office window on the second deck of the great yellow hangar at Cecil Field, Shrike could watch the flight line. She could see the pilots in their gray-green flight gear, carrying helmets and navigation bags, strapping into the FA-18 Hornet fighters. She didn't know when—if ever—she would join them.

★

Angelina "Rambo" Morales received orders to a Hornet squadron, based at Cecil Field, which already had one woman pilot on its roster. Since there were still fewer than a dozen women pilots in the entire strike fighter community, she suspected the assignment of *two* women to one squadron was more than coincidental. Had the Navy decided to assign multiple women pilots to certain squadrons to make the women feel less isolated? Or to keep other squadrons men-only?

In any case, it didn't matter to Angie. Angie was confronting a modern dilemma. She liked the Navy just fine, and loved flying the FA-18. But there was something else she wanted even more.

Though she was a product of the new age of feminism—women as warriors *and* nurturers—Angie Morales didn't think it would work for her. She wanted a traditional family. She had three and a half years of squadron duty ahead of her. And during that time Angie would have to make a decision: could she be a career naval officer and a seagoing fighter pilot—*and* a mother?

★

J. J. "Sniper" Quinn was still the oddball among the nuggets of Class 2-95. Before he reported to his new Marine FA-18 squadron at Beaufort, South Carolina, J.J. had already pinned on his major's leaves. His elevated rank only accentuated his uniqueness. As a senior officer in a fighter squadron, he should have been one of the most experienced. Instead, he was as much a nugget as the newest graduate of flight training.

But J.J. was a survivor. He had passed with a qualifying score on every test that he took—eventually. He had gotten to the cockpit of a Hornet fighter by tenacity and guts.

On the inside of J.J.'s locker door was taped the same motto that had gotten him through strike fighter training: CUNNING AND TREACHERY WILL TRIUMPH OVER YOUTH AND SKILL.

★

Chip Van Doren, like all the Navy nuggets of Class 2-95, wound up in a Cecil-based squadron. Since his squadron was not scheduled to deploy overseas for nearly a year, Van Doren had ample opportunity to indulge his *other* passion—computers. With a fellow techno-geek, a Hornet pilot in another squadron, he started a small Jacksonville-based computer company specializing in optical data storage devices. During its first nine months in business, the company's revenue swelled to nearly a quarter million dollars.

Once upon a time, Van Doren had considered himself a lifer. He would fly fighters for as long as the Navy let him. Now he had changed his mind. He had other things to do.

★

They were clustered on the concrete ramp at Maxwell Air Force Base, all four hundred of them, squinting upward at the hazy sky. Their mouths were open. Their eyes were fixed on a dot low against the horizon.

It was Memorial Day, 1996. The Tuskegee Airmen Association—the black fighter pilots from World War II—had brought in this bunch of minority kids from all over the country to Tuskegee, Alabama, for their annual convention. Tuskegee was a place where black kids interested in aviation could find a support network. It was where they could find mentors and role models.

One such role model was just arriving. Four hundred young faces tilted skyward like sunflowers, following the blurred image of an FA-18 fighter streaking toward them.

Vrrrrrroooooooom! The jet ripped across the field at six hundred feet, then broke sharply to the left. Vapor from the moist morning air spewed from each wing. The sleek jet entered the traffic pattern, slowed, and glided down to the runway. When it had landed, the fighter rolled right up to where the kids stood waiting.

The engines whined to a stop. The pilot climbed down from the cockpit. He wore the twin bars of a Marine Corps captain on each shoulder of his gray-green flight suit. He waved at the kids, giving them a big toothsome grin.

Road Ammons, alumnus of the Tuskegee kids' program, was returning to his roots. It was payback time.